They Can't Take That Away From Me

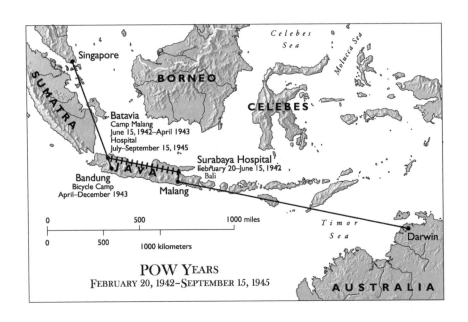

Celebes
Sea

Singapore

Molucca Sea

SUMATRA

BORNEO

CELEBES

Batavia
Camp Malang
June 15, 1942–April 1943
Hospital
July–September 15, 1945

Surabaya Hospital
February 20–June 15, 1942
Bali

Bandung
Bicycle Camp
April–December 1943

JAVA

Malang

| 0 | 500 | 1000 miles |

| 0 | 500 | 1000 kilometers |

Timor
Sea

Darwin

POW YEARS
FEBRUARY 20, 1942–SEPTEMBER 15, 1945

AUSTRALIA

They Can't Take That Away From Me

THE ODYSSEY OF AN AMERICAN POW

RALPH M. RENTZ

WITH PETER HRISKO

Michigan State University Press
East Lansing

Michigan State University Press
East Lansing, Michigan 48823–5245

Printed and bound in the United States of America.

09 08 07 06 05 04 03   1 2 3 4 5 6 7 8 9 10

           LIBRARY OF CONGRESS CATALOGING-IN-PUBLICATION DATA
Rentz, Ralph M., 1918–
   They can't take that away from me : the odyssey of an American POW /
Ralph M. Rentz with Peter Hrisko.
       p. cm.
   ISBN 0-87013-672-0 (cloth : alk. paper)
   1. Rentz, Ralph M., 1918– 2. World War, 1939–1945—Prisoners and prisons, Japanese.
3. Prisoners of war—United States—Biography. 4. Prisoners of war—Indonesia—Java—
Biography. 5. United States. Army. Air Corps—Biography I. Hrisko, Peter. II. Title.
   D811.R464A3 2003
   940.54′7252′092—dc21
                                                                        2002153574

Cartography by Ellen White
Cover design by Erin Kirk New
Book design by Sans Serif, Inc.

Visit Michigan State University Press on the World Wide Web at:
www.msupress.msu.edu

DEDICATION

During many of my medical checkups, doctors would ask me why I had so many scars on my body. I didn't know how to tell them at the time, but at the age of seventy-five, on the second anniversary of my second marriage, my wife, Ellie, persuaded me to tell my story. This book is dedicated to her and to my beautiful granddaughter, Alexandra.

Also, I thank Marge Mikleman for her support and for having faith in my writing this book.

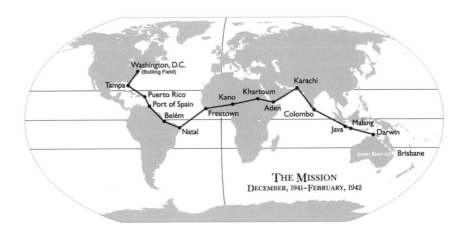

THE MISSION
DECEMBER, 1941–FEBRUARY, 1942

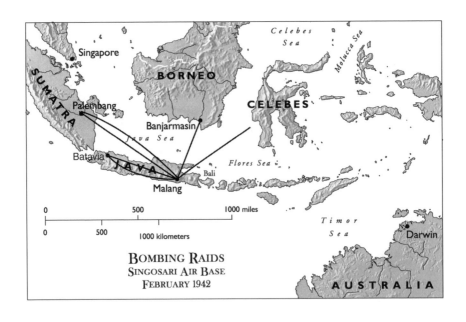

BOMBING RAIDS
SINGOSARI AIR BASE
FEBRUARY 1942

CONTENTS

"I Can't Get Started"

June 1946

Clothed in shit and piss, I looked up and saw them again. They formed a ring around me, laughing. Eyes slanted. Arms folded. Beardless.

Standing, I shivered in my eight-foot grave, surrounded by teeth and eyes. I dropped to the ground, scrubbing myself with the dirt. This jeering team of Jap doctors now started chanting: "He will die. He will die. He will die. He will die. He will . . ."

"Ralph," someone touched my arm, and I woke up.

It was my youngest brother, Zeldan. "You okay?" he asked.

I nodded, realizing my pajamas were soaking wet. No matter how many sleeping pills I took, it wouldn't keep the nightmares away. It was my first day home.

I heard some rattling downstairs in the store, and I knew it was my father. Zeldan went back to bed; my other brother, Joe, was still asleep in this same small room. Both of them were in college, but my parents wanted them in Lansdowne for my homecoming. Both were on their way to becoming professional men like my father wanted.

As I walked gingerly down the staircase, I saw my mother in the kitchen, making breakfast. My father was already dealing with the early customers. They had gone through the same routine for as long as I could remember. Their world hadn't changed much.

My father, Izzy, was a Russian Jew who emigrated to the United States in 1904 at the age of fourteen. He spoke Russian, Polish, German, and Yiddish. When he first came to this country, he would get up at four in the morning to deliver eggs, milk, and butter by horse and wagon. He was a professional man who took pride in his work and appearance: my father always wore a shirt and tie underneath his white apron; his shoes were always shined.

My mother, Minnie, was born in the United States of German parentage. She was only four feet, eleven inches tall, but she was the boss. She would handle much of the busy walk-in trade at our store, Rentz Market, while my father worked the register; later in the day, my parents would make cream cheese, cottage cheese, and other dairy products for sale. Both of them had little education, but they insisted their children would have better opportunities.

I hid in the doorway, watching my mother crack eggs. She had her back to me.

"Lynda called yesterday to find out how you were doing out at the ranch," my mother said.

Lynda. Just the sound of her name almost crushed me.

"That's what she called the hospital you were at in Denver," my mother continued. "She said she was surprised to hear you were now a civilian on your way home."

I didn't move. I knew my mother, who wasn't one to make small talk, had more to say. I braced myself as she cracked another egg.

"I haven't had the chance to tell you, Ralph, but Lynda has been married for the past two years."

A weak smile crossed my face. I inhaled, feeling every bit of my collapsed right lung—another souvenir from the Japs.

That explains it. No letters. No phone calls. No visits. Married. Lynda was married. My Lynda.

"I can't say I blame her for not waiting for me," I said, trying to remain calm. "She didn't know I was coming back."

"She was a very good friend, but you were missing in action for a long time, Son."

"She must have finished university and needed someone to love. She must have fallen in love with this fellow she married." I was babbling now. My mother changed the subject.

"Dad and I have a great surprise for you, Ralph."

"I hope it's not a family get-together with all the relatives," I said. "Because I don't want to face all those questions. I don't want to remember; I just want to live each day as it comes along."

"It's a road trip across country," my mother replied. "You don't have to face anyone, Son, or be pushed to speak about your bad dreams."

"Who's going to run the store?" I asked.

"We've made arrangements."

I didn't question her. My mind was still on Lynda. "She had to make a life for herself," I said.

"Right, Son."

"I hope she's happy."

My mother put the eggs down on the table for me as I left the room.

I shuffled back upstairs to the second floor. Zeldan was in the shower, but Joe was still in bed. I sat on my mattress, my mind running like a train—forward and backward—thoughts of my future, nightmares of my past. Lynda. I couldn't stop the train. I couldn't rest.

I closed my eyes, then reached down under my bed and touched one of my music cases. I pulled them both out, one brown leather, the other black, and placed them on the bed. Both were engraved with the letters *RR*. The cases had been dusted. My father, probably.

I opened the brown case and saw my sax and flute. I opened the other case, and there was my clarinet. I couldn't touch them. It was as if they belonged to someone else. If I even dared to lift them to my lips, I would have slit my throat.

When I left the house later that morning, I wore one of my old suits, and it swallowed me up. Forty-five pounds of me were gone.

I climbed into my father's Chrysler and placed the music cases in the passenger's seat. My father told me he had sold my 1935 Ford while I was gone because it was getting damaged during the Pennsylvania winters with no garage to store it. I wondered if he thought that I was never coming back. The morbid pleasure I derived from this indecent notion soon fleeted, and I suddenly realized that I was headed toward Lynda's old house. I eased up at an intersection, but my mind kept going. The last time I was in my Ford with Lynda . . .

. . . *I was ecstatic from getting word from my parents that they were allowing me to put off school in favor of pursuing my dream as a musician. It was 1937. I explained to them that I would have sufficient funds to pay for part of my schooling next year if I could just have one more year on the road. My parents were very unhappy, my father in particular, but I kissed them both, thanking them for their understanding. I drove to Camden, taking the Franklin Bridge into New Jersey. Lynda was looking out the front window when I arrived.*

She ran down the steps in a gorgeous, baby blue dress. Lynda wore her hair up, which was something different. I liked it. Lynda wrapped her arms around me, and without hesitation took my hand and introduced me to her father and mother.

I knew most of the nightclubs in Philadelphia because I had played in many of the joints. I selected Club 77, hoping the owner would give me the royal treatment. Almost every guy in the place was wearing a tux, and I was no different. It fit me perfectly; it was one of the four made for me by a haberdasher known to my father.

A waiter escorted us around the spacious dance floor as I kept my eyes on Lynda's high heels, working my way up to her stunning string of pearls. She turned around and winked at me.

The moment we sat down, Lynda pulled out a cigarette, and I ordered some drinks. I surveyed the room quickly; each table was softly lit. The place was packed.

I leaned in and smiled at Lynda. I didn't care if there was another woman in the place, and I didn't even notice the sixteen-piece band. Lynda had all my attention. Then I heard a trumpet blast.

"Goddamn," I said. "That's Harry."

"What?"

"No one else plays like that."

Lynda followed my eyes to the stage, and there he was, hair slicked back, eyes open, blowing that horn.

Harry studied the new rhythms coming from South America. He wasn't a great player, but he had his own sound. Slim. Six feet tall. A thin mustache. Harry was articulate, too. And the ladies liked that.

I met Harry on my first road trip with the Eddie Hamp Band, and he took me under his wing. We got along like brothers. When we used to call the musician's union to book a job, they called us "the couple." Harry didn't want to do anything else with his life but play music. His parents had money, and he was an only child.

Listening to Harry play, however, gave me mixed emotions: of course I was pleased to see him again, but I was jealous that he was doing what he loved, and I had just one more year of "the life" before I had to attend school. Something ate at me inside, but I kept it in check. After Harry's set, I excused myself and reunited with my old pal. We caught up on where he'd been playing, and then Harry spotted Lynda from across the bar.

"Nice looking girl you got there, Kid," he said. Harry knew Lynda from when I first met her in Atlantic City.

"You seeing anybody?" I asked him.

"If I want cheese, I get cheese. If I want milk, I get milk. I don't want the same plate every day, you know what I mean?"

"Harry, what do you do? Eat it all?"

Harry laughed, then said, "I got to get back to work, Kid. See you around."

Lynda and I danced a couple of numbers but didn't stay too long. Lynda said she knew of a quiet place where we could talk and not be disturbed. I knew what she meant, and I parked. We jumped into the backseat and started to kiss and caress each other, and then Lynda began to shake a little.

"Darling, are you afraid?" I asked.

"Baby, I want you so much that I can't control myself when you touch me," Lynda said shyly. "I seem to be very moist inside, and from what I've read of this condition, I must have climaxed already. I couldn't wait."

"Lynda," I said softly. "Just let me hold you. I want to make love to you and teach you how to love without having intercourse. We can have a great time without you becoming pregnant."

We took off the rest of our clothes, and soon the car windows were fogged up. After this session, I held Lynda close, and she whispered, "Where in the hell did you learn to do that?"

I laughed but didn't give her an answer.

"We have to do that all over again," Lynda said, "because I think I missed a few things."

Suddenly, a car horn beeped, jolting me. I punched the accelerator and flew through the intersection, catching the music cases with the back of my hand before they tumbled onto the floor.

✳ 2 ✳

"But Not for Me"

June 1946

MR. PUSELLI WAS A SMALL ITALIAN MAN WITH NO NECK AND A SQUARE BODY. He had owned the La France Music Center for years, and my father bought my instruments here. I came to his store often to buy new mouthpieces and other supplies. It was a huge place, with drums, bugles, pianos, trumpets, and all kinds of equipment.

"My God, you've been real sick," Mr. Puselli said as he approached me in his short-sleeve shirt. My head was down, and all I could see now were his expensive shoes on the cheap carpet.

"I was a POW for three years. I got shot up, and I can't play anymore," I told him.

Mr. Puselli studied me a bit before he called for the appraiser in the back. My instruments were the last ties to the world I loved, and I couldn't stand the thought of them around the house, decaying. In Denver, Dr. Gibson told me my right lung would never return to full capacity. I could never play music again. Maybe getting rid of these things would start a new future for me.

The appraiser came out and flipped open the cases with no ceremony. "Selmer. French, huh?" he said, examining them quickly.

I nodded and thought of Yasha. My music teacher. My mentor. "Only buy French equipment," he used to say.

"Three hundred dollars," said the appraiser flatly.

I stood there, my face blank. Three hundred dollars for a lifetime of memories and a future unrealized.

I took the money and cried in my father's car the whole way home.

Before I went back inside our house, though, I stared across the street at Yasha's old house. He was gone now; my father told me Yasha had moved to Europe. Two children were now running on his front lawn.

When I wandered into the dining room, my mother stopped me. She knew where I had been.

"Ralph, you did the right thing," she said. I kissed my mother, then sat down. She stood beside me and glanced at my baggy clothes. I knew she was displeased without her saying a word. My mother had her own clothes made specifically for her, and I felt she didn't like to see me this way.

I took my eyes off her. My head hurt. I put my hand on the table, and my fingers found a nick. A groove. Then another one. Then another nearby. I turned my head, and I saw the Vitaphone player in the corner. An opera record, *La Traviata*, one that my mother liked, was now playing. A gust of wind blew the curtains open. Then suddenly, I saw myself as an eight-year-old boy with drumsticks in my hand . . .

. . . *"I'm going to kill that kid, Izzy," yelled my mother from the kitchen. "Look what he's doing to the brand-new furniture."*

"Leave him alone, Minnie. We'll have it refinished," my father yelled back.

My father had bought me a pair of drumsticks for my birthday. I used to bang on a tin pail, chairs, drawers, anything in sight, making dents and nicks while keeping rhythm to the opera and jazz records that Yasha gave us. I enjoyed finding the empty sound, the hollowness, in a piece of furniture.

"Izzy, what is he building?" said one of the customers in our grocery store. They thought I was hammering something.

"Get him out of here, Izzy!" my mother shouted again.

With the windows wide open in the summertime, the neighbors could hear every word coming from our house. One day, Yasha came over to investigate.

"What's Minnie screaming at that kid for?" he asked in Russian. "She's having a fit."

"Ralph wants to be a drummer, and he's banging up the dining room set that just came two months ago. I don't know what to do with the kid."

"Well, maybe I can get him interested in something less destructive."

A meeting took place that night on the enclosed porch, where all the serious discussions were held. My father told me to get my drumsticks.

"What do you need them for?" I said defensively.

"I want you to do something else," my father told me.

Yasha, meanwhile, just sat there quietly with a small, black case on his lap. I handed the drumsticks to my father.

"You know Yasha plays in the orchestra," continued my father. "He would like to give you lessons on the clarinet."

My father had told me before that Yasha was a child prodigy. He was a serious artist who played first-chair clarinet for the Philadelphia Symphony. He would get my family tickets to his concerts, and we all loved to watch him perform.

"You really want to be a drummer?" Yasha asked me.

I studied his high forehead, his piercing eyes.

"Yes, I want to be a drummer," *I replied.*

"But do you know that drums have no sound but noise?"

I didn't answer him. I never thought of it that way. Yasha went to the table and opened the small, black case, revealing a clarinet. He put the pieces together, carefully instructing me not to break the reeds. Then Yasha reached for his own clarinet. A Selmer. And he played for me.

As Yasha's fingers danced over the black holes, his soft, sweet sound woke me up. It was something between opera and jazz. It wasn't noise; it was beautiful.

Later that night, I showed my mother how easy it was to put the clarinet together, explaining each part, how fragile the reed was, and how only your lips and tongue should touch the mouthpiece.

"After my first lesson, I will be able to play the clarinet," *I said proudly.*

My mother laughed. "Of course, you will. You are a brilliant . . ."

. . . "Son? Son?"

I turned my head, and my father was now standing next to my mother at the dining room table.

I couldn't move my mouth. I just stared at them, still caught in my reverie.

"Are you ready to go to Rubin's?" my father asked me.

"Yes."

I looked at the Vitaphone, then back at the open window. The curtains were still. The breeze was gone.

✭ 3 ✭

"Rhapsody in Blue"

June 1946

MY FATHER MADE AN APPOINTMENT AT RUBIN'S CLOTHIER, A MEN'S STORE IN South Philadelphia, about five blocks from the Delaware River. I'd never been to Rubin's before, and according to my father, it was about a thirty-minute ride. My father, a balding redhead, wore glasses and drove with both hands on the wheel. It was odd to see him without his apron on.

Before we headed in that direction, though, my father took me on a little tour of Lansdowne, pointing out all the new storefronts that had popped up while I was gone.

"Remember this?" my father asked, gesturing to a brick building.

I squinted and tried to think. "No," I said.

"It's your grade school."

I didn't answer him, but the alley nearby looked familiar.

My father made a turn and idled near a house. "How about this?"

I stared at the house, but nothing came into my head.

"I don't—I don't remember," I said.

"It's Ruth's place."

Ruthie. A smile crept over my face. "Really," I said. "I never knew where she lived, anyway."

"Oh," said my father. I don't think he believed me.

Ruth had been my childhood sweetheart. She was Catholic, and of course that was forbidden for me, but that didn't stop us. My father told me that Ruth had married a fireman and moved away to Boston.

"Chestnut Avenue?" my father asked.

"Yeah, I remember Chestnut," I said. My father's mood improved. He seemed happy to revive my fragile memory. He had made contact. My father

9

made a sharp left and headed down another road that looked vaguely familiar.

"There?" my father pointed again at a storefront that was closed.

He idled the car again and waited for my response.

"The haberdasher. Mr. Stein."

"That's right," said my father, excited that I had gotten another one correct. "He used to make all your tuxes and suits, remember?"

"What happened to him?" I asked.

"He passed away some time ago. His wife sold the business."

My father made a turn and spotted another street sign.

"Stewart Street," he said.

I froze. Every time I heard that name, it set me off. My mind was suddenly blitzed with *close-ups of Stuart's head, dismembered body parts, his shoulder, his arm, scattered in bloody pieces on the floor of the plane.* . . .

Dr. Gibson told me that I would always live with that flashback. I shook my head, and my father must have noticed I was disturbed. He didn't speak. He drove on.

Moving down the Baltimore Pike, we passed the police station, the fire station, and the church. I remembered these places.

"Father Marque died, you know, but I still come out three times a week," said my father. "I deliver the groceries out here now."

My father was referring to the Catholic church that was one of his largest accounts. Most of the families around my neighborhood were Catholic, and I wound up knowing more about their religion than my own. Father Marque was a kind, gray-haired Frenchman in his forties who was the head pastor at this church, which Ruth attended. One day as I was coming home from high school, Father Marque pulled me aside and told me to cut out the hanky-panky with Ruth because if she got pregnant, our family would have to move away. I figured Ruth must have told Father Marque about our little adventures when she was in confession. It didn't stop us, though. Ruthie. God love her. I sure did—many times.

I never told my father about this conversation with Father Marque, and I also never told him about what I saw one morning when I was delivering groceries to the church. I was only thirteen years old. As I was carrying in a box of eggs, I peered through the kitchen door, which had a window in it, and I spotted a nun on the floor. She was on her hands and knees, scrubbing the tiles with a water pail beside her. I didn't think anything of it until I saw a priest enter the frame with his pants down. At first, I thought they were playing leapfrog, but then the priest lifted up her brown habit and started giving her the business. I couldn't hear what they were saying, but they both seemed to be having a good time. I was watching them in profile, so I could see her bare ass and his penis disappearing inside it. The harder that priest pumped, the harder the nun scrubbed the floor. That was my first introduction to sex. How could I ever take Father Marque's advice about Ruth and me seriously when I had seen one of his fellow priests doing this? The hypocrisy of it all wasn't lost on me.

Now heading down Broad Street, my father passed some of the old burlesque houses I used to play in the heart of downtown. The names of these joints used to change all the time, but now everything was boarded up. Everything in Lansdowne looked old to me. Very little and very old.

My father parked at the corner of Fifth and South Street, and we entered Rubin's Clothiers. Four salesmen huddled nearby, waiting for the next customer.

Rubin, whose office had glass walls and was near the door, jumped up and rushed toward us. Rubin was a wide man with a bad hairpiece. His face was red from drinking, and he talked a lot. After Rubin asked my father a few questions, I caught him slanting his eyes at me as he pulled my father off to the side.

"The kid's in bad shape," I heard Rubin say.

Rubin then pointed for one of the other salesman to assist me as he and my father disappeared into the back room.

The salesman escorted me to one of the many racks of suits that filled the main floor. He got up very close to me, narrowing his eyes, as he measured my shoulders. The salesman quickly put several sets together: slacks, shirts, ties, jotting everything down on a small notepad. Then he grabbed a suit that he liked and took me in to see the tailor. I didn't offer much resistance.

I tried on the suit pants, and they hung on me. The tailor went to work with his chalk as the salesman assisted me with the jacket. I had been a forty long before the war; now even a size thirty-six needed major alterations. As both men busied themselves around me, pinching and poking, I stared in the mirror and didn't recognize myself. I looked damaged. Disappointed in life. Frightened.

"There, you look as good as new," the salesman said after they finished operating on me. They were still holding me together with their hands, stretching and tucking. It had been years since I had worn anything but hospital gowns and filthy tan shorts.

I looked back into the three-way mirror, and the threads did indeed fit. I recognized myself again. I was young and innocent. I was at . . .

☆ 4 ☆

"What a Diff'rence a Day Made"

January 1941

. . . The Thirtieth Street Station in Philadelphia. Like the other confused kids there, I wore a suit, tie, clean shirt and a pair of shined shoes. We were all huddling near our families, unsure of what was about to happen next.

My father slipped me twenty-five bucks and some advice. "Look," he said. "You're caught in the army. Make the best of it. Don't try to fight it. Enjoy what you can. Take it as it comes, all right?"

I hugged my father, knowing this was not easy for him. "Tell Mom I'll be okay," I said. "I'll see you in a few months. I'm really sorry, Pop."

My father kissed me on the cheek and said, "I'll see you next time when you come back."

"The train is waiting!" shouted the enlisting marine. "Follow me and bring your belongings."

None of my twenty-two college classmates who had enrolled in the National Guard knew where we were being sent. The army never told us where we were going. And we certainly didn't know the marines were going to be in charge of us.

The train was deathly quiet. Before we shoved off, I looked out the train window, searching for my father in the crowd, but he must have left already. How had I gotten myself into this mess? I let my mind wander.

Because I was the oldest son, my father had big ambitions for me. He wanted me to be a chemical engineer, and after years of resisting his wishes for me to attend college, I finally conceded to his way of thinking.

"The music business is no way to make a living," my father would say. "Struggling on the road, plugging for your next gig, flopping in hotel rooms. Forget it."

My mother agreed with him, but she disliked the musician's life for another reason—marital instability. The fact that my mother wouldn't marry my father until he learned to speak English only reinforced the idea that my parents valued *education. They wanted me to become a professional man, not a professional musician.*

My parents couldn't have been more pleased with me when I entered the University of Pennsylvania. Surprisingly, school was a breeze for the first six months, but I was bored. I sneaked away to play at burlesque clubs a few nights a week, and the sexy women rekindled my desire for show business.

My father planned to secure me a job through a contact of his at Du Pont after I graduated. However, my father soon discovered that no Jews worked at Du Pont, and that was the end of that. Since I abhorred physics and all the other dull classes tied into the engineering major, I transferred into the Wharton School of Business with my father's blessing.

Months passed, and it was June 1939. I was twenty-one years old. I found a gig in New Jersey during the summer, while the other kids at school were getting more agitated about the war. We all listened to President Roosevelt's chats on the radio, and we knew that the United States was shipping war materials to England. At this time, I started hanging around with a bunch of fellows from business school. We all received our draft numbers, and mine was pretty low on the list. However, these fellows came up with a surefire plan.

"The National Guard stays at home," said Charlie, the big mouth of the group. "It stayed home in World War I. We can be soldiers at home and still go to school. If we enroll, the draft can't take us."

Charlie was the most articulate kid in school. He could sell bullets to the Indians who had no guns. I didn't want to go off and fight, and Charlie's impassioned words sounded good to me. Lynda wanted to get engaged after we graduated, but I told her I didn't want to make plans three years in the future with the world in turmoil. Lynda let the idea drop, but I could tell she wasn't happy.

Then just two days before Christmas, without notifying my parents or Lynda, I followed Charlie and a group of classmates down to the National Guard headquarters. That evening, I made the biggest mistake of my life.

Enlisting with the National Guard, however, gave me a good feeling at the time. Like the other fellows, I figured I could finish school before the government caught me in the draft. I signed my name, thinking I was part of some special society that had outwitted the government. Three days later, there was a letter waiting for me at home. My mother pulled it out of the stack and showed it to my father.

"You joined the guard?" shouted my father. "Are you nuts? How do you know they're not going to send you to war?"

I explained Charlie's rationale to my father, and he wasn't impressed. While my parents worried, I remained nonchalant about the whole thing, thinking this letter to report for a physical was just routine. I passed my physical, and then ten days later I got another letter, and so did all twenty-two of my business school pals. A week later all of us reported to the same room in downtown Philadelphia; however, the mood was a little different this time. I glanced over at Charlie, and he looked white as a sheet. An officer stood at the front of the room and announced, "Welcome to the National Guard."

We all sat there, stunned.

"I congratulate all of you on stepping forward and protecting your country in this time when national defense is vital," continued the officer. "Within a week, we will notify you by telephone to pack your belongings and report for departure."

"My father's gonna cut my balls off."

"My mother's gonna put a knife in me."

"My father's gonna throw me into bankruptcy."

These were some of the milder things my classmates were saying. They were scared. And so was I.

I stopped off at a corner bar and got good and drunk. "What am I going to tell my parents?" I thought. My father had worked and saved his entire life to send me to college to make something of myself, and now I had ruined everything. Still wobbly, I climbed into my father's delivery truck and lined up the wheels on the trolley tracks. I couldn't see straight. I just let the tracks take me as far as they could.

Later that evening, I gathered my mother, my father, Yasha, and my grandmother, Nana, on the enclosed porch, and I dropped the bomb on them. "Oh, God, did I screw up," I said, and then I mumbled through the rest.

At first they just stared at me, and then my father erupted. "Here I send him to a big-name school, and they're all a gang of dummies," he hollered as he was pacing the floor. I had never seen him so angry. He looked like he had just shoved his head into an oven.

"Why did you do this without telling us?" asked my mother.

"I went to school with twenty-five dummies," I said, "including me."

I stood there, humiliated, but I didn't think it was the end of the world. My parents and grandmother, however, saw it differently. My father had witnessed the devastation of World War I and had escaped from Europe. They felt I was returning to the place my father had fled. I couldn't tell who was the most upset with me—my father, my mother, Nana, or Yasha, who didn't say a word. He just looked at me. Yasha looked right through me. I could tell by his stare, however, that his dream of me becoming a classical musician had ended.

My family tried to contact every politician they could think of, but my parents were simple people without those kinds of connections. For seven frenzied days, they tried to pull some strings, but to no avail. I requested that I be sent into the army music section. Negative.

Finally, I called Lynda. When I told her of my predicament, she cried all night, then begged me to stay over and sleep with her.

"Are you crazy?" I balked. "Your father would throw me in jail and your mother would help him. There's nothing we can do about this, Lynda. I'll be back. I made a mistake. I think I made a big mistake. I don't know, really."

Lynda suggested that we get married right away to avoid this whole disaster. I told her five guys from our business school had tried that route but were denied. Why hadn't I done more investigating before signing that paper? How had I gotten so turned around? Why had I followed the mob? I guess I was impressed by the fellows at business school, who were rich, smart, and sophisticated.

As the city of Philadelphia whizzed by my train window, I looked away and spotted Charlie, the genius who had masterminded this whole fiasco. He looked like he was about to cry.

"I wonder what's the best way?" said the young kid next to me, pulling my eyes off Charlie.

The kid was fiddling with a rosary. "I wonder what's the best way?" he repeated.

"What are you talking about?" I said.

He made a gesture across his neck.

"Cutting your throat this way or cutting it that way."

I laughed, not knowing how else to respond.

"I wonder if I'll go to purgatory first and then to hell," the kid continued, "or maybe I'll just go straight to hell."

"What's the use of worrying?" I said. "Every one of us is soft right now, so take it as it comes."

The kid looked at me, his fear somewhat arrested by my father's parting words to me.

A door opened, and the enlisting marine from the train returned. McCarthy was his name.

"Did you guys bring your own food?" he barked.

Jake, a Jewish kid from business school, stood up. "Whatta you mean—bring our food? We're in the army now. You're supposed to feed us."

"Well, we ain't draggin' a kitchen around with us," McCarthy yelled back.

"Hold it. Hold it," Jake responded, surprisingly loud. "I'm in. But I want to tell you something. You gotta feed me three times a day."

"Siddown, soldier," said McCarthy. "They didn't give us any orders to feed you."

"Well," said Jake, unshaken. "The orders are coming from me."

Jake's remark broke the place up, but McCarthy wasn't laughing. His face was leathery, like he'd been out in the sun too long. No brains, I thought. But who was I to say such a thing? Why had I listened to Charlie? I thought, "What a fuckup you are, Ralph. What a fuckup."

Two and a half days later, we passed a sign that said Jackson. The train stopped. Besides the guys from Penn, there were about two hundred other fellows—draftees and enlisted men—who piled out. It was cold. I overheard somebody say we were in Mississippi.

They herded us into several trucks. I studied my muddy shoes the entire ride. No one spoke. The truck stopped, and then the back curtain flipped open.

"Welcome to Camp Shelby," shouted McCarthy. "Now do as you're told, and you'll have no problem."

They told us to walk, and we walked and walked. Then we walked some more. We passed a battered World War I tank and several empty tents. The whole place was soggy. "What a fuckup you are, Ralph," I mumbled again under my breath.

"Leave your luggage here," said McCarthy when we reached our bunks. He led us into another room, where about twenty servicemen stood behind a giant screen. We received our clothes, along with felt hats, wrapped leggings, and knee-high shoes to combat the foul weather.

Still in our suits and ties, we looked like we were off to a fraternity party or a homecoming dance, but as we fumbled with our new gear, tripping over ourselves, it all seemed surreal. We knew that the moment we put on the wool underwear and fatigues, things would never be the same. Just five minutes in uniform, and it began to sink in: we belonged to them now. There was no going back. Civilian life was over.

We climbed back into the truck. It was the same truck as before, but everything was different now. The guys from Penn were all from good families, from parents who could afford to send them to the university, but this was like going to jail, working on a chain gang. We had been caught.

"Gonna make men outta you," screamed McCarthy, who turned out to be my topkick, my master sergeant. "Watch your partner. Watch his back, or you'll die by friendly fire."

Friendly fire was all McCarthy talked about. Thin and wiry, McCarthy evoked fear even in the captains. After the first week of marching in his company, all the soldiers thought we had gone to hell and were never coming back.

"This is the easy part of the training," McCarthy said after a typical sixteen-mile hike. "I'm going to make sure that every mother's son will be a fighting machine by the time I get finished with you."

We ate our slop out in the cold while the officers took the road back to the kitchen to eat off of tables with fine linen.

I had four weeks of basic training before the communication division, the 102nd Signal Corps, unexpectedly called me up.

Camp Shelby was a new site, and the communication system was not yet running. My new master sergeant was named Schultz, and he seemed to have a slightly better temperament than McCarthy, which wasn't saying much. Schultz explained that our first task was to string cables across the telephone poles linking everything up to central headquarters. How the hell I got on that detail, I'll never know.

We wore gloves and kneepads and tossed leather straps around the poles to raise and lower ourselves to connect the cables. But half of the poles were old and rotten, making climbing very treacherous. In the first week, two men lost their balance when the wood tore away from their dig-in cleats. Both men dangled in the air and then smacked back into the pole, breaking their pelvises.

The next day, one soldier climbed up the pole and panicked. "Motherfuckercocksuckermotherfucker!" he screamed.

The soldier wouldn't settle down. He wouldn't come down. He wouldn't shut up. Finally, Schultz got to him: "If you don't come down, Soldier, I'm gonna shoot you down!" The soldier descended the pole, shaking. I never saw him again.

After two weeks of craziness on the telephone poles, I needed to find a release. Growing up, I had read All Quiet on the Western Front, which depicted the harsh impact of war. In comparison, Camp Shelby was a comedy outfit. We didn't have guns; we practiced marching with broomsticks. Trucks broke down left and right, and tank treads occasionally rolled off and went spinning down the road.

My experience as a musician had taught me about organization, precision, and harmony—and all these ingredients were missing from Camp Shelby. As a musician, I celebrated self-expression. Feeling the notes. Following the changing rhythms. Now I was being beaten down to feel nothing, to think nothing—merely to obey.

Fortunately, I discovered the camp's indoor swimming pool. At four o'clock every afternoon I would escape from the noise. When I was in the water, I wasn't in the army anymore. Swimming was my sanctuary. I forgot about marching; I forgot about the telephone poles. I transported myself to another place, and as I swam laps, I hummed my favorite big band tunes. Breathing in the water reminded me of playing my clarinet. One day it would be "I'll Never Smile Again" on the way down, then "This Can't Be Love" on the way back. I got up to a mile a day, and my playlist was growing. With my humming, breathing, and kicking, I created my own little orchestra. And I would always finish my workout with "Stardust."

. . . Tho' I dream in vain . . .

✷ 5 ✷

"I've Heard That Song Before"

June 1946

. . . In my heart it will remain,
My stardust melody of love's refrain.

AFTER I RETURNED FROM RUBIN'S CLOTHIER WITH MY FATHER, I DECIDED TO lie down in the enclosed porch, listening to our Motorola radio.

"That was Hoagy Carmichael with 'Stardust,'" said the announcer.

I knew I was torturing myself by listening to this music, but I couldn't stop it. I had been in here for hours.

"Now here's the Glenn Miller Band with 'I Got a Gal in Kalamazoo,'" the announcer continued.

I heard after I returned to the States that Glenn Miller had died in a plane crash during the war. They never found his body, but his band kept on playing for a while. In a way, that's how I felt: my music days were over, but I needed to keep hearing the sounds. Song after song, I let the music take me back—"Woodchopper's Ball," "I'll Get By," "Skylark," "Mood Indigo." A number with a trumpet solo like "Begin the Beguine" reminded me of Harry and our week in Havana. Then, when "Let's Dance" came on, my fingers automatically became liquid. I was onstage again. I was in . . .

. . . Atlantic City. 1937. Steel Pier. I knew my solo was about to come up. I had an arrow drawn on my music sheet. I put down my sax, and about four or five bars ahead of the arrow, I picked up my clarinet. On my feet now, I made sure the reed was wet. I took a breath, then took off.

When I started to blow, I tried to do my best Benny Goodman impersonation. He was my idol. People would come to dance to Glenn Miller, but when Goodman played, people would crowd around the stage. He was the pied piper. A showman.

18

After three numbers, the fellows took a fifteen-minute break. Our band, the Steel Pier Band, played at one end of the dance hall, while a popular big band—the likes of Artie Shaw, Benny Goodman, and Tex Beneke—played at the other. This constant flow of music kept the dancers moving. These pros would storm in for a two-week gig and then hit the road for another venue.

I grabbed a smoke with Harry, who was scouting the dance floor, which accommodated about five hundred couples. I had more than girls on my mind, though; I listened to the old pros as they worked the room. They weren't young kids like me up there; they were grown men in their late twenties and early thirties. As I drifted closer to watch them play, I thanked Yasha in my head over and over again. He had gotten me into the musician's union when I was only fifteen; he had gotten me this gig when my parents wanted me in school.

Steel Pier was a vacation spot, one of the most fashionable places to play in Atlantic City. And since there was no gambling at this time, the whole shore was just a fourteen-mile stretch of hotels that played big band music. Our Steel Pier Band was led by Stan James. Our fifteen-piece band had been practicing together for a couple of weeks, and I thought we were really in synch. But after hearing these old pros, I knew we had a long way to go.

But I wanted nothing more than to be a part of this business. I loved the energy, the spontaneity, the creativity. I even liked the long hours. For thirteen weeks, we played every night from nine in the evening until about three in the morning, and then we'd go out for breakfast.

I used to hang out with the older musicians, listening to them talk about music, about women, about life over eggs, coffee, and sweet rolls. When they spoke about their children, though, there was a certain sadness that came over them. They couldn't seem to get up the courage to go and see their families. They showed pictures of their kids to strangers like me. These men had tears in their eyes; they had freedom, but they were torn up inside. I didn't want that.

Working nine to five wasn't enough for these fellows. They loved show business, and they needed to display their talent. When they stood up and played, they loved life, but when they sat down and the music stopped, they felt sad. A lot of them were boozers. Many of them touched up the gray in their hair. They had no future; they were going to play until they dropped. They were exactly what my mother and father didn't want for me. I wondered if Harry was going to be like them.

On my off time, I used to get away from the fellows and go swimming. Being alone in the water was good for me. It was soothing. I asked Harry to join me, but he wasn't much interested in that kind of exercise.

One afternoon, as I was pushing out into the deep water, someone caught up to me and swam alongside. Curious, I wanted to get a glimpse of her body. She stood up and shook her long brown hair. The wet strands scattered across her high cheekbones. She smiled as if I was supposed to say something. I couldn't. What a knockout.

We walked through the surf and sat down on the sand.

"I have been looking for a partner to swim with for the past three weeks," she said. "You're the first person I have seen who swims the ocean the way I do. Oh, by the way, my name is Lynda."

I shook her hand, still mesmerized.

"It's always safer to swim with a buddy in case you get a cramp, don't you agree?" Lynda asked.

I would have agreed to anything she said. Lynda's large green eyes sparkled in the sunlight. And those cheekbones again. They didn't make girls like this in Lansdowne.

"I'd love to have you by my side any time," I said. "My name is Ralph. I'm a member of the Steel Pier Big Band."

There was something about Lynda that oozed both confidence and kindness. I struck a close bond with her immediately, sensing that this young woman had the drive to go after anything she desired.

Lynda told me she had just finished high school and was attending college on a swimming scholarship. She was staying with her mother at the Claridge Hotel on the boardwalk; her father was chief of police for the city of Camden, New Jersey.

"I hope I'm not headed for the jailhouse," I joked.

Lynda laughed, "Don't worry, I can take care of myself."

I bet she could.

"I'll meet you tomorrow, Lynda. Same place, same time."

Lynda nodded, then stood up like a goddess and disappeared into the water.

I walked back to my hotel along Atlantic Avenue, recalling my new swimming partner's green eyes. A few black boys were pulling three-wheeled carriages that could hold about four people each. The women wore long dresses and big hats, and men were dressed in blue sport coats, white slacks, saddle shoes, and straw hats.

That evening on the bandstand, I heard someone calling my name. I looked up and saw that Lynda was dancing with a tall fellow. I couldn't wave because my hands were busy on the sax, but I smiled at her. I looked over and, sure enough, Harry had spotted her as well. He winked at me.

When the band took a break, I found Lynda, and she introduced me to the man she had been dancing with—her cousin. I was relieved.

I felt good about Lynda coming to see me play. She looked gorgeous in her white dress and high heels. Her figure was outstanding.

"Don't forget tomorrow. Same time," she said.

"How could I forget?"

The following morning, as we walked together into the surf, something possessed me, and I gave Lynda a kiss on the cheek. She smiled, and we both dove in. We swam for close to an hour without speaking, using only head signals to communicate our delight, like two seals at play.

Later, lying on the sand, Lynda asked if I would dance with her that night. I explained that I was forbidden to dance with anyone during working hours.

I rolled toward her, looked into her eyes, and drew her softly into my arms, kissing her for the second time. Lynda pulled me down toward her and kissed me with the same tenderness.

In that moment, I realized that one feels a certain loneliness in show business. It's a sadness, really. The road, with all its distractions and adventures, inevitably reminds one of being away from home. This homesickness, this loneliness, is a yearning for companionship—not unlike swimming with a stranger.

"Honey," Lynda whispered, as she took my hand and squeezed it. "I have never been kissed with so much feeling in all my life. I got the shakes. We better double-date because I don't trust myself. And I can't depend on you to stop me from doing what I would like to do."

I had no intention of missing work or getting fired. However, I was more than infatuated with Lynda. She wasn't like the girls I had met with Harry on the road. I didn't want to lie to her. It was a strange role reversal for me. Usually, I was the aggressor. Now, Lynda's engine was running, and I had trouble shutting her off.

"Let's become very good friends before we become lovers," I said.

Lynda smiled.

It was eight weeks into our thirteen-week gig when I met Lynda, and we were spending many pleasant afternoons together. But like every other musician, I was always hustling for my next gig. Labor Day came rushing in on us and on our last day together, Lynda and I decided to spend the day where we had met, on the beach. I was exhausted from another long night of playing, so I put my head on Lynda's stomach and fell asleep. I must have been out for hours when I felt someone kicking my foot. I opened one eye, and I had my nose between Lynda's legs. She was sound asleep, with a newspaper over her face.

"What the hell are you doing down there?" said my father, who was blocking the sun. Lynda scooted back, and I jumped up, nervously introducing her to my father.

My parents' visit was a complete surprise. Lansdowne was only seventy-five miles away, but I had never expected them to show up.

"I have registered you to take the entrance exam at the University of Pennsylvania," my father declared later, as my parents and I sat down on the boardwalk for a drink. "I want you home as soon as your contract is completed."

I sipped my iced tea and didn't answer him. All through my adolescence, it seemed like my father wanted to straighten me out and I wanted to go off in my own direction. Like jazz.

"Dad told me how he found you and Lynda on the beach," my mother cut in. "How could you do something like that, Ralph?"

I tried to explain, but they just shook their heads.

"I'm sure Lynda is a very nice girl, Ralph," continued my mother. "But you are only nineteen, and first comes your education, then comes the girls, understand? I think it's time to put your instruments away for a while."

On the closing night of Labor Day weekend, my father invited Lynda and her mother to have an early dinner with us. I had met Lynda's mother, who was slim and attractive, weeks earlier. Lynda's mother was pleased that her daughter had found a swimming partner, and she knew that Lynda was in love with me.

When my parents came to the pier that evening, it was the first time they had ever seen me play professionally. I knew my first solo, "Blue Moon," was coming up, and I wanted to show my parents my talent. I wanted to dazzle them. Perhaps if I could impress my father with my brilliant clarinet, he would change his tune.

Before a solo, I often heard Yasha's voice in my head: "Are you starting to feel the notes, Ralph?"

Yes, I was.

"Can you feel the exhilaration?" Yasha would ask.

Yes, I was.

"If you can't feel where the notes are falling, then you're just blowing, Ralph. If you can't listen to the music, then you're no musician, and you don't belong in the business. Music always talks back."

I eyed my parents' table, then saw the arrow on my music sheet. I put down my sax and picked up my clarinet. I took a breath and made sure the reed was wet, and for a brief moment, I was inside Yasha—the way he held his clarinet, the way his fingers danced over the black holes. I played the hell out of that clarinet in a slow, lower octave.

After this set, I noticed my parents walking toward me, smiling. They said they had to leave, they wanted to beat the traffic home. They never said a word about my solo. My hopes were dashed. . . .

. . . "Supper's ready!" I heard Zeldan shout from the dining room.

Startled, I caught myself holding an imaginary clarinet to my lips.

I turned off the radio.

That night my mother was serving brisket with heavy gravy, mashed potatoes, and string beans—my favorite meal as a child. However, when I was a kid, Nana did all the cooking. The table seemed empty without my grandmother.

My parents sat at each end of the long, rectangular table. Joe and I sat next to each other, while my older sister, Sylvia, and Zeldan sat across from us. I immediately felt all their eyes on me, scrutinizing me—how I held my fork, how I gulped my milk.

All of them wanted to know the same thing: what had it been like to be a POW. I couldn't talk about anything that had occurred, and I could not understand why they wanted to know so much about death. My family quickly became aggravated with my one-word answers, my shoulder shrugging. After some more questions about my medical condition, my father said, "Ralph is still a sick man."

The table went silent, but I continued to eat in a hurry, still thinking—always thinking—that a Jap guard might call me back to work at any second. My table manners and dinner conversation needed improvement, but I didn't care. My plate was clean.

I excused myself from the table and went up to my room. Perhaps this cross-country road trip wasn't such a good idea, I thought. How could I tell them I didn't feel like laughing? Or ever smiling again? How could I tell my mother her food wasn't as good as Nana's? I couldn't give them any answers. Nothing seemed the same anymore, not the brisket, not my family. They all felt like strangers.

I got undressed, ready to climb into bed early, when Joe surprised me.

"You all right?" he said. Joe must have heard me laboring up the stairs.

I nodded, noticing that Joe's eyes were locked on my bare right shoulder.

"Man," he sighed. "What happened there?"

Joe stepped closer to examine the eight-inch caterpillar scar that slanted across my shoulder blade.

"Operation," I said, as I pulled my pajama top over my head.

The conversation ended. Joe said good night.

I lay there in bed, hiding in the dark. I closed my eyes, and suddenly there was Stuart again, *his bloody body parts all over the floor*. I shook my head, trying to scare that one away. I started to sweat. Dr. Gibson sure wasn't lying. I wasn't even asleep yet, and the nightmares were already starting. I reached for my sleeping pills. I was up to five milligrams now. I took just enough to put me out but not so much that it would put me out for good.

☆ 6 ☆

"I'm in Love with the Honorable Mr. So-and-So"

July 1946

I DID AS LITTLE AS POSSIBLE THOSE NEXT TWO WEEKS. MY FATHER TOOK ME TO the Veterans Administration Hospital in Philadelphia to give them duplicates of my medical history, and he encouraged me to renew my driver's license, but mostly I stayed away from people. All my friends had either moved or married.

Since it was summertime, Harry was on the road. I called him at home anyway. There was no answer. I must have let the phone ring fifteen times before I hung up. I hadn't spoken to Harry in more than five years. The last time I had talked to him was after I graduated from Camp Shelby. Harry mentioned his draft number, and I told him to try to get into the entertainment section of the service. I wanted to spare Harry what I had been through; he was the only tie I had to the music I loved, and I needed to see Harry continue to play. I was keeping my dream alive by living through him.

"I think I'll go to Canada," I remember Harry saying. He was scared shitless about being sent to fight. "Maybe take up residence there."

I wondered if he had gone to Canada. Harry. Old Harry. Just then the phone rang, and I jumped. I didn't want to pick it up, but my mother was busy in the kitchen. I lifted the receiver.

"Rentz's market," I said.

"How you doin,' Honey? This is Lynda."

I melted.

Lynda wanted to meet for lunch. At first I said no, but she pleaded with me until she was near tears. I met her at the Bellevue Strathford Hotel on Walnut Street the following day.

I dressed in one of my new suits and got there early. I hid in the lobby as she walked toward me in a gorgeous, baby blue outfit. That was her color. She still had her stunning figure, but her walk was different: she was a woman now.

Lynda gave me a big kiss, then turned to the maître d' and said, "George, give me the small table near the window." She flashed him a smile and slipped him a bill in one fluid motion.

As I followed her, I noticed that her shoulders were broad and tan, recalling the glory of an Olympic swimmer.

"We should have married when we were so much in love," Lynda said the moment we sat down, as if she had rehearsed this line for years. "My husband, Sam, is on the road three weeks out of the month. The bit of love I had for him has run its course. I'm seeing an attorney the first of August."

Lynda looked at me for some type of response, and I turned away. To look into her face reminded me of all that I could never have again.

"My brother offered Sam a great job running a tire store, but he refused to consider the offer," Lynda continued. Her face tightened when she mentioned her husband. "Ralph, would you consider dating me after the divorce?"

Her directness shook me. I patted my sleeve, trying to choose my words carefully, but the idea of us together again, after all I had been through, rendered me inarticulate.

"Lynda, honey, let me tell you why I can't consider loving anyone for quite a long time."

"What do you mean?" she cut in.

"I'm very ill right now, and I would not burden anyone with taking care of me. The doctors tell me it is going to take five years to get my right lung back. I won't be able to work for a long time. I'm so sorry that your marriage hasn't worked out."

She started to cry. "My God, what did those bastards do to you?"

"Lynda, I can't talk about those things right now."

"Maybe in the future we can talk again?"

I got to my feet, kissed her on the cheek, and then walked out, leaving Lynda with a strange expression on her face.

When I arrived home, my mother stopped me at the side door. "You have been crying," she said. "Your eyes are all bloodshot. Did you sleep last night?"

"I screwed up the whole meeting with Lynda," I replied. My mother gestured for me to sit down, and I told her what happened.

"You did it right, Son, because you told the truth. Lynda understands now that it's impossible to go back. Those days are over, Ralph. You have to forget Lynda; she's the wrong train. Stop remembering the good times."

My mother went into the kitchen to fix me something to eat while I walked over to the window, wondering what else would be cut out of my old life that I loved so dearly.

I looked down the street, to the house next to Yasha's old place. When I was a boy, a sailor and his wife had put a birdcage outside the window in the summertime. They had a parrot that was about eighteen inches tall. When a man walked by, the parrot would repeat, "Another son of a bitch, another son of a bitch." The sailor had brought the parrot home from one of his trips to South America. "What the hell was that parrot's name?" I wondered. I couldn't remember.

Just then, my mother returned with some pea soup and a chicken salad sandwich; she had to notice the weird smile on my face.

"Soup's getting cold, Son."

"What happened to Gus, the parrot?" I asked my mother. The parrot's name had suddenly come to me.

"Gus died, and so did Bill and his wife," my mother told me. "There is a young couple with two children living in that house now."

"Oh," I said, then sat down and ate in silence.

☆ 7 ☆

"You'll Never Know"

July 1946

A DAY BEFORE THE ROAD TRIP, I TOLD MY MOTHER I WANTED TO VISIT NANA'S grave. I had discovered over the past few days that whenever I wanted to deflect my mother's questions about my war experiences, I could bring up Nana, and my mother would always cry. This was my only defense other than silence. I felt bad about my behavior, but I couldn't help myself.

Nana, unlike my mother and father, had been a very affectionate person. Gentle, slim, and a fabulous cook, my grandmother spoke in a voice just above a whisper. Nana and I had our little secrets, and I missed the way she rubbed the back of my neck when she knew I didn't want to do something.

So as my parents and I drove out to Larchmont Cemetery in Delaware County, I wanted to pay my respects to the woman who had probably known me best before the war. Maybe saying good-bye to Nana would help me get started again.

My father went into the mortuary and received permission to pray over Nana's grave. We put on our yarmulkes, and a rabbi lead us outside through an old iron gate, then down a walkway. We didn't stay long. My mother placed lilies by the grave, and we left with tears in our eyes.

Nana always believed in me as a musician. She loved to hear me practice the clarinet and sax on the enclosed porch. One time, I came home drunk early one morning after playing a college party. I pressed our broken front doorbell, and since there was no answer, I sat down on the steps and opened my clarinet case. I put the stick together carefully and played "In the Mood." Nana heard me, and she marched downstairs and immediately realized that I had booze on my breath. She dragged me up to my room and dumped me into bed with my clothes on, placing my clarinet by my side. She knew music was my mistress.

I packed for the cross-country trip, leaving my baggy clothes behind. Before we left, I said good-bye to my brothers, kissed Sylvia, who was minding the store, and tried Harry one more time, knowing full well that he wasn't anywhere near his small bachelor apartment in Upper Darby.

Proud of his new red Buick, my father announced that he wanted to do most of the driving. My parents were working people, and this was their first vacation. For the first 150 miles, all they talked about was the new refrigerator they were planning to buy. They were always talking about the store and how to increase business.

"Minnie, we're going to go over the side of this mountain and get killed," my father exclaimed as he steered the wheel tentatively around a curve. My father could never drive through the mountains, where there were only two lanes.

"Izzy, cut the baloney," replied the boss, who always sat in the passenger's seat. "Pull over and let Bob drive."

My mother had invited Bob Resner along for the journey; otherwise, I would have been in the backseat by myself, and my mother didn't want that.

Two years younger than me, Bob was my mother's nephew. He was very dark-skinned for a Jewish man, and he was in excellent physical shape. Bob had his own practice as an optometrist.

My mother thought that Bob would be good company for me, but springing him on me wasn't a good idea. Even though my parents meant well, I sensed that this was going to be an awful experience.

Terrified of the Appalachian Mountains, my father now stopped at a rest area and climbed into the backseat. He then slid down on the car floor and mumbled prayers in Hebrew to calm his nerves. I had never heard my mother laugh so loud. Bob nearly had to pull over to wipe his eyes.

As we traveled out of Harrisburg, I started counting trees, which kept my mind off the fact that I had no Lynda, no Yasha, no Nana, and no music in my life. When I got bored with the trees, I started counting road signs.

My father soon returned to man the wheel, and I knew the questions would soon start coming from Bob. I presumed that my mother had briefed him on my background before I became a POW; she probably told him that I made a fast decision to enlist into the Army Air Corps after a captain convinced me of the benefits of air rather than ground duty.

I had made that decision during the 1941 Louisiana maneuvers. After graduating from Camp Shelby, our company was sent to the swamps of Louisiana for war games. On the first night, we slept outdoors in sleeping bags because our pup tents, which hadn't been unpacked since World War I, reeked of mildew. I nearly vomited. That night, a soldier in our company was bitten on the neck by a coral snake. He was rushed to a jeep and was reported dead on arrival at the hospital. This scared the shit out of me.

I had been trained at Camp Shelby to be a ground-to-air communicator in an antitank unit. And for the Louisiana maneuvers, I was given orders to be in charge of radio contact with a spotter plane. The job of the pilot, Captain Martin, was to spot tanks and then report them to me. Then I would pass on the information to the ground troops. As the games began, though, I received word from the captain that all hell had broken loose: the red team—the invaders—never invaded, which caused mass confusion in the air and on the ground. Tanks were stalled and men were running in circles, while others were playing cards or sunbathing on the side of the road.

I distinctly remember my conversation with Captain Martin. During our radio communication, he was laughing. He said, "If you're going overseas with guys like this and no new equipment, you'll get wiped out in a day. Why don't you join the Army Air Corps instead of rolling in the mud, Private? Anybody could beat this army. You could have a great time. You'll have a bed with sheets, Private. Eat off linens. Live like a human being."

This sounded like a better deal to me, and when I returned to Mississippi, I signed up for four years with the Army Air Corps.

I didn't find it peculiar at the time, but I never met Captain Martin in person. Maybe it was the tone of his voice—it reminded me of Harry. I didn't think I was being impulsive, just practical. I was saving my own life. My father didn't agree.

"You're betting again," I remember my father saying, shaking his head. "You're betting it's going to last four years, and we're not in the war yet. I think you're a little meshuga. But you've made your decision now, and you're gonna have to live with it."

After being with my father for five minutes, I thought my brains were up my ass. "What are you gonna do when you get out of the air corps?" he asked, now pressing the issue.

"I don't know. I may stay in the Army Air Corps," I said, trying to convince him that I had made a good decision this time. Was I a little meshuga, like my father said?

"Four years," my mother sighed. "That's four years of college, Ralph."

"I know, I know," I repeated.

My parents looked at me like I had lost my mind.

It wasn't until now, sitting in the backseat of my father's new car, that I finally realized what a deep blow my joining the Army Air Corps must have been to him. For the second time, I had not consulted with him about the direction of my future, and for the second time, I had disappointed him greatly, spoiling his dreams for me. Just looking at the back of his pink neck as he was driving, I could sense his disdain for me.

Suddenly, Bob rolled his shoulder against the window, opening his chest toward me; he was making his move.

"So, Ralph, tell me, how long were you a POW?"

The conversation went dead in the front seat.

"Three years and seven months," I answered.

The question didn't stun me. It was one of the two most common questions asked of any POW. The other was:

"How were you captured?" Bob asked, right on cue.

"I—don't remember," I said, knowing that this wouldn't be the last of Bob.

My father remained steady at the wheel. He wanted to hear the conversation. They all wanted to hear how brutal the Japs were, but I wasn't going to tell them about the camps. But I felt like I had to tell them something, so I mentioned my first few months at Langley Field in Army Air Corps. I told them how I had joined the aircrew, how I had become a radio operator. I told them that the B-17 bomber had four engines, while the B-25 only had two. My mother turned around, slightly intrigued, as if I was revealing government secrets. She had never heard all this before.

"The Army Air Corps never took risks with classified information," I explained. I didn't mind talking about these days. These were the good times, when I was effective.

"I was on a crew with Captain Wyatt that delivered official documents in a locked briefcase."

"That must have been exciting, Ralph," my mother said, happy to see me talking again.

"After we made our delivery, the rest of the weekend was ours. Saturday nights, we never slept. Captain Wyatt would get us tickets to shows—to the air races in Cleveland, nightclubs in Boston, and USO parties up and down the East Coast. I swear the USO was running a whorehouse."

"Now that must have been exciting, Ralph," said my father. My mother threw him a look.

"Some fellow—I didn't know who the hell he was—would introduce me to one gal, and the next thing I knew I had three girls to choose from. We were a close-knit crew. It was like belonging to a country club."

"This Wyatt sounds like a decent fella," Bob chimed in.

"He was," I said. "He was the one who suggested that I apply for cadet school."

"Did you take the exam?" asked Bob.

"Yeah, I took it."

"What happened?"

"Pearl Harbor happened."

"Where were you?"

"Playing cards," I said. "At the base. All of a sudden, the radio cut off, and they made the announcement. One of the fellows I was playing with had been in the service for four years, and he was heading out the next day. His discharge was rescinded. Poor bastard. Everyone was on stand-by."

"Well, how'd you get over to Java, then?" asked Bob.

I looked at him quickly, then down at the car floor. Again I had a sudden flash of Stuart's scrambled body. I didn't answer.

"That's where you were captured, right?" Bob continued to pry. "I heard your plane—it was—"

"That's enough, Bob," my mother said, rescuing me.

We rode in silence for the next few miles.

"Seventy-eight, seventy-nine . . . ," I said to myself. I went back to counting trees. I wasn't going to tell this jerk my story. Who was he? He hadn't been there. I didn't want to talk to anybody. Not about my POW years, not even about the mission.

⋆ 8 ⋆

"Sentimental Journey"

December 1941

CAPTAIN WYATT HAD AN ENVELOPE IN HIS HAND.

"Sorry to see you go, Ralph," he said. "I'll miss you."

For the past ten days, Captain Wyatt and our crew, along with eight more B-25 crews, had been in Garden City, New York, patrolling three hundred miles outside New York Harbor for German subs. The captain now told me I had received orders to report to Bolling Field.

"Why me?" I asked the captain.

"If I knew, I'd tell you, Ralph," he said matter-of-factly. "I don't know what the hell's happening, but someone's going to walk up to me tomorrow and introduce himself as my new radio operator."

I shook Captain Wyatt's hand and said good-bye. I never saw him again.

Two other men in Garden City—a pilot and a navigator—received the same orders as I did. They had more radio experience than I did. Why was I the only one from Captain Wyatt's crew who had orders to move?

A DC-3 picked us up and flew us to our destination, Washington, D.C.

"The Army Air Corps has chosen you men because you are specialists in your particular jobs on the B-17 plane," said Brigadier General Fleming, who stood at a podium with his staff behind him.

There were a total of about fifty noncoms and officers in the meeting.

"The Army Air Corps has a research mission to perform, a secret mission," continued the general. "No one outside of these walls knows of the orders that you are going to receive. You will receive your orders when you fly to Tampa, Florida."

I was curious about why we were going to fly B-17s, not the B-25s. After testing our new plane for a few days, my commander for this "secret mission," Captain Jacque Montel, called a meeting for our new crew in the officers' quarters. Montel was about thirty years old, with reddish-brown hair. He had been in the Army Air Corps for five years, and he was a very experienced flier. Montel spoke with a slight French accent as he introduced the crew:

First Lieutenant James Frerry: copilot; blond hair; blue eyes; five feet, eleven inches tall; 185 pounds; round face; had been in the Army Air Corps for thirty months.

Second Lieutenant Carl Miller: navigator; short; compact; five feet, eight inches tall; 165 pounds; spent time in the merchant marines; high strung.

Sergeant Ray Kroll: chief engineer; slim; muscular; five feet, eleven inches tall; 170 pounds; responsible for plane being in flying condition; in charge of all men on crew except officers.

Sergeant Joe Mann: second engineer; black hair; ruddy complexion; five feet, seven inches tall; 160 pounds; quiet.

Sergeant Stuart Smith: second radio operator; sandy-brown hair; five feet, eleven inches tall; 175 pounds.

I was the chief radio operator.

None of us were married, and all of us were smokers.

I instantly hit it off with my partner, Stuart, who was a handsome kid from Cleveland. Two years younger than me, Stuart had joined the National Guard like I had, hoping to avoid the war. Both Stuart and I were confused about why we had been thrown on this secret mission, and the Army Air Corps liked it that way. They wanted to keep us all in the dark, guessing, so we wouldn't know the true nature of our trip. Germany had spies everywhere.

When we returned to our quarters, our mail had finally caught up with us. I had a letter from my mother, two from Lynda, and one official letter from the U.S. government. I opened the last letter first, and it was a notice to appear before my commanding officer. I had passed the written examination for cadet training school, which I had taken in November. I immediately ran over to Captain Montel's quarters.

"I will let you know on Monday," said Montel. He didn't look pleased. He didn't want my good fortune to break up his unit.

I understood Montel's concern. It was the beginning of the war in the Pacific, and there weren't many trained radio operators for B-17s. The captain would have trouble replacing me on such short notice.

I called my parents later and told them I had been accepted to the school. I also told them not to tell Lynda about the good news, because I wanted to surprise her when I got home. Of course, I was prohibited from mentioning the secret mission, and I wouldn't have known how to explain what we were embarking on anyway.

December 22, 1941
Tampa, Florida

My darling Lynda,

The thought of loving you every day sometimes drives me out of my mind. I want to hold you in my arms. That one thought makes me happy. Tears come to my eyes when I think of how far away we are from each other.

I cannot tell you where the crew is going, but I can tell you how much I love you. I miss you so much. When we are together, it is like heaven itself, just to hold you and be near you. Your skin is like satin, and I want to consume every little piece that I touch. You are my beautiful satin doll.

Darling, I will be back in a few months, and I will express all the love that I have for you when we are together for a whole weekend or maybe more, as long as my R and R will last.

Love,
Ralph

The next day, Captain Montel called me to his quarters. "I don't have good news, Ralph," he said. "I spoke to Brigadier General Fleming and explained your situation. Since this is a special outfit, your going to cadet school will have to wait until this first mission is completed."

I was very unhappy with this exchange, but I had been trained to follow orders. Our crew was selected as the first of the seven planes to fly on the secret mission. We received orders to fly to Tampa later that day.

Tampa was a maintenance center for all bombers. After our crew arrived, I attended classes in both marine communications and foreign communications, which gave me a fair idea about our crew's future plans. Our crew was told shortly thereafter that we were going to San Juan, Puerto Rico, and to Port of Spain, Trinidad. I was initially curious about how a B-17 could fly such long distances without more fuel tanks aboard; then, a day later, two five-hundred-gallon bomb bay tanks were loaded on the plane, and all guns were removed except a light .30-caliber machine gun in the navigator's nose compartment.

Most of the crew had had some experience with a .50-caliber, air-cooled machine gun at Langley Field, and we practiced over the Atlantic Ocean. Sometimes we would do skeet shooting, or we would drop red dye into the water and fire at stationary targets. But it seemed odd that the guns had been taken off the plane.

"Is this going to be a vacation? Why aren't we taking the guns?" I asked Lieutenant Frerry, with whom I quickly established a rapport, knowing that I would be communicating mostly with him.

"This is going to be a trial run," said the first lieutenant. "A trial run for what?" I wondered. But Frerry was tight-lipped; he wasn't going to offer anything else.

Also installed on our B-17 at this time was a twenty-foot steel rib that was one foot high and one foot wide. This rib was bolted down right behind where Stuart and I sat, and it looked like a long coffin. The engineers in Tampa said the rib was designed to reinforce the structure of the fuselage, but I had never seen anything like it before, and neither had anyone else on the crew.

My radio equipment, meanwhile, was reduced to a small, lightweight receiver and an electric key for sending radio messages, along with two prepackaged codebooks that came in little loose-leaf ring binders containing location and frequency for our two destinations, San Juan and Port of Spain. The following morning the call came to be ready to fly at 0700 hours.

The officers—Montel, Frerry, and Miller—were already on the plane when our jeeps drove up. We loaded our duffel bags and buckled our harnesses, and everyone checked in by intercom.

Stuart and I sat back-to-back in swivel chairs behind the bomb bay tanks, while the other five men sat up front. The first engine turned over, and my heart was pounding, knowing that most of our trip would be over water.

"Gentlemen," said the captain as he opened the intercom again. "We now are on the first leg of a historic flight. It will be a few weeks before we return home, so get comfortable. And good luck."

Stuart looked over at me with a puzzled expression and said, "Ralph, how can this be a historic flight? We're just making two stops."

"I know," I said, shrugging my shoulders. "Something doesn't smell right."

I didn't care. In a couple weeks I'd be in cadet school. I'd be flying.

☆ 9 ☆

"Candy"

January 1942

THERE WAS A ROMANCE TO BEING IN THE AIR, AND THE ADVENTURE OF FLYING quickly captivated me. When I took my first flight at Langley Field in May 1941, it was my first time inside an aircraft of any kind. I wasn't scared, really, but I was worried that if I became ill, I would be taken off the aircrew. The experience was breathtaking. Just three months earlier, I had been climbing up telephone poles in Mississippi, and now I was climbing up to fifteen thousand feet in a B-17. Although flying was exhilarating, it wasn't my passion. Nothing could replace my music. When we landed in San Juan, Puerto Rico, the police force took over security for our plane, and our crew was escorted to a hotel. After we showered and changed into our regular uniforms, Montel called a crew meeting at the hotel bar to celebrate the first leg of our tour.

Montel spoke several Romance languages and knew his way around a wine list. He ordered several bottles of Crystal French champagne without a trace of a foreign accent. We raised our glasses, not knowing what we were toasting but glad to imbibe just the same.

Music started to trickle in from the ballroom. Tangos, then sambas, then cha-chas, and even some American dance numbers I had played. I leaned over to Stuart and said, "I can't get away from my music days."

Stuart laughed. "Someday you'll have to tell me about your swinging years before you joined up." I nodded, swept up by the music.

After dinner, the crew went into the ballroom. At first it seemed strange when I noticed a group of young girls dancing together, but then, one by one, each man in our crew got paired up. A lovely dark-skinned girl with green eyes, no more than sixteen, approached me.

"My name is Juanita," she said in broken English. "What is your name?"

"Raoul," I said—Ralph in Spanish.

Juanita smiled, and we started to dance. After a few of the old numbers, Juanita's perfume made me forget about cadet school. With my cheek pressed to hers, I was swooning, reliving my musical past.

"Let's walk on the beach," Juanita said.

I agreed and then suddenly realized that we were the only ones left on the dance floor.

Minutes later, I was making love to Juanita on the sand. She seemed perfectly comfortable, but, seeking a little privacy, I asked her if she would like to go up to my room. Juanita nodded, and the shape of this new hand in mine fueled my desire.

I put the key in the lock, and Stuart surprised me when he quietly opened the door. His hair was wet, and he wore a sheepish grin. I could have sworn the kid was a virgin.

"I have my—my friend with me, Ralph," he said. "But if you want, you can use the bed. Just don't turn on the lights."

Juanita and I got undressed in the bathroom and decided to stay there. As we showered, I explored Juanita, who couldn't stop giggling. Her body was taut. Trim. She had developed early.

"Let's go into the bed. I'm going to explode," Juanita whispered, then smiled. I could translate that smile in any language.

Stuart and his friend seemed to be sleeping, and it didn't make much difference to me, anyway. My craving for Juanita was at a new high. She was so warm, I thought she was running a fever. We made love for hours, and even though I was inside her, it seemed I couldn't get close enough to her. Drenched in sweat, we showered again, and then I sent her on her way. It was two o'clock in the morning when I woke Stuart up.

"Your girlfriend better leave, Kid," I told him. "We have to be up by six."

While they said their good-byes, I went into the bathroom and cleaned myself up. To prevent any infection, I injected a jelly into my penis and then tied a small cloth bag around my privates to catch the excess. Pleased with the night's events, I glanced at myself in the mirror and did a little two step—cha-cha-cha.

When our crew boarded the plane that morning, we were exhausted but our spirits were renewed. The intercom crackled to life; the captain was chuckling.

"Well, it looks like you Romeos had a good time last night. Don't start thinking you're great lovers or anything though, because you know who paid for those girls, don't you?"

Montel was laughing like hell now. "That evening was on me," he snorted. "Now let's get down to business and get this plane to Port of Spain."

I heard Kroll and Mann laughing up front in the engineer's room. Miller, up in the nose, probably had a smile on his face as well. Stuart, meanwhile, looked bewildered.

"Ralph, you mean those girls were prostitutes?"

"You're damn right," I replied.

"Ralph, I've never been with a prostitute."

"You were last night, Kid."

Stuart blinked, his Midwestern innocence still intact; he didn't even attempt to mask his embarrassment. I stopped laughing.

"Was that your first time?"

Stuart wouldn't answer me.

Since Captain Montel instructed me not to contact any station unless there was an emergency, I decided to take a nap, and the drone of the four B-17 engines was like a lullaby. I asked Stuart to put on my headphones and wake me up if he heard even a slight noise. He agreed, and I could tell he was still obsessing about the girl last night, still unable to forgive himself for sleeping with a prostitute.

I went over and stretched out on the long, steel rib, and I was out in five minutes. Stuart woke me up hours later when Lieutenant Frerry alerted us that we were heading into a wet situation. I returned to my seat, but the rain never showed up. The winds did, however, and they were fierce, hitting us heavy on the right side of the plane. The captain first increased the altitude, then decided to dive into the winds at a lower altitude, which improved our predicament, but our flight was way off schedule. We landed two hours later.

We taxied up to the hangar and were immediately surrounded by soldiers. Captain Montel told us not to make any sudden moves until he showed his landing papers. Once the Trinidadian servicemen glanced at Montel's government orders, they smiled and introduced us to a group of foreign dignitaries who were quickly lining up to greet us. An interpreter informed us that our plane would be under tight security and that we would be taken to the best hotel in town. We were chauffeured to a four-star hotel and then escorted to our rooms—Captain Montel didn't even have to sign the register. It was like royalty had arrived. We were all put on the same floor, with military guards at each end.

"Don't open your doors until I call your room," ordered the captain. Since Trinidad was known to be a hotbed for spying, the captain had warned us earlier to keep our mouths shut.

Later that night, three different wines and an assortment of liquors were placed in the center of the dinner table. Captain Montel stated we could have only one drink before dinner and one drink after. Now I knew for sure that the captain wasn't himself. No one spoke during the meal.

After dinner, the mayor arrived and asked the captain if we would like to go to a nightclub. Captain Montel thanked the man but refused the invitation, explaining that we had a long flight tomorrow with an early call in the morning.

When Stuart and I returned to our room, he said, "I wonder what the problem is. The captain is acting sort of strange."

"We'll know sooner or later," I said, exhausted and full.

The following morning, a large station wagon picked us up in front of the hotel. The driver, who was in a military uniform, spoke English with a German accent. The captain got in the passenger's seat.

"Do you like to fly, Captain?" asked the driver en route to the airfield.

"I enjoy flying. Thank you," said the captain.

"Are you flying across the ocean?" probed the driver.

The captain looked hard at the driver. "How is that possible in such a small plane? We are just a weather plane," the captain replied.

Lieutenant Frerry had referred to the mission as a "trial run"; now Captain Montel called us a "weather plane." I didn't think too much of the captain's deception at the time, but I knew our secret mission had to be more than gathering information on rain, winds, and jet streams. There was a war in both Europe and Asia, and I wondered how our crew fit into the whole plan. What was our "historic flight?" Our "secret mission?" All we had done so far was get laid once and have our plane refueled twice. I gave up trying to figure it all out, and as we reached the airport, I began thinking again about cadet school. Once on board, we strapped on our harnesses, and the buzzers went off. Lieutenant Frerry came over the intercom, asking each of us if we were set to fly.

"Yessir," I responded, but then I noticed that I had not received my codebooks for our route back home. I presumed that since I had received only two codebooks before we left Tampa, we were now headed home—perhaps through Havana and then back to Tampa for some R and R.

I called Lieutenant Frerry over the intercom, and he apologized, telling me to send Stuart up to the cabin to get the codebooks.

Stuart returned and handed me a batch of codebooks. I quickly opened the prepackaged envelopes.

When we reached eight thousand feet and leveled off, the captain's voice came over the intercom.

"Gentlemen, I know you heard our German driver this morning try to get information out of me. We will have more of these delicate situations throughout our trip, so please be careful with whom you speak. The slightest slip of the tongue could cost the whole crew our lives. We are now headed to Belém, Brazil."

Stuart looked at me and said. "Where the hell is Belém, Brazil?"

"Right along the mouth of the Amazon," I said, remembering a book report I had done in grade school about President Hoover's trip to South America. Hoover was the first president to visit the continent, and I had made a presentation to the class with press clippings and all. But I was preoccupied now. Brazil meant we were not heading home as I had thought. Was Montel taking us on Hoover's historic trip? I wished that had been the case, but I didn't think so.

After scrutinizing the codebooks, I discovered that we weren't going back to Tampa for some time. Our final destination was Australia.

"Dammit!" I said to myself. Montel had deceived me. Now it would be months before I got to cadet school.

I now held those codebooks in my hands like playing cards, unable to believe the rotten hand I had been dealt. Australia? Why were we taking this eastern route when we could have just left from California and crossed the Pacific? Stuart knew I was not pleased, and he kept quiet. I was certain that I had just gotten screwed.

✶ 10 ✶

"The More I See You"

January 1942

THE TEMPERATURE MUST HAVE BEEN 110 DEGREES. AS WE PASSED OVER THE mouth of the Amazon, the color of the water changed from blue to a dirty yellow. Mud flowed through the river as smoke was rising from the shore. Just as Frerry gave us permission to open our side windows to cool down the interior of the plane, there was a sudden rattling coming from the engines.

"Look at that thing wobble," I heard Captain Montel say over the intercom. It was the cowling—an aluminum cover that fitted over each engine to protect it from the elements. When this engine started to overheat, Montel ordered an emergency landing.

Ten minutes later, we piled out of the plane and ran for the hangar, fearing that the plane might blow. Cool drinks and beer were served as the captain introduced us to Brazilian officers who spoke English. One of the Brazilian workers brought us straw hats and heavy gloves, while other men rolled out aircraft ladders to reach the engines. The captain instructed us to help Kroll and Mann remove the troublesome cowling and place it in the air-conditioned hangar. Montel anticipated that if the cowling cooled, it would return to its regular size.

During the ride to our hotel, disease and squalor crept in through the car vents, making the foul air hard to breathe. The groups of tin shacks along the road, called shantytowns, were an eyesore. And the view didn't get any better as we reached the heart of town. Belém was a dump.

Our accommodations weren't four-star hotels like in San Juan or Trinidad, either—just a plain room with ten old iron beds, a shower, and toilet. In Belém, this was considered a deluxe hotel. Montel was irate, and he chastised our Brazilian officer, who immediately arranged for us to stay elsewhere.

As we traveled along a newly paved road, then up a mountain that had lights along each side, I was starting to feel less resentful toward Montel. I slowly let go of my anger, welcoming this unexpected adventure, secretly pleased that things weren't going according to Montel's hidden agenda. But this was small of me. Montel was only following orders. Who was I going to complain to, anyhow? "Maybe this will be exciting," I thought. I could visit Australia, then go to cadet school when I returned. I tried to put it all out of my mind.

"It's gonna be a while before you get back, Ralph," said Stuart, who seemed to be reading my thoughts.

"I know, Kid," I said. "A couple months ain't gonna kill me."

A uniformed soldier stopped us at a large gate, asking for identification. Our Brazilian officer spoke to the guard, gaining us entry, and then a man appeared from one of the larger buildings to greet us.

"Gentlemen, come into the hall. Come. Your bags will be brought in for you," he said.

Our host was the administrator of Belém University. He explained that an English-speaking family residing on the university grounds would pick up each crew member. When Captain Montel flashed those government documents, people sure moved in a hurry.

The crew was told that wealthy families who supported higher learning had established this university just two years earlier. I was amazed by the architecture. The entire area was surrounded by high stone walls and had more than a hundred security guards on duty.

After dinner on the campus, a Dutch husband and wife, Mr. and Mrs. Van Amsterheld, picked me up and took me to their home, which was a glorious stone structure with a large swimming pool. As I entered the front doorway, their daughter, Jhannella, was winding down the circular staircase. Golden-blond hair and blue eyes, Jhannella was a vision. Even her name was seductive. I stopped.

"Welcome," she said, coming toward me.

Jhannella was twenty-one and spoke perfect English, like her parents. I politely thanked them all. Jhannella's father, John, then showed me to my room.

As I followed him upstairs, I glanced back at Jhannella, and she smiled. She had a tiny sparkle in her eye. I smiled back.

The following morning at the airport, our orders were to get the cowling out of the hangar and put it back on the engine; however, the cowling never contracted, meaning that it was useless, and we could not fly without it.

Captain Montel immediately called Tampa and discovered that it would be another seventy-two hours before a new cowling could be shipped. The Army Air Corps maintenance center had to make four new cowlings with the exact specifications and serial numbers. All four engines had to be calibrated, or our B-17 wouldn't fly properly. This was an uncommon breakdown.

Lieutenant Frerry was angry because this delay would push back all our future stops. But Captain Montel seemed unfazed; he ordered us to pull *Dolly*, which is what we called our B-17, into the shade to cover her up.

Meanwhile, Lieutenant Frerry contacted Washington, D.C., with a coded message about our plight.

"He's certainly upset," said Stuart, referring to Frerry. "Let's get a couple beers and cool him off."

Stuart had a kind way about him. He was both observant and a good listener. "Is there anything I can do to help, Lieutenant?" Stuart asked.

Frerry finally smiled, disarmed by Stuart's gesture. "Son, we're all in the same boat, but thank you for asking," he said.

Stuart returned with several beers, determined to make the best out of this situation. "Do you have nice quarters where you're staying, Ralph?"

"Just lovely."

"What the hell are lovely quarters, Ralph?"

"Well, they have a daughter," I said. "And she is a beauty."

"Oh, God, Ralph—keep that thing in your pants or all hell will break loose."

"Stuart, you should know me better than that," I said. "Of course, I will be a gentleman and watch my manners."

Stuart laughed.

Four beers later, Lieutenant Frerry had calmed down. He asked Kroll and Mann if there was some way to resize the cowling. Kroll and Mann played with all four cowlings, trying and retrying each one on each engine every which way, but they had no success. Both men were frustrated and embarrassed.

Knowing we had to remain in Belém for three days, Captain Montel quickly worked out an arrangement with our Brazilian friends. The same families who were our hosts the night before were laughing when we returned with our luggage. My khakis were dirty from handling the greasy cowling, and I was afraid to sit on the furniture. Jhannella, meanwhile, went into the kitchen and came back with a warm, wet towel. As she bent down to remove the grease from my face, I saw that her blouse was open.

"Doesn't that feel better?" she said.

I nodded. It sure did.

"Ralph, you had better keep your distance from this one," I thought.

Jhannella then escorted me upstairs, and I took a shower. When I stepped out of the tub, there was a Turkish bathrobe on the back of the door waiting for me. I put it on and felt like a king. Jhannella knocked on the door and entered with my luggage before I could answer it.

I nodded and thanked her. All I seemed to do around her now was nod. I was under her spell.

That night after dinner, Jhannella wanted to show me the university grounds. During our walk, she mentioned that her father was a sales executive for Shell Oil. He handled shipments of rubber around the world for the company. Belém, she told me, was the largest rubber port in South America.

"Your dad must be a very intelligent man to hold such a position," I said.

Jhannella surprised me with a kiss on the cheek. She sure was brazen. I made no advances, but I didn't stop her, either. I was enjoying the spider and the fly.

The following morning, Jhannella woke me at 0700 hours with a message from Captain Montel to report to breakfast wearing fatigues and a hat.

The captain informed the entire crew that he wanted us to clean and inspect the entire aircraft. Suspicious of sabotage, Montel told us to check every wire, including the inside pumps on the fuel lines. This was tedious and agonizing work because of the intense heat, and after three hours, we sought refuge in the hangar, throwing cold towels around our heads and necks. We dozed for the rest of the day.

I soon discovered why most of the population in South America slept during the day: it was just too damn hot to move around or work. Even the university shut down its classes after one o'clock in the afternoon.

"You crazy Americans try to beat the heat, and that's impossible," Jhannella said when she picked me up in her car. "Did you get some rest this afternoon?"

"Yes," I told her, sensing her accent for the first time.

"Good," she said as she patted my knee. "Because after you finish supper, we are going to go dancing tonight."

"How many languages do you speak, Jhannella?" I asked, welcoming her touch.

"I speak Dutch, English, Spanish, and Portuguese."

"You are a very bright girl, just like your father," I said.

Jhannella suddenly stopped the car and put her arms around me. She kissed me on the lips.

"What was that spontaneous emotion all about?"

Jhannella released me and then said, "You were sent to me only for a very short time to enjoy myself, Ralph. We will have lots of fun tonight. I promise you."

The spider caught the fly.

At dinner with the crew that evening, Captain Montel informed us that we would meet again tomorrow at 0600 hours to continue inspecting the aircraft. There wasn't much conversation at the table except for the impending cowling delivery, until Stuart spoke up: "Well, I assume the one person who is having a great time is our radio operator."

I looked around the table, a bit embarrassed by the attention, and said, "Stuart, I think you're jealous, but believe me, there is nothing going on."

"It's the luck of the Irish," Captain Montel quipped.

Everyone at the table burst out laughing, knowing I was Jewish.

The nightclub wasn't far from the university, and the owner knew Jhannella and sent regards to her parents. In a room littered with college students, Jhannella made quite an impression strolling in with an American soldier on her arm, and she soaked up the attention. We sat at a quiet table in the corner. I ordered some drinks and then asked Jhannella to dance.

The band was playing a samba, and at first I had a little difficulty getting into the rhythm. The Brazilians smooth out their steps and make their turns much closer together than Americans do, which makes for constant body contact.

"You've never danced the real samba like we do here, have you?" asked Jhannella, who was now a whirlwind.

"This is the closest thing to sex with clothes on," I said.

Jhannella laughed. Our bodies now were glued together; we never missed a step. Intoxicated by the rhythms, I lost myself in the music. Perhaps this was the new adventure I was looking for. Rather than being the traveling musician, I was now the traveling radio operator, bopping from one foreign town to the next. Dancing, romancing my way, on a secret mission to Australia.

Just then the band kicked into a rumba, and Jhannella pulled me even closer to her. I could feel every crease, every curve of her body. I looked around discreetly—there was a sea of bodies moving as one.

Hours later, the heat, booze, and dancing still didn't seem to affect Jhannella. "Let's go," she said, shouting over the crowd. "You have to get up early in the morning."

I wanted to pay the bill, but Jhannella signed a tab and gave it back to the waiter.

"We have an account at this club. We don't pay cash," she said.

I smiled at her. "Ralph, marry this girl. Right now," I told myself. "Do it."

When we returned home, Jhannella's parents had retired for the night. We went into the den, sat down on the couch, turned off the lights, and started giggling like kids.

"Let's go upstairs," Jhannella whispered.

We tiptoed into my room. With the rum running through my veins and this goddess in my hands, I became an animal. And she enjoyed it more as I became more physical. Jhannella wasn't interested in ordinary sex. I could tell by the way she sounded, by the way she let me handle her. "This could be the last time I ever have sex," I thought. Our plane would soon be flying over the ocean to Natal. We could land in the drink. This could be my last fuck. "I'm going out with a bang," I thought.

The thought of Jhannella's parents just a few rooms down the hall did nothing but heighten this passion. The wild sex I had had with those burlesque girls was working on me, and now I was working on Jhannella. I made it last as long as I could. We made love on the floor and on the couch and then finished each other off on the bed. Spent, we lay in each other's arms, kissing.

After this amazing session, I asked Jhannella if she had used any safeguards.

"Of course, silly," she said, as she popped up beside me. "I use a soft rubber ring. All the girls at the university are fitted with them if they want to be safe."

"If I lived here, I would marry you in a minute," I said.

It wasn't hard to get these words out of my mouth. It was a lie, but she was so beautiful.

Jhannella smiled. "I'll wake you up in the morning. I had a wonderful time," she whispered as she pulled on her robe and disappeared.

I rolled over and pulled the pillow under my arm, my mind jogging now. After playing with both Juanita and Jhannella, I had no guilt. I had made love to both of them, but I was in love with Lynda. I knew this. I knew the difference. Like many men I had met during my band years, I was able to put the woman I loved into a neat compartment while I enjoyed a fresh moment with another lover. Making love was like making music. It was discovery. Self-expression. Jazz.

The next day at the university dining hall, Captain Montel informed us that he had received a coded message for us to be packed and ready to fly the next day. The delivery would arrive in the morning. I looked over at Stuart, and he smirked.

When we returned home, I thanked Jhannella's parents for their hospitality. Captain Montel had already informed the crew that the U.S. government would be reimbursing the Van Amsterhelds as well as the other hosts.

I went upstairs and started to pack. I showered again—my third of the day—then flicked off the lights and went to bed. When I turned over, I found Jhannella lying beside me.

"What are you doing?" I said softly. "Are you crazy?"

"Darling," she said, "I have a feeling that tomorrow is the last I will ever see of you. I couldn't sleep until I had you in my arms."

"We got away with it last night, but this is really taking chances."

She took off her robe, and my balking ceased. My hands started to move over her body, softly touching her breasts, then her hips. But tears were now rolling down Jhannella's face.

"Why are you crying?" I whispered.

"My heart is crying," she said.

I wiped away her tears. "I'll be seeing you in my dreams," I told her.

As we kissed, I squeezed my eyes shut, trying never to forget the moment.

✫ 11 ✫

"Taking a Chance on Love"

January 1942

THE CREW WAS ALREADY IN THE STATION WAGON WAITING FOR ME WHEN I arrived at the university. When I got into the car, Stuart noticed my khaki shirt.

"Someone's been crying on your shoulder," Stuart grinned.

I wanted to punch him, but Captain Montel was standing beside me.

"Good morning, Sergeant," he said, letting me know he didn't appreciate my tardiness.

"Good morning, Captain," I replied.

Stuart suppressed a laugh.

As we arrived at the airport, a DC-3 landed, and two pilots and two aircraft engineers got out. The four men had flown all night, carrying the four new cowlings. Kroll and Mann assisted the aircraft engineers, and within an hour we were ready for takeoff. While our tanks were being filled, Miller and I sat down on the steel rib and went over my codebooks for Africa, checking locations and time periods. One mechanical breakdown had cost us four days, and we knew we had to make up that time quickly.

Four hundred miles southeast of Belém, we landed on a dusty runway and taxied to a large fuel storage container. Our bomb bays and side tanks were refilled to the brim, while water, food, and compact rubber rafts were stacked in the rear. The crew found a small, tin hut where a table was set up with chicken and beef sandwiches. Three black girls, no older than fourteen, served us. They couldn't speak English, so we pointed when we wanted more bananas or melons. The girls were dressed in short skirts, thin blouses, and open sandals. They watched us curiously, while two elderly women sitting nearby watched them. I bagged up some nuts and raisins, and we boarded the plane.

When I looked out my window, there was only water below. We were still at a low altitude and climbing very slowly. Captain Montel ordered radio silence, so I decided to take an afternoon nap in my chair with my headphones on.

Sex was open and natural in South America, I thought, and I liked that. It wasn't considered bad; you didn't feel like you were stealing something. I dozed off.

Stuart woke me up a few hours later. "Are you going to sleep your way over this ocean or what? I'm getting bored talking to myself," he said.

"Stuart, why don't you get a book and read for a while?"

"Tell me all about Jhannella," Stuart said, "She sure was a beautiful woman."

"Stuart, what do you really want to know? Do you really think I would talk to you about her?"

Jhannella was the best, I thought. When you cheat on your girl in the States, you come quickly; when you do it overseas, you make it last. We were so hot, sweating so much, it was like there was oil between our bodies.

Stuart frowned and swiveled away, then swiveled back again.

"Well, then tell me about your music career back in the States. Tell me about the bands."

Stuart asked about the music, but I knew he wanted to hear about the girls.

"All right," I sighed.

"You mean it?" asked Stuart, who looked more like a child before a bedtime story than a side gunner.

I nodded and began.

"I went on the road with Eddie Hamp and his band."

"Never heard of him," Stuart cut in.

"Stuart? Do you want to hear this story or not?"

"Sorry."

"All right then. When I—"

"Wait. What instrument did you play, Ralph?"

"Clarinet, sax, and flute."

"Multitalented. Sorry. Go 'head."

"All right. Okay, I got my first gig on the road after my part-time work in burlesque was drying up."

"Burlesque!" jumped in Stuart again. His eyes went wide. "Ralph, you never said before that you were in burlesque."

Stuart's innocence was charming. He swiveled his chair closer, as if he had a greater respect for me now.

"The majority of my gigs were fraternity and sorority dances, Stuart," I told him. "But when I was sixteen, I went on the road with a big band for the first time. Our first stop that summer was a two-week gig at Revere Beach, just outside of Boston. It was 1934 . . .

. . . *We stayed at the Cosmopolitan Hotel, a joint that catered to show people. When we checked in, we learned we were the only men in the place. Apparently, the burlesque companies had booked the other rooms. My brain was doing flips, remembering my burlesque days, and Eddie Hamp knew that all the guys in the band were having similar thoughts.*

"You fellas are here to work," he shouted. "And I'm going to put a leash on each one of you if I have to."

With more than three hundred rooms and only one bathroom at each end of the hallway, the Cosmopolitan was like Grand Central Station. Women were walking around, barely wearing flimsy see-through nightgowns. Harry and I stood in line in our bathrobes. Harry, who was my roommate, was our first trumpet player; he was around twenty-two then, and Harry had been on tour before.

"How long you girls gonna take?" Harry asked the two showgirls in front of us.

"Oh, we're just going in for showers," said the brunette. "My name is Stella, and this is my girlfriend, Karen."

"I hope you two don't fall in love in there," said Harry, flashing a smile. "My name is Harry, and this is my kid brother, Ralph." We all shook hands, and by the end of the afternoon, everyone was chummy. Because of this bathroom mayhem, though, most of the guys dressed on the bus. If a guy was trying to put on his pants and the bus turned a corner, he would usually fall on top of someone else. Shirt studs sprayed all over the floor. It was all ass and elbows, arms sprawling, mass confusion. Once at the stage, Eddie Hamp told the porters how to set up the sound equipment, and we found our instruments in a pile.

"All right," shouted Eddie into the microphone when he was ready to roll. "You know why we're here, so let's dance."

The couples were smiling, really jumping to our sound, and they gave us a rousing ovation.

After that first gig, I was excited, and Eddie Hamp told us about a great restaurant that was open all night. The place was packed with showgirls, but we were escorted to a separate room away from the ladies, per Eddie's orders. I chowed on eggs straight-up, with toast and bacon. I was a kid surrounded by show people, and I soon learned that they lived in a different world, by a different clock, by a different set of rules. Harry and I stopped to pay our bill, and we noticed Stella and Karen were standing in line ahead of us again.

"How long you girls gonna take?" joked Harry. Stella and Karen turned around and laughed. Harry winked at me, and we walked the girls back to the hotel.

When we came into the well-lit lobby, I got a good look at Karen for the first time: she was an exquisite strawberry blonde. "You are the most beautiful woman I have ever met," I said truthfully.

"You're not so bad yourself," she replied.

The next day, Harry told me we had a problem: Karen and Stella were room-mates, too.

"Could you talk with Karen and stay with her tomorrow night?"

"Harry," I said, "I just met Karen."

"Ralph," Harry said impatiently. "Don't you realize you're in show business? This happens all the time."

Karen and I had breakfast together the following morning, and then after some small talk, she said, "You know, Ralph, Stella and Harry would like to get together in your room. Would you mind sleeping with me in our room tonight?"

I almost choked on my coffee.

"Sure. Why not?" I said. Harry wasn't kidding.

Karen told me she had a boyfriend in New York, but they had just broken up. I didn't care about her past, though; she was all I wanted now. Karen had the most graceful body, and when she walked across the room, she moved like a panther. It wasn't long before we were in love.

Karen and I experimented with sex all fourteen nights together, then discussed it later, which was even more enjoyable. All the men in the band knew about us, but they never said a word to Eddie Hamp. It was a musician's code not to rat on your buddy. Ed wasn't a monk, either, I heard.

The last evening Karen and I had together we stayed up all night loving each other. It was like we were on a honeymoon. The band bus shoved off the next morning for Old Orchard Beach, Maine. I was very withdrawn and fell asleep. Harry woke me up a few hours later.

"How are you feeling now, Kid?"

"I didn't get much sleep last night," I said.

Harry shook his head.

"Ralph, you shouldn't get so involved on the road," Harry advised. "You don't fall in love with these girls. You have a good time. You tell 'em you're in love. You lie, and you enjoy yourself. Because if you don't get enough sleep, it's impossible to function. You'll die a very young man."

I figured Harry was right, but I couldn't shake my feelings for Karen. My fatigue was worth every minute I had spent with her. I fell back asleep, loving the thought of being in love.

Just then, I stopped and looked over at Stuart; he was hanging on every word.

"You really were in love with her then, huh, Ralph?" Stuart said.

I nodded. I was.

"Stuart, I'm so dry. Please get me my canteen, will ya?" I asked.

As Stuart got up, Captain Montel's voice came over the intercom, informing us we would be experiencing high winds and perhaps a rainstorm. He then told us that we were going to stop in Freetown because we could not refuel anyplace else on the African coast.

Stuart turned around, suddenly looking at our wings, which had a tendency to flap like they were going to break off. "Ralph, we are over the Atlantic. If we get hard winds and rain, we got big problems."

"Are you afraid of dying, Stuart?"

"I never thought of dying on a plane without guns and no enemy around," Stuart confessed. "I don't like to think of dying in the ocean, but, yes, I'm always afraid of dying when I see those wings flapping up and down when the weather has taken over."

"Well, we might get thrown around and have a wet time of it. Maybe that's why we have this extra housing here—for support," I said, referring to the steel rib.

Stuart nodded.

From my codebooks, I knew Freetown, in what is now Sierra Leone, was three hundred miles south of a German Messerschmidt base. However, with this nasty weather, we were pretty certain that no German fighter planes would be flying, especially at night.

Shortly after the captain finished his transmission, the rain and wind came rushing at us as Montel expected. We buckled ourselves down while the plane was sliding all over the sky. The storm lasted about an hour, and as we came out of it, our number four engine started to stutter and smoke. It was wet. Hissing.

"Feather the prop. Feather the prop," I heard the captain repeat to Frerry over the intercom. During the rainstorm, water had leaked into one of the engines, creating electrical shorts. Frerry then had to feather the engines— turn the blades of the propeller toward the wind. This was a dangerous maneuver, and it scared the hell out of the crew because we still had some flying to do over the Atlantic.

Now flying on only three engines and with blackness all around us, I heard the captain trying to call the Freetown tower. No luck. After the fifth try, he made contact, and the crew heaved a sigh of relief, knowing we had been flying blind, relying solely on our navigator, Miller, who was up in the nose.

Freetown was in a complete blackout because of the storm, and the only light I saw came from the quarter moon and the burning oil drums that illuminated both sides of the dirt runway. A runner holding a flare guided us to the three-story tower.

Frerry gave us orders: no smoking and no talking to anyone once we deplaned. It was near midnight. As the local engineers used small flashlights to check the fueling, we were escorted into the hangar. There were no planes in Freetown, just two British officers who ran this operation. They approached us and shook our hands.

"That was a good show, fellows, bringing that ship in," said one of them. Captain Montel spoke to these officers about our number four engine, while Stuart and I found some cots on the other side of the hangar. We pulled the blankets over our clothes, escaping into a sound sleep.

It was 0500 when I noticed Lieutenant Frerry and Miller sleeping on two other cots near us. Captain Montel, Kroll, and Mann had worked through the night to fix number four: all four engines were now turning over in the foggy dawn.

After breakfast, I walked onto the dirt runway and noticed something odd in the morning light. The whole area was infested with large, red ants as far as the eye could see. They were crawling over ten-foot-high mounds. The place looked like it was under siege.

✷ 12 ✷

"Swinging on a Star"

January 1942

As we were flying across the belly of Africa, the captain informed
the crew that number four was singing, and we wouldn't have any more
problems with her. We were now headed to the city of Kano, located in the
Belgian Congo (now Nigeria).

Captain Montel put the plane on automatic pilot and had Frerry take
over once we reached ten thousand feet. Kroll and Mann headed to the back
of the plane, pulled out some blankets, and dozed off. Meanwhile, I told Stuart to take over my chair because I wanted to go down to talk to Miller.

I squeezed between the bomb bay tanks, passed the engineer's turret, and
opened the floor door behind the pilot's seats, and then I dropped down into
the nose of the plane. Miller, a little man, fortunately, was sitting in his tiny
cubicle, checking his instruments as he watched the scenery go by.

"Sir, you have the best seat in the house," I said. "What a panorama. You
have at least two hundred degrees to scan."

"And I need every degree of it when I shoot the stars at night," Miller
said, as he tapped his surveyor's gun, which he used to determine our location and arrival time by computing longitude and latitude.

"You must have had a hell of a time when we were in that rainstorm, trying to bring us back on course."

"Half the time I didn't know where we were. What were you worried
about? We were only flying sideways!" Miller laughed. "After the storm, the
visibility was pretty bad. We were flying by the seat of our pants. God must
be with us."

Miller's reference to God was odd, I thought. I hadn't met anyone reli-
gious in the service—or anyone who prayed, for that matter. God wasn't

something men talked about because we were trained to kill, and that didn't jive with religion.

"Carl, why do you think you were picked for this assignment?" I asked.

Miller paused and looked at me as if he knew something I didn't.

"I happened to be there," he said.

"What do you mean?"

"Someone was trying to get rid of me. Someone in D.C. who picked this crew. I found this out when they put the crew together."

Confused, I wasn't sure if I wanted to hear anymore. I changed the subject.

"What is our ETA for Kano?" I asked.

"If the airspeed, tailwind, and elevation remain the same, we should be over Kano at 1700 hours—if we're lucky."

I nodded, studied him some more, and decided to head back to my receiver.

My conversation with Miller left a sour taste in my mouth. Why the hell didn't someone tell me why I had been picked? Did someone want to get rid of me too?

As I climbed up the hatch, I noticed that Kroll and Mann were still sleeping. Stuart was half dozing in my chair, and he put his fingers to his lips for me to be quiet.

As Stuart moved over to his chair, I sat down, perplexed. I hadn't pissed anybody off at Camp Shelby or Langley Field—nobody I could remember, anyway. The whole thing was a mystery, some kind of riddle I couldn't figure out.

"So tell me more about Karen," Stuart whispered as he rubbed his hands together. Stuart's curiosity for my love life became a welcomed distraction.

"Karen?" I said.

"Yeah. What happened next?"

Now I swiveled my chair toward Stuart, my mind racing back. Stuart noticed the searching look on my face.

"Old Orchard Park, Maine," Stuart said.

"Old Orchard Beach," I corrected him. "Right. People were coming from all over. It was now July 1934 and . . .

. . . *the town was putting on a fireworks display. Tickets were sold out for the ballroom. Apparently, this was the first time a big band had come to Old Orchard Beach, and the city didn't have enough facilities for the influx of people. Folks were sleeping in their cars, in the movie house, or in the woods just to hear us play. Old Orchard Beach Pier was smaller than the piers in Atlantic City, but the entire place could hold about three hundred couples.*

There were plenty of nice, young women on the dance floor, but I was a little gun-shy, still holding onto my feelings for Karen. I just danced and talked with a few of the girls between sets, while the other fellows in the band were on the prowl, flirting, screwing anything that would sit still. Harry was off with another girl, laughing it up—another town, another woman. But I still couldn't stop thinking about Karen, even after we headed southwest for a gig in the Catskills.

Harry and I sent out our tuxes for cleaning and then grazed by the large swimming pool nearby. As the girls drifted by in their bathing suits, I looked up and realized I was in the middle of the mountains. Performing here was like a badge of honor, a dream come true for an entertainer.

By now I had memorized our playlist. I didn't know the names of the tunes: everything in our music book was done by numbers rather than titles. After a few gigs, the routine became so natural that I didn't even have to look at the book. Instead, I would study the shape of other women's legs, the bend in an elbow, the slope of a neck, as the women floated on the dance floor; my feelings for Karen soon started to disappear. She was out of my system. I moved on. And the band moved onto West Virginia, where we hit a place that I think was run by the—

I noticed Stuart wasn't listening anymore. He was asleep, perhaps dreaming of his Puerto Rican sweetheart. The look on Stuart's face reminded me of mine when I was on the bus with Harry. "You don't fall in love with these girls. You have a good time. You tell them you're in love. You lie, and you enjoy yourself," was indeed Harry's little nugget of wisdom. But why was it so hard for me to learn that lesson? I had shaken off the residue of Juanita after my morning cup of coffee in San Juan, but Jhannella wasn't so easily dismissed. And Lynda. What about her? I leaned back in my swivel chair, and as the engines throbbed on, I fell asleep.

It must have been 1600 hours when we hit a downdraft that shook everyone up. Fortunately, all of us were buckled down, and there was no damage. We must have dropped three hundred feet. Even though the weather was beautiful, a sudden downdraft could occur at any moment, and its force could toss onto the ceiling any man who wasn't strapped down. After Montel checked to see if we were safe, I heard him calling the Kano tower to put us on the homing device to guide us in. Our plane was far enough south not to be picked up by German planes.

As we landed on the dirt field, I noticed farms, thatched huts, oxen, and scores of animals in cages near the airstrip.

"Stay close to your quarters tonight, Gentlemen," said a Belgian officer who escorted us to a tiny shack, "because the animals stroll around at night looking for food."

Another officer then apologized for the black bread, rice, chicken, and cooked tomatoes that were served, stating that this was the best food that they could obtain in this part of Africa.

I looked down at my plate. "If the animals want this slop, they can have it," I said to Stuart.

"Also, carry a sidearm with you wherever you go," said the other Belgian officer in broken English. "Animals travel close because they smell food. Congo has lions, panthers, snakes—man-eaters. Even when you're going to the outhouse, carry your gun. And watch out for large rodents, because some will attack if they think they are in danger."

The crew looked at each other warily, and then Miller spoke up: "Let's get the hell out of this hole before the rats take over."

"I know the way you feel, Miller," said Captain Montel. "But one night is not going to kill you." Each of us packed a .45-caliber pistol on his hip, just to be safe.

While the others went to bed early, I wandered into the large, screened-in porch. It was pitch-black. Quiet. Then I heard a scream. A jackal? A wild dog? The others had gone to bed, but I knew they weren't sleeping. Miller's comment about why he had been selected still lingered in my head; so did Frerry's calling this mission a "trial run." "A trial run for what?" I wondered.

The more I thought, the more I became confused. Here we were in the heart of Africa. Were we hiding from someone? Perhaps the only place where a large plane like ours could land and refuel was a bald spot in the middle of the jungle like this. As my mind searched for answers, a symphony of screams punctuated the night. This wasn't sweet music. I was frightened.

✱ 13 ✱

"Strange Fruit"

January 1942

EVERYONE WAS HAPPY TO ESCAPE FROM KANO, AND WHEN WE TOOK OFF THE following morning, Montel opened the intercom so every man could hear him.

"Our next destination is the city of Khartoum, located on the banks of the White Nile. Khartoum is an English outpost. While we are there, each man will go through a light medical checkup and get a few shots. This will be our last English stop for a while. Drink plenty of that canned water, and snack on those dehydrated fruits. That's it for the time being. Rest as much as you can."

Stuart and I were using our binoculars for a while to observe the zebras and lions that were running from the sound of our engines.

"You look like a cow chewing its cud, Ralph," Stuart said when I starting to eat some of the dehydrated bananas, apricots, and peaches.

"You should eat some fruit, Stuart. You don't want to get sick."

Stuart imitated my chewing and made a mooing sound.

"You think you got a cold in your nose?" I asked Stuart.

"What?"

"A cold in your nose. The clap."

"Be quiet, Ralph."

I kidded Stuart some more about the prostitute he was still in love with, and he simmered down. He told me he had used a condom. I didn't with Juanita. They broke too often.

"I got it," Stuart said, suddenly swiveling around in his chair, now gesturing to the steel rib. "I know why they put that thing in here."

"Why?" I asked, drinking some water, which was rapidly expanding the fruit in my stomach.

"Flotation device. When we go down in the water, it'll float. That tail will float. That's why they reinforced the tail."

"Where do you come up with this shit, Stuart?" I said, mocking him. "Reinforce the tail! Shut up!"

My scolding silenced Stuart temporarily, but then he started swiveling in his chair again.

"Hey, Ralph."

"Hey, what, Stuart."

"Tell me about burlesque, will you?"

"You fell asleep last time I—"

"C'mon!"

"I'm full, Stuart."

"I'm bored, Ralph."

"I don't feel like talking now. I'm bloated."

Stuart made a face, pouting. I laughed at him.

"All right." I said, taking another swig of water.

I waited for Stuart to stop swiveling and then began. "Timing was everything in burlesque, Stuart. It was suggestive, risqué, and erotic. It was like going to school for sex. . . .

. . . *Occasionally, when a regular musician called in sick, I filled in at the burlesque houses in the orchestra pit. Our band was small—drums, piano, trombone, and clarinet. Most of the routines were focused on sex, especially the climax. The showgirls, who were raunchy and wild, were up on a stage, and we were down in the pit.*

"There's Pus-say Number 1 and there's Pus-say Number 2," we used to say when the girls would open their legs. They never wore anything underneath. This was my first real experience with women other than being around my mother and grandmother, and I'd never seen anything like this.

It only took about four or five nights before I got laid. The shows ran from one in the afternoon to one in the morning, and I used to work from seven to ten in the evening. Anyway, after a show one night, I decided to head backstage. I entered a large room where all the performers were walking around naked. These people were comfortable being nude, but they could tell I was nervous. Two of the showgirls, who were about eighteen, smiled at me, got up, and starting pulling me away.

"Come on, Honey," said one of them.

"Well, we might as well go in here," said the other.

We ended up in a small back room that had a bed. The girls tossed me on the mattress and jumped on either side of me. They giggled as they took off all my clothes, as if I was a toy to them. I never knew that there were so many ways to have sex. It was all so natural to them, like brushing your teeth. When they were finished polishing me off, I was completely exhausted, but I knew I had had fun, and I wanted to do it again. . . .

"Man," said Stuart. "How did you do it? What did you do? How did you hold them?"

"What do you mean?

"Did you know what you were doing, Ralph?" said Stuart finally.

"Well, it wasn't my first time, Stuart."

"Oh," sighed Stuart, wanting more details. "Who was your first then?"

I laughed again, and Stuart nodded. He had a wide-eyed grin on his face, as if he was expecting something juicy.

"Ruthie," I said. "When I was a freshman in high school, I met Ruth at my parents' store. My parents own a market, Stuart."

"Hmmh."

"Ruth was a small-town girl. A Rudy Vallee fan. Pink cheeks and light brown hair. Her parents were regulars at our market. I used to stock food and make change with the customers, and Ruth's mother liked me and told my mother that Ruth could only date me. . . .

    . . . *One hot summer night, Ruth and I were sitting on a swing on the play-ground near my home, and she said she wanted me to sit on her lap while we swung back and forth. It was a small swing, and there wasn't much room for the two of us. I sat down facing Ruth, with my legs thrown over hers. Everything was fine for a while. We were swinging happily and then something suddenly exploded. My pants were soggy. I jumped off Ruth's lap and ran home and changed my clothes. Ruth waited until I came back, and I told her what had happened, and she laughed and said that we should swing more often.*

    I also used to take my father's panel truck and head up to the hills with Ruth all the time to continue our adventures. She would come over on Sunday, too, when no one was home. One time my grandmother came in and caught us in the en-closed porch as we were having a "loving good time," as they say. . . .

Suddenly, I laughed uncontrollably out loud, amused at my own antics.

"And that's the story of my old cherry blossom," I said.

Stuart now looked as if he wanted to say something.

"She must have thought I was just a kid, Ralph, because I didn't know what to do," Stuart confessed, referring to his prostitute. "She did all the work."

"Yeah," I replied. "She put it in and took it out."

I laughed like hell, and Stuart cracked a smile. It was all still a mystery to him.

The captain then came over the intercom and told the crew to put on our fatigues and leather jackets over our khakis because we were starting to climb to a much higher altitude.

"Close the side windows, and be ready to use oxygen within the next thirty minutes," he said.

We were trying to avoid another rainstorm that was in front of us, and the captain thought he could fly over the top this time. It was becoming dark and slightly turbulent. We each had a steel oxygen container pressurized for two thousand pounds. This container was attached to a small rubber hose that had an ivory pipe mouthpiece. We inserted our mouthpieces to inhale the oxygen. If you forgot to use the mouthpiece, dizziness would follow and then perhaps death. We continued climbing until about twenty thousand feet, where the captain leveled off above the storm. The winds were now helping us, and it felt like we were flying at three hundred miles per hour. With the sun now shining above and below us, Captain Montel slowly, expertly, started to make his descent. We removed our mouthpieces as well as our flight jackets and fatigues, and all of us breathed a sigh of relief.

Kroll, Mann, Stuart, and I stopped at a buffet table in a mess hall after we were shown our quarters, while the officers were escorted upstairs to their dining room.

Kroll and Mann said that we all should consider ourselves lucky that the plane was holding up under these conditions. Stuart and I agreed with them, but we said little to the engineers. They had bonded like Stuart and I had: they were up in the front of the plane, and Stuart and I spent all our time together in the back. Kroll and Mann had different opinions of themselves. They thought they were in charge of the plane, not just along for the ride, like Stuart and me.

Stuart and I were radiomen and machine gunners, but since we didn't have any guns on the plane, there was little to do. Ninety-five percent of our time so far on this mission had been spent doing nothing but talking. I did very little sending or receiving. As the radio operator, I guess I was an insurance policy in case something went wrong.

As the four of us enjoyed the lamb stew, dehydrated fruit, and tea, Montel, Frerry, and Miller arrived and invited us to walk around the area.

"Captain, if it wasn't for your expertise handling that weak plane with a heavy load, I think we would have taken a swim in the South Atlantic," Stuart said.

Everyone laughed, and then Captain Montel changed the mood. "Let's stop the backslapping, Stuart. We still have a long way to go."

Montel didn't like his crew jabbering around him. He had been growing increasingly irritable since Belém, and everyone noticed it. He made calls to Washington, D.C., throughout the trip but never informed us of what was going on with the Japs. And since he ordered me to keep the radio off for most of the trip, the crew heard updates only from word-of-mouth rumors whenever we refueled. Strangely enough, Kroll and Mann didn't seem very curious about what was happening in the war in the Pacific. Because they had been in the service longer than I was, maybe they had learned to obey orders without asking questions. Stuart, meanwhile, was just a kid, more interested in sex than in strategic warfare. To calm my restless brain, I felt I needed to become more like the engineers or more like Stuart. I didn't know which.

The following morning after showers, the crew was led into a small, makeshift hospital.

"Gentlemen, take off your shirts and bare an arm," ordered an English doctor. "You will receive shots for typhoid and cholera. You may experience some discomfort for twenty-four hours, and this may shake a few of you."

"My men have taken many shots in the States," said Captain Montel. "They can take it without fear, Doctor."

We had taken vaccination shots before we left Tampa. It was policy to receive shots before leaving the shore.

The English doctor lined us up in a row, then loaded up the hypodermic, which was a monster. Going right down the line, the doctor injected each man with the same needle.

Our next stop was Aden, Yemen, located on the Arabian Peninsula. It was one of our shorter flights, only two hours. We stopped to refuel even though our tanks were more than half full. I didn't understand this. "Don't think, Ralph," I told myself. "Just obey orders. It's easier that way."

Our accommodations in Aden—seven flimsy cots and an outhouse—had the stench of a dead horse. While the crew was sitting around, nibbling on nuts, I noticed that Kroll looked a little peaked and so did Mann. I touched my forehead and discovered that I was running a slight temperature. Then I couldn't keep my eyes open. I went to bed early.

The following morning, the entire crew felt groggy and weak. Hot showers provided no relief. After we taxied down the runway, the captain opened the intercom.

"I know everyone feels like hell this morning, but as soon as we gain some altitude, we may feel better. We are headed for Karachi, India, and will be flying northeast along the coast of Arabia." Then the intercom went silent.

Moments later, I caught a whiff of something foul coming from the front cabin. Suddenly, Mann came running into our area and vomited into a bag. He quickly tossed the bag out the window and then turned toward Stuart and me. His face was ash gray. Mann dropped to the floor, clutching his stomach. "Get me a wet rag!" he screamed.

Stuart jumped from his chair, and I realized that the smell was getting worse. My insides, meanwhile, were moving like a merry-go-round. I reached for a bag close by but never got it. I spewed everywhere. It erupted from my mouth like a volcano. I tried to jam my head out the window, which was a big mistake. My vomit boomeranged, covering my face and clothes with lamb stew. Burning with fever, my eyes felt like they were ready to pop out of my head. I became dizzy and then collapsed, clinging to the steel rib for dear life. I passed out.

I felt a cold rag against my face when I finally came to. Stuart was kneeling beside me, cleaning off my face.

"Thank you," I said, barely able to speak.

"Everyone's sick except me and Lieutenant Frerry," Stuart said. "He has the plane on automatic pilot, and Miller is trying his best, but he's running a high fever."

Just then, Captain Montel appeared. He looked worse than Mann did.

"I'm sorry, fellows," he gasped. "But we needed those heavy shots in Khartoum to stay on schedule."

From Montel's shaky confession, I gleaned that he had been warned of the consequences of taking all our vaccination shots in one dose, but he disregarded it. He wanted to press on.

But now the captain looked like he was about to tumble. Stuart quickly got up and escorted him back to the front cabin. Meanwhile, I leaned back in my chair, dying. "They've given us poison," I said to myself. "That English doctor was a spy." Delusional, I passed out again.

Hours later, I awoke with my head on my radio table. My back and shoulders were frozen together. I could hardly move.

Stuart was nursing all of us with wet towels while scrubbing the plane, which reeked terribly. Stuart helped me onto the floor to make me more comfortable. I didn't have the breath to thank him. I was out.

The stench of vomit woke me up, and I tried to focus my eyes.

"The way you were sleeping, Ralph, I thought you were gone for good. You look a little better," Stuart said.

"It stinks in here."

"I know," said Stuart. "The captain and the others are still running a fever, but they can operate."

"We were lucky you didn't get sick. Thank you," I said.

"Don't mention it. You'd have done the same for me, right, Ralph?"

Stuart smiled with that boyish grin of his. I smiled back and crept to my chair, still queasy.

We hit the ground with a thump, and Captain Montel discovered that the tiny runway was going to be a tight fit. Montel didn't land on the first approach, and his second was much lower. Rattling in my seat, I thought the plane felt out of control. The runway was coming up fast. Finally, the plane stopped, and then I heard screaming: "Get me the hell out of here! Get me the hell out of here!"

It was Miller. All of us unbuckled our belts and raced up front. The view startled all of us. The nose of the plane jutted out over a deep canyon. Miller was looking down at a four-hundred-foot drop.

Kroll slipped down into Miller's cabin and brought up the navigator, who looked like he'd seen a ghost.

"I thought I was floating on air," Miller said.

"I was praying the last hundred yards," Frerry kicked in.

"We all were," said Stuart, who looked peculiarly fresh.

Miller finally settled down, and Stuart and I went back to our cabin. As we opened the windows to ventilate the aircraft, we noticed that Sikh soldiers were surrounding the plane. The British officers in charge then ordered our crew to open the door. Captain Montel obliged, and one British officer stepped onto the plane, only to turn around in a flash and race out, covering his nose.

"Those blokes are all sick, and they look like they are dying," said the officer, who was now coughing. "Call the wagon and have them quarantined."

Another British officer commanded the Sikh soldiers in a foreign tongue, and they promptly put bayonets on the ends of their rifles.

Meanwhile, Captain Montel gathered his strength and tried to explain to the British officer what had occurred. Thinking fast, Montel returned to the pilot's cabin and informed the tower, but he was told to remain on the plane until a doctor arrived.

With the sun beaming down, caking the vomit to the fuselage, I leaned back in my chair, exhausted and delirious. I was going to die now. I was sure of it. Then a hand touched mine and squeezed it. It was Stuart.

Medical personnel rushed on board, dressed in white masks and white gloves, and told us to remove all our clothes. We changed into hospital garb and were transported to a hospital, where we were escorted to a stall of showers and provided with lye.

"These bastards are trying to kill us," Stuart said. "I'm on fire, and the rest of you look like you're being baked."

Two medical attendants arrived with bottles of body cream, which softened the sting of the soap. All seven of us were a comical sight, naked, scrubbing wildly, looking like overgrown red beets.

"Now they're putting the grease on us so we'll be brown like a turkey," continued Stuart.

"Enough of your dialogue, Stuart," ordered Captain Montel.

We were told that our bodies would absorb the cream and our skin would soon return to normal. After the doctors checked our blood and took our temperatures, dinner was served at our bedsides. Lights were dimmed early, with two armed Sikh soldiers stationed at each end of the ward.

"It was a miracle how the captain stopped that plane today," whispered Frerry. "You fellows should all thank God that your lives were saved today, especially, you, Rentz. He prays directly to the Boss; he doesn't go through the Son."

We all laughed until a British officer came in and told us to keep quiet.

The next morning, two Sikh soldiers brought in our clothes, which had been washed and pressed. Captain Montel obtained the manpower to wash and disinfect our plane, but our main order of business was to figure out how to move our plane away from the edge of the cliff. Since *Dolly* did not have enough room to turn on the edge of the cliff, she had to be backed up at least fifty yards, and turning on her engines at this point might vibrate the earth and prove disastrous.

"What the hell are we gonna do now, Captain?" asked Lieutenant Frerry.

For once, Montel looked stumped.

"Not a problem, Lieutenant," answered a British officer.

"Not a problem?" Montel shouted incredulously. "How are you going to turn a plane of that size around off the end of a cliff?"

"We'll call Betsy," the British officer replied.

Less than fifteen minutes later, as if by magic, a tiny brown man appeared, sitting atop a trotting elephant.

"Here she comes now," said the British officer.

"What the hell is this?" said Kroll.

As Betsy got closer, I noticed that she had layers of flat rope and a harness on her back. The little brown man dropped the flat rope to the ground, and the British officer ordered his men to tie the rope to both wings of the plane and then to pull the flat rope back to the tail, where a steel ring was attached. Another rope was tied to the steel ring, with the other end attached to Betsy's harness.

The little brown man patted Betsy's head and then whispered into her ear. The elephant seemed to understand every word. Once workers made sure that both ropes were fastened securely, Betsy slowly tugged *Dolly* to freedom. After fifty yards, the tiny brown man stopped Betsy and climbed on top of her, clapping his hands and kissing the elephant on the forehead.

Still amazed, Captain Montel spoke up. "Gentlemen, you have just witnessed a miracle of strength and brains from an elephant. We need some of those brains down in Washington."

✵ 14 ✵

"We'll Meet Again"

February 1942

AFTER WE REFUELED, CAPTAIN MONTEL INFORMED US THAT WE WERE NOW headed down to Ceylon (now known as Sri Lanka), an island off the tip of India, for a few days of R and R in a city named Colombo.

"Gentlemen, I'm sure you noticed that the British kept their distance from us because communicable diseases run rampant in India," said Captain Montel over the intercom. "No bother. Take it easy. Keep your eyes open and survey the skies."

Kroll and Mann had small air pumps to take the hot air out and bring the cold air in, but they had no windows. Stuart and I had windows but no pumps. After obeying the captain for a bit, I put down my binoculars. Stuart seemed to be studying something out there, though, and I studied him. Tired from doing all the talking on these long treks, I decided to ask Stuart a few questions about himself. He wasn't much of a talker, but he did tell me that he had played basketball in high school.

Just nineteen, Stuart didn't know what he wanted to do after he got out of the service—maybe go to business school and then join his father's business. No matter—from the way Stuart spoke, it was clear that his old man was proud of him, and I envied that.

After Colombo, we flew over the lower part of the Bay of Bengal to Batavia, Java (now Jakarta, Indonesia). This flight was one of the longest of the mission. We were overloaded with fuel, but fortunately, we had no hills or mountains to climb.

Flying along the southern coast of Sumatra, Captain Montel again ordered Stuart and me to use our binoculars to spot any foreign aircraft. He also told Kroll and Mann to peer out of the top turret to keep a watch of the rear.

"I wonder what the captain knows that he is not telling us," I said to Stuart. "Something is sure bothering him."

"We're getting closer to Burma," Stuart said. "Closer to the Japs."

In Colombo, we heard from the Brits that the Japs were moving south and building airfields for their supplies.

"I wonder if the Japs are planning on going all the way to Australia."

Stuart didn't respond.

Curious, I contacted Lieutenant Frerry, requesting permission to turn on my receiver to pick up any news pertaining to the Japs advances into Burma.

"Negative," said Lieutenant Frerry. "Survey your side of the skies, Sergeant."

As I obeyed Frerry's orders, looking out at the clouds, I started thinking about the red ants in Freetown, the screaming animals in Kano, the oxen shit in the filthy streets of Colombo: the deeper we went into this mission, the more ominous it felt. Stuart and I did not talk during this flight. Reminiscing no longer seemed appropriate. We were becoming less chatty, more vigilant.

From the air, Batavia seemed to be a large city. It was a major trading port in the Dutch East Indies, crowded with merchant marine ships of all kinds.

Before our wheels hit the ground, Captain Montel insisted again that no one ask or answer any questions concerning the war.

That evening, our Dutch host, Captain Heller, took us to a restaurant in Batavia where we had marathon meal in which rice was served with all seven courses. I had never eaten so much rice at one sitting in my life. By the time I put down my fork, I was ready to be carried to the truck.

I didn't sleep well because of indigestion, and Stuart was still awake. After the way he had tended to me when I was ill, I thought of Stuart differently now—probably like the way Harry thought of me.

"Why don't you take the cadet school exam when we get back, Stuart? You had some college, and believe me, the test is not too hard."

"You think so, Ralph?"

"Sure, Kid. Anybody can be a ninety-day wonder."

Stuart smiled that wide grin of his, then rolled over and went to sleep.

It was only a five-hundred-mile flight to Malang, a city in eastern Java, just outside the port of Surabaja. This was our last stop before Australia. As we continued to survey the skies, each man updated Captain Montel every fifteen minutes. We saw nothing.

When we reached Malang, however, we did see six B-17s on the airfield.

"Where in the hell did these planes come from, and how did they get here?" I heard the captain exclaim, still on the radio with the tower.

"Those planes escaped from the Philippines, Captain," replied the voice from the tower.

All of us had heard that the Japs were fighting in the Philippines and that they had taken most of the islands, but the sight of these six B-17s frightened me. It meant that many more American soldiers were now either dead or taken as prisoners of war by the Japs.

Colonel Eubank, who was an Army Air Corps commander in the Philippines, greeted Captain Montel when we landed. Eubank had retreated to Malang when the fighting got fierce. He was now in charge of the American troops on the island at an air base called Singosari. The Dutch, who had colonized Java, did not have an air force of their own; they had only a small army comprised of the local Javanese people.

While Colonel Eubank and Captain Montel met for lunch, I joined Stuart, Kroll, and Mann and took a Dutch army bus into town for some food. Our host, Captain Heller, told us that during peacetime, Malang had been a summer getaway for the Dutch.

The city was only two blocks long, crowded with whorehouses and restaurants, along with one dance hall. Most of the whores were dark-skinned Javanese girls, although a few were Eurasian. They were unkempt and uninviting, but I was amazed at how well they could dance the jitterbug.

The fellows and I decided to get a few drinks at an outside table rather than have a meal, but I found the atmosphere tense—like something was looming in the hills.

On the way back to the base, I noticed something strange; only three B-17s were now at the airfield. "Hey, let's track down Captain Montel and find out what is going on," I said to the others.

We headed to the mess hall, which was the only meeting hall at the base. Captain Montel, Lieutenant Frerry, and Miller were having drinks with some other American officers who had escaped from the Philippines. Frerry stopped me with his eyes, and I pulled Stuart and the others aside to a table.

Lieutenant Frerry looked uneasy, but Captain Montel looked worse, like he now had the weight of the world on his shoulders. I knew at that moment that I wanted to leave immediately for Australia.

Minutes later, Captain Montel sat down at our table.

"Gentlemen," he said, "The Japs have taken Singapore, and they're regrouping for Sumatra."

"Singapore? Fucking shit!" said Mann, who hadn't put more than two words together the whole trip.

"What does that mean for us, Captain?" asked Stuart.

"That means if Sumatra is invaded, Java is next—at this point in time—and it would be impossible to hold the yellow horde back," said Montel. "The Japs need Java for its oil reserves and rice. That would help their supply lines for invading Australia."

Kroll lit a cigarette and passed one to Mann.

Montel continued. "Colonel Eubank has received information by radio that it will be approximately two months or more before the Japs will have enough transports to carry an invasion into Sumatra and Java."

I pulled out my own pack of smokes now, and as I struck the match, all I thought was that it would be a long time before I reached cadet school.

Our flight time was scheduled for 0500 hours the next morning, an hour earlier than usual. Captain Montel, like the rest of the crew, wanted to get the hell out of Malang. By 0600 hours we were airborne for Darwin, Australia.

✳ 15 ✳

"Do Nothing till You Hear from Me"

February 1942

No one needed to be told to survey the skies on this flight. A rumor was circulating before we left Malang that the Japs had an aircraft carrier and other naval craft somewhere between Java and Australia.

For the first time since Ceylon, I had my radio receiver turned on, and I was rolling the dial to other frequencies, trying to hear anything. I got nothing but static.

"Ralph, if we make Darwin, we will be lucky," Stuart said. "A Jap fleet could blow us out of the sky or send Zeros to shoot us down. We have no guns to protect ourselves. I'm nervous as hell."

"Look at it this way, Stuart," I said. "If the Japs are hiding for another strike, they won't give up their position in the Coral Sea just to knock down a single plane."

Stuart nodded his head, but my theory didn't calm his nerves. Fortunately, we had no sightings, and this stressful flight ended when we reached Darwin safely that afternoon. The moment we landed, the entire crew was jumping around, hugging each other, and shouting, "We made it! We did it. We made it!"

"We're going on a fuckin' wild R and R," screamed Kroll. "What a relief."

The seven of us went to the officers' club and started celebrating. The beer flowed. All of us knew, according to our codebooks, that Brisbane was our final destination. We also knew we were heading there the following morning. Still, we didn't know the purpose of this secret mission, but at this point, we didn't care. We had been flying nearly every day for three weeks, and the stress had caught up with us. All of us, especially after escaping Malang, were looking forward to a long R and R.

The following morning, however, as we were in the showers getting dressed, Captain Montel received a coded message marked *urgent*. Montel called the crew together, then clenched his teeth. He read the message again to himself before he shared it with us. I thought he had tears in his eyes.

"That son of a bitch Eubank is putting us in harm's way," said the captain.

The crew couldn't believe Montel's outburst.

"Gentlemen," Montel continued, "Colonel Eubank has told Washington, D.C., that an extra B-17 would be a useful deterrent to an impending invasion of Java. The colonel has received authorization from Army Air Corps Intelligence for us to turn over our cargo to the Australian authorities here in Darwin instead of Brisbane. Gentlemen, we have gold inside that steel rib, and we have been ordered to hand it over to the Aussies and then fly back to Malang, Java, immediately."

"Gold?" said Stuart.

"What the hell are we doing with gold, Captain?" I asked.

Montel composed himself and then explained the details of our secret mission: "The Australian government wanted gold to convert directly into Australian pound notes to pay the growing number of American soldiers now being sent to Australia."

The captain further explained that with gold rather than American dollars, the U.S. soldiers would not have to pay an exchange rate. It was a prudent idea. Montel also mentioned that the Japs had recently torpedoed and destroyed two American ships carrying gold to Australia. Brigadier General Fleming and his staff orchestrated a deal to transfer the gold by plane. Ours was the first of seven planes scheduled to deliver gold, but since the Japs pushed south faster than expected, orders were given for the other six planes to abort their missions.

I could see that Montel was having second thoughts about following Eubank's order—we all were. I thought Captain Montel would go back to Malang now, if only to strangle Colonel Eubank. But Montel wouldn't disobey an order; he sent a coded message to confirm Colonel Eubank's order. Meanwhile, Kroll, Mann, Stuart, and I unscrewed the bolts to the steel rib, and several Aussie soldiers removed the gold bars from the plane.

That evening, we received a confirmation from D.C. of Colonel Eubank's orders. The captain called the crew together again and relayed the awful news. No one said a word. Our secret mission was over, and a new one was just beginning, one we had never expected and weren't prepared for.

* 16 *

"It's All in the Game"

February 1942

DISGUSTED AND TERRIFIED, I WONDERED WHAT LAY AHEAD IN MALANG. Certain death was my only answer. As I surveyed the skies, knowing *Dolly* was not equipped for bombing, let alone protecting herself, my mind retraced the steps of our mission, and it all seemed to make sense now. The rib. No guns onboard. The secrecy. The long, mysterious route east. We were delivery boys. It was that simple.

We returned to Malang that afternoon. As Lieutenant Frerry was exiting the side door, I heard him say to the captain, "I wonder what the colonel really wants us to do for him."

"I'm going to find out—if I can get an appointment," Montel replied.

Moments later, the entire crew stood at attention and saluted Colonel Eubank, who looked like he had been up all night.

"Gentleman, I know how unhappy you are, but I need your help," explained Eubank. "In the last forty-eight hours, my information has changed drastically. Japanese armies have invaded Sumatra. We didn't expect this invasion so soon, but the Japanese are moving troops and supplies by the hundreds down the coast of Sumatra via Chinese junks—convoys strung together like giant rafts. As I speak, we are bombing them with five-hundred-kilo Dutch bombs. The Zero fighters do not have a base close enough to give the ships cover, so we are destroying these Chinese junks and creating as much havoc as possible. If we can destroy enough of them, we may stop the Japanese invasion for a while. That is the reason I changed your orders and brought you back to help us."

Eubank could read the looks on our faces: we didn't give a shit what his problems were. Did he think he was going to be a hero by stopping a few Jap soldiers? This plan was insane. But Colonel Eubank wasn't finished.

"We will convert your plane back to a regular B-17, with twin .50-caliber machine guns in the rear," he said. "You will have forty-eight hours of rest before you take your first flight. That will give us time to refit your plane with guns and remove the bomb bay tanks. A ground crew has already started to work on it. You will obtain transportation to your quarters, and my adjutant can answer all your questions. Thank you for being so prompt. That's all, Gentlemen."

Our crew saluted and left the colonel's office.

When we settled into our quarters, it was time for supper, but our appetites were small. We picked at our rice.

"I guess this means we've lost our R and R in Australia, huh, Ralph?" said Stuart.

"I guess so," I said.

"Fuck all this rice," shouted Kroll, who now wanted to go over to the bar. The entire crew followed him.

"That bastard Eubank isn't going to throw us into the brig," said Kroll, quickly downing a shot and chasing it with a beer. "Let's go back to Darwin. Fuck this!"

No one argued with Kroll, but we couldn't go back to Australia now. Or could we? No, Eubank had seen to that—the bomb bay tanks had already been taken off our plane.

I looked over at Captain Montel, and he seemed especially depressed. The fact that his job now was to take orders from Colonel Eubank rather than D.C. rendered him almost invisible. However, Montel, like always, composed himself, ordering us to check our equipment and make sure our plane would be ready to fly by the appointed time. That night, we all got good and drunk.

The following morning, when I was speaking to the maintenance people, I saw the tail end of our plane being cut off to install two air-cooled .50-caliber machine guns. I knew then that some of us were going to get killed.

Rumor also had it that a new man was joining our crew, a tail gunner. We spoke to Captain Montel about the new man.

"It looks like the captain is the last to be given the news around here," said Montel, who still had liquor on his breath. "I'm just the man who flies the plane now."

I studied Montel's bloodshot eyes. I had never seen him like this before. The Renaissance man who once impressed me was now crawling into a bottle. Booze would keep his mind off our impending death.

Montel suggested that I review all the codes with a radio communications officer on the base. Radio codes were continually changed to avoid decoding; however, I had picked up most of the changes from our previous stop in Malang less than three days ago.

"I'll go over to see the colonel about our new crew member," said Montel, as we watched five B-17s take off into the sky. "I hope those poor guys get back," he said.

After I made the changes in my radio codebooks, I wandered off to the crew building, where Kroll, Mann, Stuart, Miller, and Frerry were sitting with one of the crews who had escaped from the Philippines. The navigator was talking, and everyone in our crew was listening intently.

" . . . it was a hell of an escape," the navigator said. "But we should have left before we did. We left at 0500 hours, just before the Zeros came in at dawn. By then, the place was on fire."

The navigator mentioned that his outfit had worked day and night for two days getting their six planes ready to escape the islands.

"We packed everything we could in those babies. Gasoline. Bomb bays. And all the men and parts we could carry. We were really flying heavy. The six planes here are the only B-17s left. We lost eighteen planes over there, all of them shot down by Zeros. The P-40 can't hold a candle to the Zeros. We were no match for them. We were sitting ducks."

Kroll and Mann looked grim, and I could see the wheels turning in Frerry's head. He was sensing that Eubank wasn't too bright.

"We thought we might stop in Java to refuel and then go on to Australia," continued the navigator, "but orders came through to go to Java and bomb the Chinese junks. We've been using the Dutch bombs to blow the shit out of those convoys. Just do as much damage as you can and get the hell out."

I looked at the men in the navigator's crew. All of them were smoking, staring straight ahead, like they'd seen hell. I nearly shit myself.

"It's going to be very rough around here if we stay too long," the navigator said. "We lost a lot of men in the Philippines, and I'm not looking forward to our next escapade. I'm scared to death that the colonel is going to overstay his visit on Java."

Shortly afterward, the navigator and his crew dispersed. Our crew hung around to discuss what we had heard, and Frerry mentioned he had heard stories of American soldiers parachuting and being machine-gunned down by the Zeros. This scared me even more.

That night, while the others were exchanging theories, I was no longer thinking "When do we get out of Java?" but rather "When do we get it?" I was certain Eubank was going to use us as gun fodder, and the thought of my impending death consumed me.

"Based on the movement of those Japs, I think we're going to get caught in the wringer," said Kroll.

"You can bet your ass we're gonna get plenty of action around here as soon as the Japs set up their airstrips," followed Miller. "I think we should run like hell as soon as we see the first Zero, but by then, I think it will be too late."

"Should we sabotage our own plane?" asked Mann.

The room went silent. No, we couldn't get off the island that way. With the bomb bay tanks removed from our plane, we wouldn't have enough fuel to make it to Australia anyway. We were all fucked, and we knew it.

As the others continued talking, I recalled my meeting with Montel in Tampa. Maybe if I hadn't shown Montel my letter of acceptance to cadet school, we wouldn't have been the first plane to go on this fucking mission. Maybe we would have been the second, third, or fifth plane.

Just then, Captain Montel showed up with Sergeant Mueller, our new tail gunner. The crew welcomed Mueller, who had been transferred from the gunnery maintenance section that flew out of the Philippines. He was a machine gun expert, a valuable man to have because he could fix a jammed .50-caliber machine gun within seconds.

The following morning, after the bombs were loaded into the bomb bay racks and the plane was fueled, our refitted B-17 was placed under an alcove of palm trees and covered with a green canvas. The crewmen then went back to quarters, showered, and sat around on our beds, not saying much but all thinking the same thing: "When do we die?"

"Ralph, have you ever had the shakes?" Stuart asked me. "Or an idea that you will be killed very shortly?"

I looked at him and tried to think of something that would calm us both. "Stuart, don't think about being hit. We're going to get out of here before things get too bloody."

I don't know if my words did Stuart any good, but they did make me feel better.

That evening, Captain Montel called our crew together along with the other four crews who were flying the next day. Most of the men were pacing, smoking, fidgeting. No one knew what to do with himself.

A fellow from another crew spoke up, "I wish that the colonel would say 'Let's get ready to fly to Australia,'" he said. "Because I need a vacation. This shit is getting to me. I'm going in for a section 8 after this trip." Everyone laughed, but the smell of fear soon returned.

Just then, Colonel Eubank entered with his adjutant, carrying a large map of the islands. Eubank proceeded to show us the mission for tomorrow: Palembang, Sumatra, was the first bombing target.

Our mission was simple: find the Chinese junks and blow them to bits. If Palembang was unoccupied, our planes would then split up, with three flying to the southern coast of Sumatra and the other two flying east along the northern coast of Java. Each plane was also instructed to jettison its bombs out at sea before landing back at the base. It was customary to unload unused bombs for safety reasons. If a bomb dislodged from its fuse on landing, a plane could explode.

"Good luck, Gentlemen," Colonel Eubank said when we finished, "and good hunting."

Our five planes took off at 0700 hours, flying in a V formation along the northern coast of Java. Flying at ten thousand feet, we reached Palembang and immediately spotted the convoy of Chinese junks just as Eubank had described. There must have been at least a hundred of these ships tied together, and they were sailing about five miles off the coast, turning toward the port.

Captain Montel, however, called our attention to the skies rather than junks. Watching for Zeros, we stayed by our guns. Moments later, our V formation broke up, and the bombing runs were ordered to be at six thousand feet. Our five planes formed a straight line. There wasn't a Zero in the sky when we dropped a portion of our bombs. We made direct hits on the front of the convoy, which quickly vanished under the flames. Hundreds of Jap soldiers leapt from these burning junks into the water, while others started shooting at our plane.

Montel leveled out, and we made another drop, but since we had passed our targets, I couldn't see anything.

"We got a complete hit!" Captain Montel shouted over the intercom.

All five planes had made direct hits and quickly lined up for the next run. More than half of the convoy remained. As we made our second run, I noticed that the water had changed from blue to red. And there was splashing.

"Fellows, that is what you call a feeding frenzy," exclaimed Montel. "These waters are the home of the great whites."

Montel sounded exuberant, but the notion of being eaten alive by a shark gave me the shock of my life. What if I dropped into that water? That was a little heavy to think about. Nevertheless, at least today, the Japs were dead and we were still alive. That was the score. Much credit went to Miller, whose bomb dropping was fabulous.

"Besides being a great navigator," I screamed to Miller over the intercom. "You have become a number one bombardier. The drinks are on me. You were fantastic!"

"The luck of the Irish," Miller responded.

I laughed like hell and turned off my transmission.

"Ralph, that was a piece of cake," said Stuart, now brimming with confidence. "I was scared to death when we took off, but I'm not afraid anymore."

I nodded and smiled at my partner. Stuart had forgotten all about the Zeros that might be giving those Chinese junks cover the next time we planned to bomb.

"Gentlemen, we are now headed back to base," said Captain Montel over the intercom. "But keep your eyes open because we might run into some angry Japs."

That evening over drinks, Colonel Eubank congratulated all the crews on our first run. Eubank thought our five planes had curtailed the advance of the Japs, and he now believed it would be weeks before the Japs would reach Java.

The next afternoon, several of the crews went into town and did some drinking.

"We have the greatest crew that I've ever flown with. This round is for the captain," said Kroll, who was half bombed himself by now. At twenty-seven, Kroll was an old-timer. He'd been in the service for ten years.

"Thank you, Kroll and the rest of you guys," said Montel, who now stood up. "Remember, don't let your guard down. Our time will come when the Zeros hit the skies. Every one of you will be very busy then."

"We'll take care of those mosquitoes, Captain," Stuart jumped in. "We have enough guns on board to blow them apart."

"Always keep that idea in your minds, Gentlemen," replied the captain. "Never forget we have superiority, and we will get through this war."

No one really wanted to talk about tomorrow; we had won today, and we cherished it. Perhaps we could head back to Australia sooner than I had thought possible.

The five aircrews and one maintenance crew met with Colonel Eubank later that evening to receive our new orders. Only three planes were going to fly the next day, while the other three crews were excused. Our crew was chosen to fly the same route in hopes of finishing off the remaining Chinese junks if we could find them.

That night I went to bed and dreamed about trying to outswim a shark that was chasing me.

"I can't sleep, Ralph," said Stuart, waking me. "Too much action today. How can you sleep, Ralph? I don't know how you put it out of your head."

"What do you have it in your head for, anyhow?" I said.

Stuart rolled over.

The next morning, we were in the air again at 0700 hours. Captain Montel was leading two wing planes heading northwest to Palembang. With my binoculars, I could see that the harbor was littered with floating bamboo—the remains of yesterday's bombings.

Just then, Montel opened the intercom when he spotted the Chinese junks in the harbor, unloading soldiers and supplies. There were more of them today.

"Gentleman, we're going to make low-level bomb runs so we will hit everything, then we'll strafe what's left. Let's let them have the whole dose."

In a flash, all three planes dropped half their loads on the defenseless ships, then quickly circled back to dump the rest. Belching smoke and spitting fire, the harbor looked like hell. This whole place would take months to rebuild, I thought, as I used my gun, strafing at will.

On our way back to the base, the captain explained that to prevent the Japs from taking Java, we would eventually destroy every operational port, harbor, and utility that the Japs could possibly use on their way south.

As Montel said this, I wondered what would happen if the Japs attacked our base. Before the war, Singosari air base had been a small Dutch air cadet training site. The original dirt runways now had to be expanded, and workers were building another runway. There were no ground lights, which meant there were no night landings. Also, there were no guns or antiaircraft equipment, which were absolutely vital in case of an enemy attack. The base didn't even have a machine gun nest around the perimeter. Singosari was for takeoffs and landings only. The more I thought of all this, the more I thought we should be in Australia. Even though we had killed some men during the past two days, I knew the Japs had thousands more to take their place.

When we landed at the base, the three crews were debriefed, and we went back to our quarters. That evening, there was another briefing on the next day's operations. Colonel Eubank was very pleased with the past two days' events, but he wanted to expand. We were now going to fly four hundred miles north, across the Java Sea, to Banjarmasin, located on the southern coast of Borneo.

Colonel Eubank wanted to know if the Japs had reached Banjarmasin and if there was an airstrip located nearby. For this assignment, only our crew was selected. The other crews were sent on other operations.

"Why us?" I asked Captain Montel. "Why are we the only plane going on this bombing mission? We will be all alone, and we won't know what is happening behind our backs."

The captain replied. "We have a good navigator and more experience flying from country to country than any of these other crews, Sergeant. The colonel thinks we are the best crew to handle it."

For a fleeting second, I thought about Charlie, then Captain Martin. Hell, I could be a chemical engineer right now. "Nothing wrong with being a chemical engineer," I thought. "Hell, no. Oh, Dad, what I am doing here? I'm not supposed to be here. Somebody made a big fucking mistake. I'm a musician. I'm a goddamn musician."

It would take us about three hours to reach Banjarmasin. Rather than flying directly into town, Eubank instructed us to circle around the city to the north and then fly south. At fifteen thousand feet, with oxygen tubes in our mouths and using our binoculars, we spotted bulldozers building an airstrip near several thatched huts. Montel explained that we would not bomb these sites because he didn't want to alert the Japs to the fact that we had spotted their airstrip. So we dumped our bombs into the ocean about twenty miles from the coast of Java and returned to the base.

Before being debriefed that evening, the crew sat around the mess hall, discussing the Japs' next move. Our triumphant mood, however, had changed considerably.

"We have to get the hell out of Java before we see the first Zero in the sky. It's only a matter of time," said the captain. Montel now thought the Japs were planning to set up small fighter bases on Sumatra, Borneo, the Celebes (Sulawesi), and the other surrounding small islands so that Zeros could take off and land closer to Java.

What really confused me, though, was that five thousand British airmen had recently landed in Batavia, seven hundred miles to the west of us, but these troops were waiting for fighter planes and equipment to arrive. Then, another thousand American soldiers from the cruiser *Houston* turned up, but they too had very little equipment on board. All these soldiers were now just sitting around in Batavia, playing cards, catching suntans, and drinking beer. They were waiting for their equipment, while we were sent on bombing missions.

Later that evening, our crew received orders from Colonel Eubank for the following morning. We were to fly to a small town named Tanjungpandan located on the southern tip of the Celebes to destroy more Chinese junks.

Stuart looked at me after the colonel left and said, "Are you second-guessing what Colonel Eubank is thinking concerning the Jap advance on Java?"

"It's not so hard to figure it out, Stuart. If we stay here too much longer, we are going to be caught in a trap."

That night everyone concocted a new theory about our predicament.

"We're running short of bombs," Miller said.

"Maybe if we run out, we'll have no choice but to leave this shit hole," added Kroll.

"Steal all the fucking bombs," Mann suggested.

"Yeah," Kroll continued, liking the idea. "Then we could leave for Darwin."

"Are you crazy?" said the new tail gunner. "How do we get the bombs out of the ammunition dump? And where are we gonna hide 'em?"

I finally jumped in. "Have all the pilots make a demand to the colonel that the next flight is the last," I said. "We have no ground troops to stop an invasion, and we're all gonna wind up dead."

My words hung in the air. No one wanted to respond. No one wanted to be a hero except that bastard Eubank. We all snubbed out our cigarettes. The meeting ended.

By 0700 hours we were flying over the Java Sea, heading for Tanjungpandan. We took the same route as the day before, flying around the town, then heading down into the city from the north.

"Ralph, look," said Stuart, calling me to his window. Just like in Borneo, the locals were constructing an airstrip and thatched huts. Flying a little lower than we had the last time, our crew could see the people on the ground waving at us.

"Little by little, they're closing the trap around Java," I said.

"When we get back to the base, let's find out what the range of a Zero fighter is," said Stuart.

"Good idea," I said, thinking that the two airstrips we had spotted were too far away for a Zero to fly without stopping for fuel. Then another thought came to me: perhaps these two airstrips were just refueling stations for flights to smaller islands closer to Java.

Later that night, the crew got together as usual.

"Those thatched huts aren't a mirage," said Kroll. "Those are bases that can be ready in a week. Those fucking Japs are setting us up, I tell you. We're gonna be fed to the sharks."

"No, we're not," cut in Montel. "We will be moved to Australia within a week."

Montel's words seemed very optimistic. According to the captain, Eubank had said that he was sending all of Montel's reports to Melbourne, where General MacArthur was headquartered. Montel learned from Eubank that it was MacArthur's idea to do enough damage here to give the troops in Australia enough time to gear up and protect themselves. The general wanted us to remain and fight in Java, then flee at the last possible moment.

Just then, Colonel Eubank's adjutant entered our quarters, and I could tell by his expression that it wasn't good news. He told us that Sumatra was now under Jap control, and the Japs were now bombing and strafing Batavia. The Chinese junks we had been pummeling had last been seen traveling down the Sunda Straits, near Batavia, our bombing target for tomorrow.

"How in the hell are we going to stop thousands of Japs that have already started to land in Java?" asked Miller, wild with anger, after the adjutant left. "The Zeros will be all over the place."

"The colonel didn't even have the nerve to give us the orders himself this time," I said. "This is a death sentence."

Later that night, none of us could sleep. Stuart leaned over and whispered to me, "I'm scared, Ralph. I'm really scared."

"This Colonel Eubank is the most stupid bastard I ever met," I said. "We should ask him to ride with us tomorrow morning. If we die, he dies. That's all I have to say."

"I'm going to go crazy tonight and go over and see the doctor," Stuart threatened.

Stuart never pulled this maneuver, but if he had, I might have headed over there with him. It wasn't a bad idea.

The following morning, we test fired the B-17s over the Java Sea before we headed toward Batavia. Later, at ten thousand feet, our crews suddenly spotted Zeros about twenty-five miles in front of us. Captain Montel gave orders to increase altitude to fifteen thousand feet.

The Zeros rushed at us and fired. We returned fire, but they zipped past us. Captain Montel continued toward our targets, and we spotted the Chinese junks, but they were all separated. There must have been five hundred ships. We unloaded, hitting approximately eighty of the ships before we ran out of ammunition. We could have bombed all day and never hit all of them. Several Zeros were now flying at eight thousand feet, and without hesitation, Montel consolidated our formation and led us back to the base.

"Those Zeros are not coming up to engage us," shouted the captain over the intercom. "And we are not going down there to be shot up. We will stay at fifteen thousand feet, because if they follow for too long, those Zeros will run out of fuel."

Captain Montel gave orders to the other planes to hold their altitude, anticipating that the Zeros would have to turn back after another hour or so. However, a pair of Zeros stayed on our tail. Finally, fifty miles outside of our airbase, those two pesky Zeros bent off and retreated.

Meanwhile, two of our five planes were suffering engine trouble, so we changed formation, allowing those two planes to land quickly somewhere in the hills. We didn't know whether they made it.

After we touched down, our crew was informed that those two B-17s had landed just southeast of Batavia near Bandung. That's all the information we could get. We asked if there was a place to land there, but we didn't get any answers.

"Those poor bastards must have caught it from the other Zeros, and the colonel's office won't tell us," Stuart said.

Later, Stuart and I wanted to ask Captain Montel if he had received any more information, but we saw him and Frerry head in for dinner that evening with drinks in their hands. Their faces were drawn. We didn't want to approach them.

The next morning, three B-17s headed again toward the Sunda Straits and Batavia with the intent of bombing the Chinese junks. Again, ours was the lead plane. However, there were fewer targets in the water today, and the junks were spread very far apart, making them even more difficult to hit from fifteen thousand feet. Consequently, Montel decided to head back to the base, hoping the Zeros wouldn't appear.

About seventy miles away from the base, both our wing planes began having engine trouble again, just like the day before. Captain Montel had to slow down, which created a continuous drop in altitude.

"Watch for Zeros at every level of flight," the captain said sternly.

I turned on my radio, searching for any frequency, listening intently for a Jap voice. Spinning and listening. Spinning and listening. I leaned forward. Concentrating. Clutching my headphones. Nothing.

Then as we reached about twenty miles from the base, "Bandits on our right at three o'clock," shouted Captain Montel. I shut down my radio and jumped to the open window. I slipped into my harness and pulled back on the loaded ammunition handle. With my feet in the slots and both hands on the gun, my .50-caliber was set to fire, I made sure my grip was tight, so the gun wouldn't run away from me and cut Mueller to pieces when I fired.

I turned my head and saw five Zeros coming in from Stuart's side. They were headed straight for us.

Stuart was ready for them when they fired. His tracer bullets smoked, burned, and curved right into their target. Boom!—a Zero dropped out of line.

"I got one!" Stuart shouted. "And I think it's a complete hit!"

"The other four aren't in my sights. I can't see them," I said.

We must have been flying at five thousand feet and dropping fast. The four remaining Zeros changed course and moved toward the rear, rendering Stuart and me useless.

Meanwhile, Kroll and Mann were firing from the top turret, and Mueller was lying flat on his stomach and firing the twin .50-caliber machine guns. Stuart and I were caught in the middle, helpless.

The wind and the chatter of machine guns were deafening, but I heard the captain over the intercom.

"We're going to fight these Jap bastards until both of our wing planes are on the ground," screamed Montel, who wanted to cover our wing planes so they could land first because of their engine trouble. "See how many of those dogs you can bring down before we approach the runway."

Stuart and I jumped back to our guns, and as Montel swerved to the left, I suddenly saw two Zeros. I fired. Then I heard an explosion behind me, which threw me onto my twin .50. When I lifted my head, I saw an arm hanging over the barrel of my gun. I tilted my gun downward and the detached flesh slid down the hot barrel. I looked up, thinking the top turret had been hit.

"Another six Zeros coming in at eleven o'clock!" shouted the captain over the intercom.

My gun kept pounding out bullets, but the Zeros had already vanished.

"Everyone all right?" shouted the captain.

Confused, I turned around to see if Stuart was okay, but all I saw was blood and a puzzle of body parts.

"They killed Stuart!" I cried into the intercom.

I looked around and started to gag, but nothing came up. Then I realized I was soaked in Stuart's blood.

"Come on, you bastards!" I suddenly screamed out the window. "Where are you? C'mon!"

A Zero whizzed by us, but I had no chance. The sky now seemed littered with them.

"Where in the hell did they come from?" I heard the captain say over the intercom. "We've got to land this bird. It's got the shakes. Here goes."

With the Jap reinforcements swarming in on us, Captain Montel tried to land right behind our last wing plane. Falling fast, about fifteen feet from the runway, *Dolly* took a hit in the front.

Suddenly, the plane crashed onto the dirt runway, and I was tossed like a rag doll. The plane was now sliding on its belly, out of Montel's control. Dazed, I squinted and saw a light at the rear of the plane. The dust from the runway was kicking and swirling. The rear portion of the plane was gone, and so was Mueller.

Speeding wildly, we collided with something that scraped along the fuselage. *Dolly* stopped abruptly, and her side door fell off across from me. My head was spinning, and I heard an explosion then another, and another.

Metal was flying all around me, and I felt something rip my right leg. I was hit. I had to get out of the plane.

My hands were shaking so badly that I couldn't squeeze out of my harness. I finally wiggled free and began to crawl, swiping aside Stuart's bloody head and then his raw shoulder, snaking my way to the door.

I dropped onto the ground. Blood poured from my thigh. Gasping, I gathered my strength and started to drag myself along the runway.

Another explosion riddled the aircraft.

Another.

Shells bursting.

And closer.

Bursting.

Closer.

I was hit. Again.

"My back!" I screamed.

Blinded by fear, I saw nothing and passed out.

⋆ 17 ⋆

"Don't Get Around Much Anymore"

February 20, 1942

I LOOKED UP AND SAW A LARGE NEEDLE BEING PULLED OUT OF MY CHEST, AND then Stuart's head flashed before me.

"We nearly lost you," said the Dutch officer who was withdrawing the needle. He had a slight accent. "One of our doctors pulled you off the dead wagon just in time. He saw you move your fingers and brought you over here."

I looked down and realized I was propped against a building. There was something wrong with my shoulder, but I didn't know what.

"We are waiting for the ambulance to take you to the hospital," the officer said.

Moments later, I was carried a short distance and put inside a black vehicle where other men were moaning and crying. When this ambulance started to bounce around over a bumpy road, I couldn't breathe. I couldn't move either. Two men were lying on either side of me. I passed out.

When I awoke, two nurses were washing my body, and I was complaining about the severe pain in my right leg and right shoulder. One of the nurses gave me a shot. I was out again in minutes.

I woke up during the night, feeling groggy. I was lying on my stomach with two pillows along the sides of my face. There was a hole cut out on the bed so I could breathe. I heard the man lying in the bed next to me call a nurse to give me another shot. The needle went into my hip. I was asleep again, passing in and out of consciousness.

Transferred by hospital cart, I was taken to an X-ray room and placed on a cold table. The pain was so intense that I lost consciousness once again. When I woke up, I found myself back in bed. A dark-skinned Javanese nurse in a little white hat was taking my vital signs, recording them on a clipboard.

"Water," I whispered.

She returned with a cup and a straw.

"Where am I?"

"At the hospital. In Surabaja," she said. "You will feel better with a few days of rest. It looks like you lost a lot of blood by the amount they gave you when you arrived."

When I tried to turn my head, a spasm of pain shot up the back of my neck, nearly putting me out again.

"You must not move because you will have pain," the nurse said as she left. I raised myself slightly and looked down, noticing a catheter in me. I didn't remember it being inserted.

"Ralph, Ralph," called the man on the bed beside me. "Can you hear me?"

"My God, you sound just like Lieutenant Frerry, our copilot," I replied.

"Ralph. It's me," said Frerry. "I was in the same meat wagon that brought you in. From what I've been told, we're the only two left of the crew."

Tears came when I thought of Montel, Miller, Kroll, Mann, Mueller, and Stu—.

I couldn't even say his name. If I didn't think about him, maybe I wouldn't remember what I had seen.

"That fucking high-pressured oxygen bottle took a bullet and blew the lower part of my right leg off," Frerry continued. "The doctors told me that you sure were walking the thin line when they picked you up. I thought you had passed out or passed on. The doc showed me the X-rays. You will have to be operated on as soon as your blood gets back to normal, Ralph."

"What happened to the rest of the men?" I asked.

Frerry paused to find the right words. "I took a hit and went out when we were already on the ground," he said. "Kroll and Mann were killed before we touched down, and Mueller was killed when the tail came off."

"My God," I whispered.

"Miller and the captain were killed when *Dolly* took it in the nose as we were sliding down the runway. The fucking Zeros came out of Bali and surprised us. Eubank, that fuck, didn't know the Japs had an airstrip there. They were on top of us. There was nothing we could do about it. I don't know why I wasn't killed at the same time," said Frerry quietly.

I closed my eyes, trying to digest the news. Why hadn't God taken me with them? Why was I still alive? Why me? I was scared to death. I got the shakes. I should be dead, but I wasn't. It would have been better that way; they're killing me now by letting me live. Why?

For some reason, my mind went back to the priest and nun having sex in Lansdowne. They were laughing, having a good time. "Shit. I shouldn't have done it," I thought. "I took advantage of all those girls. Jhannella, Juanita—and Ruthie in the enclosed porch. I wasn't fair to them—those burlesque girls—and what's her name—I can't remember now—Karen—my music life—my wild sex life. It was all coming back to haunt me now. I knew why. I knew why for sure. I was being punished. That was it. And I had lied to a priest! Father Marque. This had to be the wrath of God. Shit. I know I'm going to die. I'm making peace with God. I'm sorry, God. Forgive me. Oh, shit. There are many more sins, but right now I can't remember them."

I passed out.

February 21, 1942

While the nurses were changing my bandages, the Dutch doctor told me that my wounds had become infected and I needed to be operated on immediately. The nurses wheeled me down to the surgery room, where they shaved my entire body except my head. They gave me a shot in my shoulder and upper leg, and then the Dutch doctor came in with some pills. He explained that I was to be semiconscious while the surgery was taking place.

"You mean you are going to open me up, and I will not feel the pain?" I asked.

"Very little pain," said the Dutch doctor with a smile. Then he left the room. Two attendants lifted me onto an operating table and placed me on my stomach. There was a split at the end of the table where my head could rest, just like my hospital bed. I saw the base of the operating table. The tile floor. Everyone was muttering in Dutch and Javanese. My right arm was then strapped underneath the table.

"I'm going to pull your right arm a little more under the table so we can pull this long piece of steel out of you," said the Dutch doctor, now speaking very slowly in English.

"Steel?" I thought. I didn't know I had a piece of shrapnel in me. I thought I had a broken shoulder.

Someone pulled my arm, and the doctor made a deep cut.

"You no-good son of a bitch!" I yelled. "You're butchering me!"

Another cut.

"You brought me in here to stab me to death! You are from the world of death, you fucking bastard, you!" I shouted.

"I got it," the doctor called out as he removed the shrapnel from my shoulder. Delirious from the pain, I passed out again.

February 22, 1942

The pain was pulsating from my head to my feet. Rolling side to side, I moaned, then screamed. I was ready to throw myself out of the bed. I wanted to kill myself because the pain was so bad. It felt like I was being tortured.

"Give him another shot," hollered Frerry to a nurse.

A Javanese nurse came in and put a cold pack on my forehead and gave me a shot, telling me to stop moving.

"I will give you a shot every three hours to make you sleep. No more," she said. This procedure went on for three days.

February 25, 1942

I could not turn my head, and my right arm was tied to my body with heavy bandages. As the three nurses removed the cotton pads from my back and shoulder, one of the women ran out of the ward. She quickly returned with the Dutch doctor, who put some antiseptic on the incision.

"Shit. I was wrong," I said to myself. "This doctor isn't a butcher: he's a fucking welder."

"We are trying to stop the infection around the stitches," the Dutch doctor said, trying to calm me. "Your bandages will have to be changed every day, and the incision must be cleaned. In the tropics, most incisions become infected. Ralph, you must move around as little as possible so that the stitches will not pull. I also want you to take some food every three hours, after your shot. I want you to eat and drink as much as you possibly can hold, Ralph. That is the only method of combating infection."

"How can I eat when every fiber in my body is on fire?" I thought.

I just nodded, and the doctor went away.

February 26, 1942

They didn't want the ward disturbed with my screaming day and night, but there was nowhere else to put me. There were no postoperative rooms in this hospital, just fourteen unlucky bastards stuck in this room. How was I going to keep my mouth shut?

Two nurses held me up in bed while the other one changed the bloody sheets and spread the covers.

"Could I lie on my stomach?" I asked them.

"No," they said in unison.

These Javanese nurses didn't understand much English, but when they heard *stomach*, they knew what I meant.

The nurses propped me up with pillows, and when I went to sleep in the evening, the pillows were removed one by one. Since I couldn't move my head, all I could see were the huge, filthy windows that loomed behind the seven patients on the other side of room. But most of the time, my point of view was the ceiling. I remembered being in my bedroom as a child. I thought of my mother and father. My mother was teaching me how to swim. She was paddling in a rowboat, calling me. She vanished, and then my father appeared. I was with him. We were driving down to the produce market. We put on heavy white coats and went into a large cooler, where they kept the hunks of meat.

I couldn't concentrate or hold these images. I was so doped up, and with that IV in my arm all the time, I was slipping in and out of consciousness. I had a flash of Yasha; he was upset with me. They were all upset with me.

February 27, 1942

After a few days of having some food in me, I was able to hold a conversation with Lieutenant Frerry. He was also in a lot of pain, but he took it much better than I did. He was also calling me *Ralph* now. He only called me *Sergeant* when he was angry.

"Ralph, do you remember asking the doctor if I could put you out of your misery?"

"No," I said with a laugh that pierced my shoulder. "I don't remember that request, Lieutenant. But maybe it was a good idea."

"Do you hear the Jap bombing in the distance?"

"No, I can't hear it right now. How many days have you heard it?"

"Oh, about two days. I think they are bombing the air base at Sangosari. It seems to be getting closer and closer."

Once Frerry mentioned it, the bombing was clearly audible to me.

February 28, 1942

A nurse came running in and informed everyone that the Japs had invaded Batavia, killing and capturing the Dutch, Americans, and Australians who were fighting around the outskirts of Bandung.

That night I had a dream: I was in battle with a gun and a bayonet on a huge field. The Japs were coming at me. I was mowing down Japs left and right, but I was always scrambling for more ammunition. They were dead, but then they started coming at me again. They kept approaching, and I kept scrambling for more guns. When I woke up, my bed was soaking wet.

March 1, 1942

The planes flew over us, alarming everyone, but the bombing had stopped. The nurse informed us that there were large red crosses on the roof, and the Japs wouldn't bomb a hospital. I asked Lieutenant Frerry about this.

"Ralph, who in the hell knows what those people will do?" he said. "We can't do anything about it, anyway, lying on our backs."

Two more Americans were brought in. One had his head covered with bandages and the other had his leg in traction, hanging from a wire. Both soldiers seemed to be sleeping, so Frerry and I couldn't get any news.

That evening, the Dutch doctor sat on a stool next to me and began to tell me about my operation. He had something in his hand.

"I pulled this out from underneath your shoulder blade. It was lodged deep between two ribs," he said.

The piece of steel was four inches long and a half inch wide, with jagged edges.

"It's from a twenty-millimeter cannon shell," said the doctor. "It took quite a long time to find it, and it's going to be a long recovery before you can use your right arm again. So have lots of patience."

I nodded my head, grateful.

"Would you like to have this as a keepsake, Sergeant?"

I looked at the piece of steel, then rolled it in my left hand. It gave me the chills.

"Thanks for the memento, Doc," I said. "And thanks for saving my life."

When the doctor left, Frerry saw me examining the shrapnel, and he told me more about our secret mission. He said he had known gold was on board the plane when we left Tampa. Frerry mentioned that the price of gold at that time was thirty-two dollars an ounce; however, the U.S. government charged the Aussies five hundred dollars an ounce. Our entire mission—our "historic flight"—was nothing more than an eighteen-thousand-mile business transaction, and the government made a killing off of us.

March 2, 1942

The doctor went over to Frerry's bed and asked him how he felt.

"I would like to take the next plane for Australia because those Nips are getting too close," said Frerry.

"There's no way to escape from this island, Lieutenant. We are completely surrounded by the Japanese navy, and their marines are now landing from all sides," the doctor said. "We were just told an hour ago to stay in the hospital. The Japanese have broken through the lines of defense, and everyone will be a prisoner of war within ten days."

The ward went silent.

"A prisoner of war?" I thought. "I'm paralyzed. I'm never gonna walk again. How am I gonna walk again? How?"

When the doctor left, I heard another patient say what we all were thinking: "We're dead meat."

March 3, 1942

The spasms of pain came less often, but the incision in my right shoulder seemed moist. A foul smell persisted underneath the bandages. I called for a nurse, and she appeared with a doctor about an hour later. "This man must be moved to surgery," the Dutch doctor said as he removed my bandages. "I will clean the wound there. Just roll him in as is."

Two nurses pushed my bed down a long hall and through some swinging doors. I asked for a shot and then was lifted onto the surgery table and held there. The doctor began to flush my shoulder wound with a brown liquid. I became dizzy. Two more attendants came over to hold me up. The shot did its duty, and I passed out.

Hours later, I woke up. A nurse was soothing my body with cool water.

"You all right, Ralph?" Lieutenant Frerry asked.

"I think so," I muttered.

"Fever. Infection," said the Javanese nurse, who spoke little English.

"How long will it last?" I asked her.

She shrugged. I tried to use hand signals to communicate with her, but she didn't understand.

The nurse left, and Lieutenant Frerry told me I had slept through the morning bombing raid. The Japs continued to bomb Surabaja and the Sangosari air base.

Frerry then mentioned that Colonel Eubank and the other crews had escaped to Australia a week earlier.

"That fucking bastard Eubank should be court-martialed," I thought. "He used us. I will die because of him. That motherfucker! I will never make it in any kind of prisoner of war camp. My life is over. Fuck. Fuck him. Fuck."

March 4, 1942

A plane skimmed the roof of the hospital. Minutes later, the Dutch doctor burst into the room with a notice that had been dropped from the plane. It was to inform all hospital residents that the Imperial Japanese Marines would visit the hospital soon. No one should leave. Leave? Where the hell was I going to run off to?

March 17, 1942

At 0600 hours, while doctors and nurses were changing shifts, gunshots rang out. Then screaming. Windows breaking. The Imperial Japanese Marines entered the hospital. Since the Japs now had Java, I suspected that they would move through the Coral Sea and go after New Zealand and Australia next.

No one in our ward was ambulatory, so we were scared to death. All we could think about was when would the Japs shoot us.

A ward door flew open, and a Jap officer appeared.

"I am Major Samaguchi of the Imperial Marines," he said in perfect English. "I understand that you men are all Americans wounded in battle. I salute you." The major lifted his hand to his helmet.

"This bastard is a spy," I thought. "He'll try to get secrets out of me, but *he* will be interrogated before this whole thing is over. He will!"

"This ward is my responsibility and under my guidance," continued Major Samaguchi. "There will be guards at each end of the ward. Now, the gunshots and screaming you heard just a moment ago were from civilians, nurses, and patients who were mistaken for people trying to escape our friendly takeover of the hospital. As long as you follow my orders, you will have a quiet recovery from your wounds."

A cocky smile crept over the major's face, and he informed us that he was a graduate of the University of California at Los Angeles.

"This could very well be true," I thought. He spoke just like an American from the States, but I still thought this little fucker was a spy. Everybody was a spy. I was really doped up, but I knew my mind was working normally. I didn't trust anybody except Frerry because he called the nurses for me.

"I was raised by my aunt and uncle in southern California from the age of five," said the major proudly. "I was visiting my birth parents in Japan when the war broke out between Japan and the United States. The Japanese government gave me no choice and put me into the service."

Interesting. A better spy than I originally thought. "How can this little bastard already be a major?" I thought. "It's only been three months since

Pearl Harbor. How can this tiny fuck move up so fast? I don't believe him. He's a liar. They're all a gang of liars."

After the major left, the ward went dead until Lieutenant Frerry spoke up: "Not for one instant should any one of you drop your guard with that major. If you believe that propaganda that those people were shot in the takeover of this hospital, you are very naive. Don't believe a thing they say. Those people were murdered to put fear in the hearts of the rest of us. The major came over loud and clear. Even though he seemed very friendly, remember, he is the enemy."

March 18, 1942

My bandages had been changed only once the previous day. My shoulder and the right side of my leg were again having spasms. The Dutch doctor told me that all fourteen American patients would be visited by a new Jap staff.

Later, Major Samaguchi and a Jap doctor came to my bedside. The Dutch doctor explained my condition to them in English while the Jap major translated for the Jap doctor. As a nurse removed the old bandages, the Japs had no reaction. Actually, they had no interest. "They're animals. They like to see blood, especially American," I thought. They didn't care. They were ice. Cold. Their faces were made of stone.

The Dutch doctor told me that my shoulder was inflamed again and that pus was oozing out of the incision. I couldn't see it, but I could smell it. Major Samaguchi walked away from my bed and the foul odor, taking the Jap doctor with him. They returned, speaking in Japanese. Their faces never changed expression. Stone again.

"We will have to take this patient to surgery to clean the wound and put a small drain in the shoulder to relieve the infection," said the Dutch doctor to the major, who was still a study in granite.

I was given a shot and pushed into surgery. Two orderlies lifted me onto the table, facedown. I took another shot in the shoulder, grunted, and passed out. I thought I was passing to the other side.

March 20, 1942

It must have been late that afternoon when I became conscious again. The pain was intolerable. My shoulder felt like it had been torn from my body.

March 21, 1942

Lieutenant Frerry notified the nurse that I was awake and needed a shot. The nurse came in with the needle, and I was asleep again. Later that night, I awoke in pure agony, and a new nurse would not give me any more injections. She misread my medical chart.

"Hit me! Smother me. Fucking kill me!" I shouted. "I can't take this. I can't take much more pain."

I knew Frerry had a .45 under his pillow, but he wouldn't honor my request. He kept trying to distract me, and I kept telling him to shoot me. I fell asleep from exhaustion.

March 23, 1942

I remember little except for shots and feedings. But the pain had subsided to a bothersome ache, and my head and eyes were improving so I could hear and see more clearly.

"Well, you finally came back to visit us," joked Frerry. "You sure produced enough excitement around here."

I gave Frerry a weak smile. "I think I'm back to stay," I said. "I need some water."

Frerry called a nurse, and she and the doctor came into the ward. They propped me up so I could drink and then changed my bandages. I was so weak I needed help just to move my arms.

"Remember our stay in Belém, Brazil?" asked Frerry.

"What?" I said, surprised.

"That great time you had with Jhannella."

"How did you know what was going on between the two of us?" I asked, more alert now.

"All we had to do was look at both of you when you were together," said Frerry. "It was obvious. You were in love with each other. If we hadn't needed you on the crew, we would have told you to take Jhannella home and get married."

I tried to laugh, but it hurt too much.

March 28, 1942

The nurses were still feeding and cleaning me. I still couldn't use my right arm, and my left arm was shaky. I couldn't turn my head. All I really could do was sleep and take shots. I was turning into a druggie.

April 15, 1942

The Japs took the Philippines. They were winning everything now. They'd have Australia soon. We didn't hear any reports. We didn't need to. If the Japs had taken Java so easily, we all knew Australia was the only safe place left. In an effort to try to protect ourselves, Lieutenant Frerry and I would take turns sleeping and keeping watch. After almost a month of this vigilance, I noticed I was starting to get stronger. I was beginning to dream about Lynda and the great time we had had together swimming in Atlantic City. I knew I was getting better because I remembered our long, lazy afternoons at Steel Pier. I made my time with Lynda last as long as I could in my mind. I let it linger. I was smiling more, thinking of these memories. I was learning to live with a certain amount of pain. But I kept seeing the kid, Stuart. His scrambled body on the floor. Why him? Why not me? To combat this gruesome image of Stuart, I would imagine torturing Eubank. I would cut his throat slowly and watch him bleed to death.

April 26, 1942

I don't know what kept me going, but having Frerry alongside me was a big help. In addition to being my friend and inspiration, Frerry was also my news source. He told me that many American and Australian soldiers had been taken as prisoners of war. I wondered how all this was going to affect the hospital. I couldn't go to a prison camp in this condition. I would die within weeks. I couldn't walk. What would they do with me?

May 10, 1942

We heard many things swirling around the hospital, unable to distinguish truth from rumor. Frerry overheard that all patients who couldn't walk or work would be shot because they were useless to the Imperial Japanese Army. Another patient told me that all patients would be sent to Japan to show the Jap people that they were winning the war. The Dutch doctor mentioned that he had heard that we would be put on the front line with guns and ordered to shoot American soldiers. A Javanese nurse said that the Jap major said that we would be used for medical experiments.

May 15, 1942

The radios were taken away, and according to Major Samaguchi, if one was found, everyone within earshot would have their head removed.

May 19, 1942

I asked Frerry if some of the patients from our ward had been taken away.

"Half the fellows have been moved, but I don't know where," Frerry said. "The nurses, doctors, and personnel are living at the hospital, and the whole area has been electrically wired, except the gates to the entrance."

The Jap major also told Frerry that the Javanese soldiers had been sent to Japan in support of their cause. "Asia for the Asiatics" was the new slogan. The Javanese believed the Dutch had exploited them as slave labor for many years, and since the Japs would feed the locals and give them work, they were in a state of euphoria.

I asked the lieutenant if anyone had mentioned what was next for us. Frerry shook his head and said, "I think we're here for the duration of the war, Ralph."

Frerry thought all of us would be held as prisoners. Even on one leg, I thought Frerry had what it took to be a POW. He'd make it. I didn't know if I could.

May 22, 1942

I was gaining some weight back when the Dutch doctor surprised me by saying that he was going to remove the three-inch piece of shrapnel that was still in my right leg.

"Why wasn't it done before?" I said, ready to shoot the son of a bitch. I was under the impression that that procedure had been completed during my shoulder operation.

"You were too weak to handle another operation, Ralph. It would have killed you," said the doctor.

More torture, I thought. God isn't through with me yet.

May 23, 1942

I was sent for X-rays that afternoon, and a fluoroscope located the piece of metal. My leg was marked with purple dye.

May 24, 1942

I was taken to surgery, and my right hip and thigh were numbed. The doctor was sitting at a desk with my X-rays lit up in front of him, and then he stood and approached me. "This surgery should only take a short while, Ralph," he said. "I'm waiting until all feeling in your leg is thoroughly anesthetized."

While the surgery crew waited for the doctor to return, I thought I was going to die right there. My whole life flashed before me: my father in his white apron at the cash register; my mother taking orders on the store phone; her gray hair; my lessons with Yasha; swimming with Lynda; showering with Juanita; dancing with Jhannella; Nana making breakfast; Ruth on the swing; those jam sessions in Havana with Harry; Stuart's smile; Stuart's body on the floor; Eubank with his throat cut. Blood everywhere.

The Dutch doctor returned, and I was flipped on my left side and strapped to the table. I heard the doctor ask for an instrument and felt some pressure on my thigh. I was out again.

May 25, 1942

I couldn't feel any pain in my leg. It was still numb. "They just can't kill me," I said to Frerry. "I keep popping back for more torture."

"I think that's the last operation you'll undergo," the lieutenant said. "I spoke with the doctor, and he told me that all you have to do is to heal and get your strength back."

"That's gonna take some time because I hurt all over."

"Ralph, the doctor told me that you would heal real fast."

I looked at Frerry and said, "Do you believe that horseshit? I have a feeling that something is going on at this hospital, like they want to rush us into the work camp."

Frerry didn't answer me.

May 27, 1942

Major Samaguchi saluted us as he asked how everyone was feeling. No one said a word, but those who could raise their hands saluted him back. The rest of us bowed from our beds.

"The Imperial Marines are leaving the hospital," said the major. "The new head of the hospital is now touring the grounds, and he will be visiting the ward sometime today. The new administrator is going to make a lot of changes. I know that you will cooperate with him, and I hope you will survive to return to your country."

The major bowed this time before his exit, and all of us turned to Frerry for his commentary.

"Gentlemen, you heard the major," said Frerry, who was the only officer in the ward. "He explicitly stated that there will be a lot of changes made, and you had better cooperate, or else. Also, the major is warning us that the shit will hit the fan before we get out of this jam. Let's wait and see what this new administrator has to say."

Suddenly, there was shouting in Japanese. The ward doors swung open, and two Jap soldiers appeared with bayonets attached to their guns. Our new administrator, Colonel Tarasuchi, dressed in an open-collared shirt and high brown boots, walked between them. He also wore a uniform coat decorated with ribbons, and he carried a long sword on his hip. The colonel faced us, then bowed with a slight grin. One of the other Jap officers acted as an interpreter for the colonel, who spoke at length, shaking his fist and hitting his chest repeatedly.

"Colonel Tarasuchi wants you to follow his instructions," the interpreter translated. "You will bow to every Japanese soldier and officer who speaks to you. You will not speak to anyone, except to the doctors or nurses who are attending to you. If you have any firearms, you must turn them in immediately. If you do not follow instructions, you will be beaten or shot. When you are considered cured, you will be taken to an outside camp. The colonel and the doctor will make the decision when you are ready to leave. If you suffer too many beatings while you are here, you will be sent to an outside camp. This hospital is now a Japanese hospital for sick and wounded courageous Japanese soldiers, not for prisoners of war. You will be fed and clothed and you must keep clean as long as you are here."

The interpreter then turned to the colonel, made a wild sound, then bowed before him. The colonel bowed at us. Those patients who were sitting up bowed in return.

After the colonel and his entourage left in single file, Frerry looked over at me, shook his head, and said, "Well, I'll most likely be sent to the officers' camp and given a desk job."

I tried to laugh, but I couldn't. At this point, I thought the Japs wouldn't wait for me to heal. I'd most likely be taken out to the POW cemetery and shot.

May 29, 1942

We noticed that our menu was changing. The patients were now receiving larger portions of rice and much less chicken and vegetables. However, I was still being served the same diet, protein and various vegetables with fruit. I spoke to the Dutch doctor about why I was still receiving a more substantial diet than most of the men, and the doctor informed the entire ward, "Very shortly, many of you men who are ambulatory will be taken to a prisoner of war camp. I don't know which camp. Those who will be taken first are receiving more rice and less protein. You know who you are, so be prepared for the move. And please be very humble and bow. We have already had two employees beaten in the administrative office."

May 31, 1942

Most of the ward had been moved to a POW camp. They trickled out two at a time. Not only was the ward getting smaller, but so were the meals. Everyone started measuring their food.

June 1, 1942

My shoulder wasn't healing properly, and the Dutch doctor was growing concerned. He asked Colonel Tarasuchi if I could have more fresh fruit and vegetables, and the administrator agreed. However, the Dutch doctor told me that I would soon be moved to a POW camp.

"You better start eating as much as they feed you, Ralph, because they will ship you out of here in whatever condition you are at that point," said the doctor.

June 4, 1942

Lieutenant Frerry was moved out on crutches. Before he left, Frerry gave me a hug while I was sitting up in bed.

"I'll see you in the States, Ralph," he said, shaking my hand. "Take care of yourself and get out of that damn bed."

I had made it this far because Frerry had talked me through it. If Frerry hadn't been here, I don't know if I would have made it. I don't know. I might have talked to someone else. I needed companionship. Now I felt lost.

There were only two of us remaining in the ward—a man named Jeffrey and me.

June 7, 1942

Jeffrey did not talk. He had a head injury, and I never heard him say a word. He might have lost his voice or his tongue. He used sign language with the nurses and doctors. I couldn't walk, and Jeffrey couldn't talk—what a team we made.

Each morning, I started forcing myself to get out of bed and stand up straight. I needed to hold onto the side of my bed for support, and since my right arm and right leg were still semiparalyzed, I was having a difficult time trying to take that first step. The nurses were helpful until I got my balance, but I was still badly dragging my right leg. The doctor had had to cut a muscle to remove the shrapnel.

June 9, 1942

My right arm was getting stronger, but as I shuffled across the empty ward, I was still hunched over, with my shoulder bent forward. A wounded animal.

June 10, 1942

Jeffrey was moved out. When he left the ward, he just raised his arm toward me and was gone.

June 11, 1942

Now I was alone. The nurses and doctors seldom entered the ward. With no books, no radio, and not even a deck of cards to play solitaire, I exercised more, dreading the day I would be taken out of here. I made friends with some of the nurses, and they sneaked food to me so I would gain more weight and get stronger. I vowed to walk out of this place. What came after that, I couldn't let myself think about.

June 13, 1942

I decided to exercise until the tears came. When I wasn't walking, I was exercising my arms and shoulders in bed or on a chair. I shuffled across that floor for hours. I had my balance back now, and I could swing my right arm back and forth.

June 14, 1942

I received notice that I would be leaving the hospital the following morning. The administrator and the doctor came to see me that evening to say good-bye and to watch me hobble around the vacant ward. I was still bent over and dragging my right leg, but I thanked Colonel Tarasuchi for being so kind and letting me stay so long. I also thanked the doctor again for saving my life.

Speaking through his interpreter, Colonel Tarasuchi told me, "You have been a good soldier and have followed all instructions."

Without hesitation, I looked at the colonel and bowed. My humility was false, but I didn't show it. Bowing in bed was easy, but on your feet? That was different. The lower one bowed, the more the Japs liked it. What else could I do, though? They had the upper hand. At this particular moment, this is how I viewed the Japs: It's your turn to make me bow, but I don't bow to anyone, not even in temple. I will get better, you fuckers—and look out when the Americans come in and take over. I must continue to hate to make me feel better. About myself. About my condition. "It's all in your mind," I told myself. "Hate will make you walk, Ralph."

After the colonel and the interpreter left, I shook hands with the Dutch doctor and said good-bye. The nurses came in a little later, bringing me a new set of tan clothes and sandals. I thanked the Javanese nurses, who for the most part had been very kind to me. Each one of them held my head in their hands and pulled me close to their breasts, a way to express love in their culture.

When the nurses left, I asked myself how I would be able to get along with my disabilities in a prison camp. I had to become an actor in a play. I had to become the nice guy and do everything the way the Japs wanted it. All the bowing and ritual would be an act. "Play the game, Ralph. Don't let your eyes or body show the hate you have for them. You were in show business before—you can play this part."

But what I was really thinking was how I was going to cut their nuts off someday. I'd do it slow, too. With scissors.

Unsure if my act would work, I called the Dutch doctor and told him my fears.

"Sergeant, that problem has already been addressed," said the doctor. "You will be taken care of by a Dutch physical therapist who is also a prisoner at the camp."

"I don't believe it," I told him.

I was astonished that the colonel had made this arrangement for me. Did he want something from me? What was his angle?

June 15, 1942

At 0500 hours, the night nurse awakened me to change my bandages. "You are leaving us today, and I was instructed to get you ready for an early breakfast," she said.

This nurse was Dutch, and she spoke English very well. I asked her where she had come from, and she told me she was the wife of the Dutch doctor who had operated on me. They lived at the hospital and were on call twenty-four hours a day.

After the Dutch nurse left, the nurses changed shifts, and there was no one around to inquire about my breakfast. Fortunately, a Javanese nurse came in and asked me what I was doing in this ward. I tried to explain to her, but she didn't understand English.

"Doctor," I said in frustration, and she understood that word. The Dutch doctor appeared, surprised to see me still here.

I explained the mix-up, and he thought it was very funny.

"I will get your breakfast to you immediately, Sergeant."

"What a comedy of errors," I thought. "They don't even know I exist. If I could walk, I might escape, but where would I escape to—a Javanese kampong?"

My rice cakes and tea showed up, and then a nurse helped me get dressed. Alone again and afraid, I sat in a rocking chair and waited.

The door opened, and a Javanese nurse pushed a wheelchair toward me and beckoned me with her hand. I got up gingerly, holding my rocking chair with whatever strength I could muster, but the chair slipped away from me. As I was falling, the nurse quickly shoved the wheelchair under my ass. I landed hard on the seat and felt a sudden pain in my leg and shoulder.

The nurse giggled, and her laughter made me forget my pain for a moment. I laughed along with her.

A Dutch jeep was idling outside. The Javanese nurse wheeled me to the front gate while the fears of the prison camp tormented me. I drank in the fresh air.

The nurse called over two Jap guards, who lifted me inside the vehicle. I kept my head down, trying to adjust to the harsh sunlight. Six more Jap guards with guns were nearby. I bowed graciously to them, and the jeep took off. I thought the worst was over.

✸ 18 ✸

"Look for the Silver Lining"

July 1946

"ARE YOU SLEEPING, RALPH?" MY MOTHER ASKED AS SHE TURNED AROUND TO face me.

"No," I said. "I guess I wasn't listening."

"Dad has to use the restroom. Do you have to go? Hungry? Want anything to eat?"

I shook my head.

My father pulled off the road. We got out of the Buick, and I wandered off to get a better view of the Midwestern scenery. I was so used to traveling by plane that being in a car for such a long distance was confining, especially with Bob, who was still trying to extract the source of my deepening depression. He had been pestering me for the past three days. When we stopped at night at a motel, I told Bob I just wanted to brush my teeth and go to sleep. I didn't want to talk about anything. I think he was finally starting to get the message.

Bob stayed near the car, looking a little foolish doing jumping jacks. I thought I heard him say he was over in Europe in the medical corps but took ill or something. They sent him home after two months.

My mother, meanwhile, had followed my father into the roadside diner to get some sandwiches. She carried her maps, brochures, and auto club materials with her. My father was excited to visit the Budweiser plant in St. Louis. My mother also had been calling ahead to make dinner reservations. She booked three different restaurants at a time. "Tentative reservations," my mother called them.

My right leg was a little stiff from all the riding. I tried to walk it off and found myself stopping near a roadside cliff. Maybe traveling to California would be good for me. The weather would benefit my recovery, I told myself.

Then I looked down, staring into the brown abyss, searching for answers to the question of what to do with my life. How was I going to put it all behind me when I had nothing to look forward to?

I stepped closer to the cliff and noticed a small stone nearby. I pulled the stone near me with my foot, rolling it under my shoe.

Just then, I looked over my shoulder and saw my mother watching me, clutching her travel materials to her chest. I quickly kicked the stone over the edge, watching it dribble down the cliff, disappearing. I returned to the car.

✶ 19 ✶

"Body and Soul"

June 1942

THE JEEP NOW CUT ALONG A DIRT ROAD THAT HAD RICE FIELDS ON BOTH sides. We passed several Javanese kampongs, where twenty or thirty locals lived and raised their food. A dark-skinned girl with hollow eyes stared at me as we pulled through the front gates of Camp Malang.

Once inside the barbed wire, I saw Jap guards carrying rifles with fixed bayonets. Machine gun towers peppered the perimeter.

When the jeep arrived at a small building, the driver pointed for me to get out. As I attempted to lift myself out of the vehicle, a tall blond man appeared.

"I have been instructed to carry you into the camp commandant's office if you cannot walk," he said with a Dutch accent.

"I can walk," I mumbled, "if there aren't any steps."

"Let me see you walk," the Dutchman said as he hoisted me out of the jeep. Intimidated, I almost lost my balance. I was only 130 pounds. As my right arm dangled against my side, I proceeded to show this stranger my gait, dragging my stiff right leg along the gravel, sweeping stones along the way. As I finally reached the steps, the Dutchman scooped me off my feet.

He then carried me into the camp commandant's outer office and stood me up against a wall. When the Dutchman smiled at me, I knew I had a friend.

The room was bare, and the Dutchman and I must have waited for thirty minutes until a door opened. A Jap officer motioned us to enter. The camp commandant, a tiny man in his forties, sat in a bamboo chair dwarfed behind a massive desk. He bowed. The Dutchman and I did the same.

After reviewing my hospital papers, the commandant smiled knowingly and addressed the Dutchman in Malayan. From their facial expressions, there seemed to be a difference of opinion over some matter, but the Dutchman quickly conceded. We bowed again and exited.

"Don't speak," whispered the Dutchman as he carried me back outside. He placed me in a small, two-wheeled flatbed and pushed me to his quarters, a medium-sized hut consisting of four small bamboo beds with mosquito netting draped over each one.

"I'm Captain Van Doren," said the Dutchman. "I'm a physical therapist for the Dutch Armed Forces. Welcome to the Ritz."

Van Doren was twenty-nine years old and big as a gorilla. At six feet, five inches tall and 235 pounds, he was an imposing figure, but his disarming smile and fading blond hair softened him a bit.

"The guards are the ones who stole all this equipment from a doctor in town," Van said, referring to the three therapy tables, dumbbells, and the most bizarre sight—a jungle of bamboo ropes that dangled from the roof.

"This is where I work on my patients until they scream," Van boasted, "and I love it."

Van had been working at the same hospital where I was in Surabaja, but he had recently been moved to this prison camp, primarily to work on the Jap guards. Small men carrying big rifles all day made for aching backs, necks, and shoulders.

Van told me he employed rough massage and other unorthodox techniques, channeling his hate through his hands.

"How long will I be staying here?" I asked.

"The commandant said you should be ready to work in six months."

"Van," I said, "I think I'm a hopeless case. They butchered me at that hospital. You're gonna make me work in six months?"

"Yes," Van replied. "And if I don't get you to work, he's going to send *me* to another camp. I know when he gives me one of those smiles, he's pretty sure I can't do something. But I can, but I'm gonna hurt you, Ralph. Now let's see what you can do with that arm."

I tried my best to raise my right arm, and Van saw the pain in my eyes. He knew my right side was nearly paralyzed. I could barely grip a bamboo pole.

"I can help you, Ralph," the Dutchman said, "but it will be up to you whether you can take the pain."

Rice and something smelly was on the menu that first night. When Van brought back our dinner in clay dishes, I was surprised that he had been able to score some meat. He explained that since he worked on the guards, the commandant allowed him to eat from the Jap kitchen.

"I consider myself lucky to be in your hut," I said.

"Starting tomorrow, you may not have the same opinion," Van replied.

Lights were out at ten. Since I couldn't toss or turn in my condition, I just lay awake in my bamboo bed for hours, feeling each pole cutting into my back. And every time I closed my eyes, Stuart's head was there again. Then Eubank. Then Stuart. Then Eubank. Then . . .

Van found me asleep the next morning, curled up against the wall. I got up and examined the colored jars on one of Van's therapy tables. The bright orange and green oils he used for massages gave the hut a glow of a mad chemist's laboratory. Van returned with two small bowls of rice, dried fish, and bananas. We sat down, and as we ate in silence, I noticed that Van's high, chiseled cheekbones reminded me, oddly enough, of Jhannella.

Van, who had been a prisoner here for four months, explained that Camp Malang was a holding camp for the leftover prisoners who hadn't been sent to the larger camps in Batavia and Singapore. Camp Malang, Van mentioned, was the only place that would take me because there was room in his med hut; otherwise, I would have been shot.

"We don't have much time, Ralph," the Dutchman said after he finished his breakfast. "If you don't do what I say, you will die here. So let's get to work."

Van carefully picked me up and laid me on the therapy table, turning me over on my stomach.

"Whew, they really tore you up," he said, removing the pad from my shoulder. "I think the cut nerves have to heal first. We'll start on the arm, and once we get it liberated, the shoulder will heal much faster."

Van located the nerves in my right arm and applied some pressure. I winced. He then took my right wrist, pulling the blood into the fingers. I grunted, the sweat beginning to roll off my face. Spasms followed. I jumped.

"This is going to take longer than I thought," Van decided.

Van sat me up on the table and placed his hand on the inside of my right elbow, finding the tendon. He then instructed me to curl my arm to my chest. I could barely do it. Just six months earlier, I had been playing five-card stud at Langley Field; now I couldn't even deal.

After ten repetitions, Van threw me facedown on the table and pulled my right arm behind my head. It felt like he was pulling my arm out of its socket. Van could see my face turning purple, but he just kept his cool and smiled. It was the same smile he wore when he talked about torturing the Jap guards. Was this big Dutchman a spy? I thought the Japs had made a pact with him to kill me slowly. Was that the plan? Or did the devil send him? I didn't trust anyone. I couldn't.

Days later, Van got to work on my right leg, pulling and straightening the muscles. I screamed this time: "You evil son of a bitch! I'm gonna quit this goddamn shit. I mean it!"

But Van would just look at me and smile until I calmed down, and then he would go back to work. I couldn't scream too loudly either, for fear of rousing the Jap guards who patrolled outside our hut. One of those bastards might come in and give me a beating—or kill me—just to shut me up. "The more pain your right leg takes, the stronger it will get," Van told me. "You will walk on this leg, Ralph. I'm not here to torture you; I'm here to save your life."

That night I looked at Van, and he reminded me of a man I had met when I was eight years old. John Foreman owned a gym near our family store in Lansdowne. He was six feet, two inches tall and muscular, and to a kid, he seemed enormous. A goddamn mountain.

I remember roller-skating one Saturday morning in front of our store when one of my mates asked what religion I was.

I thought a few moments and said, "Presbyterian."

I didn't see my mother standing on the store steps. She immediately called me to practice my music. That evening at dinner, my mother raised the topic with my father: "Izzy, do you know that your son is a Presbyterian? I heard him tell the boys."

My father gave me a smile, but it didn't look like his real smile. The next morning my father introduced me to Rabbi Matt, and I became a regular at West Philadelphia Temple. However, once the kids at school found out I was a Jew, they no longer wanted to associate with me. During recess, I would run around the playground by myself. I quickly became an outsider, but I wanted in. Then, one day after school, a gang of kids surrounded me. The leader of the gang called me a dirty Jew, and they all beat me up real good.

I ran home bleeding and crying. My mother cleaned me up and explained to my father what had happened. My father then took me into the enclosed porch and plotted a strategy. "If you want to live in peace, Son, you have to beat those boys at their own game," I recall my father saying.

I was confused. All I wanted was to enjoy myself, but it seemed that my Jewishness was preventing me from having a good time with the other boys.

My father sent me to see John Foreman. "John will teach you the art of defense," my father told me.

My father advised me to stay away from the "director," the name he gave to the ringleader of the gang. I obeyed my father's wishes and studied with Foreman for three months.

After my sessions with Foreman, I would come home with bruises all over my body. I hated him, and I hated my father for making me go through this. I was alone. I had no friends my own age. I didn't belong.

As time went on, however, I began to enjoy my progress with Foreman because I was getting some of my punching, tripping, and self-defense techniques to work for me. I was becoming more aggressive. Finally, after six months of seclusion and training, Foreman sat on our enclosed porch and announced, "Your son is now ready to take on any of those little rats."

Shortly afterward, I concocted a plan to catch the director. I wanted to get him alone, someplace quiet. I stalked my prey for two weeks and selected the spot where the fight would take place. It was an alley that the director took home every day. Sensing my newfound confidence, I confronted my adversary.

"I guess you need another beating," smiled the director.

I didn't wait for him to swing. I rushed him, hooking my right foot around the back of his knee. When he tried to move, I hit him with a right hook to the chin. He collapsed.

I saw the surprised look on the director's face, and I waited until he got up. He staggered toward me, and I hit him again, straight in the nose. Thrilled by the sight of his blood, I picked him up and wrapped my arm around his neck, then repeatedly rammed his head into a wooden fence. The exhilaration was glorious. My aggression amazed me. I didn't know I had this anger in me. I was surprised by my own strength and the damage I could do—and I liked it. I was empowered. I was proud of myself.

Now I understood. I didn't realize that I was weak until they beat me up. I went from weak to strong. I discovered that I could change my situation. At eight years old, I felt I could take on anybody. I could take care of myself, and I could dispose of them within minutes. I left the director there, bleeding and crying.

I strutted home and told my father what happened. He told my mother, who became irate. She thought I had gone too far. She believed I had taken advantage of the bully.

"I don't want to hear about this again," my mother said to me. "Forget about being an animal and using your strength. You are going to be a social animal, not a wild animal."

I let that comment go over my head. The following day, the director and his father came to see my father. "You've got a killer for a son," said the man. He was furious.

My father calmly explained what the director and his pals had done to me prior to the previous day's beating, and the battle of words soon died down. The director and his father quietly left our home.

It wasn't more than a week later when another boy, the biggest in the gang, confronted me after school with his pals.

"Rentz, you ain't nothin,' and I'm gonna take you on single-handed," the kid said. I knocked his front teeth onto the concrete before he could say another word. From that day on, I became a respected member of the playground.

I told Van I was a Jew. It didn't matter to him. There were Dutch Jews on the island. He didn't care. I was his project. To keep myself going, I told myself, "I did this before with Foreman. I can do it again."

Van worked on me four times a day for nearly two hours a session during those first weeks, then he increased the intensity until he saw an improvement in my arm and leg. To keep me busy in the afternoons while he worked on the Jap guards, Van gave me a book of Malayan words with English translation, which he suggested I memorize.

The Malayan language, which the Dutch had invented, was useful to know since it was spoken throughout the islands. I heard the doctors speak it often with the Jap marines while I was in the hospital, but I didn't know then that there were two variations of the language. One, spoken by the Jap soldiers, was considered the low speech. Educated Jap officers spoke the other, the high speech. Van taught me the latter.

"Survival here depends on more than just being able to walk, Ralph," Van instructed me. "Your life depends on speaking this language."

Van believed that if I could communicate in Malayan, the Jap guards would acknowledge my effort and perhaps be less violent. Van would tutor me into the night. One of the first phrases Van taught me was *teta ba goose*, which has a dual meaning: "no damn good" and "tastes like shit."

Van kept me at a cool distance that first month, but during the evenings, we started talking more openly—whispering, actually—about the politics of war, about the Germans.

Being from Holland, Van hated the Germans, but he thought the Japs were worse—more brutal, more savage. As Van and I became more comfortable with each other, the Dutchman wanted to know more about me. Van hadn't worked on many Americans in the hospital at Surabaja, and he was curious about the States. He wanted to know about my life before the war.

I told Van that I was a professional musician. I told him about how Yasha had trained me and how angry he would get when he had to retrain me in classical music when my execution became sloppy after my long gigs with the big bands.

Like Yasha, Van was a teacher, but his style was very different. Where Yasha concentrated on my musical gift—my soul—Van worked on my body and mind, like Foreman.

"Go to another world, Ralph," Van said when he pressed his knuckles deep into my shoulder. "Go to another place. You don't know what the hell's happening on this table. Think very intently. Put your mind in another world, Ralph. Think."

And as Van would dig deeper into my body, I would dig deeper into my past.

I shut my eyes, seeing only blackness. Van now tore into my back and shoulder—deeper and deeper—but I didn't scream. Then the blackness began to move. Undulating. Waving. Suddenly, she appeared in the water beside me, her hair strewn across her face. I was swimming with Lynda at

Steel Pier. We floated together, wordlessly. She swam out further, deeper and deeper into the waves, her eyes inviting me to chase her. I followed. She was the one that I wanted. She was the one. Lynda.

"All done," Van said, rubbing me down with the oil. The session was over. I had somehow bypassed the pain.

I gradually began to look forward to the therapy sessions with Van. I started to welcome the pain, knowing that pain was what I needed to recover. Once in a while, when Van would take my shoulder and press it into the table, I actually saw stars. Van said that meant my mind was enjoying the pain. The Dutchman had seduced me into transporting my mind, and the sessions became less torturous. The bamboo pole bed was no longer giving me fits. The tears were no longer there. I also started to gain some weight back as a result of the fresh bananas, papayas, coconuts, and mangos Van brought me each day. I was 155 pounds now.

During these sessions, Van never spoke much about himself. He did mention, however, that he wanted to go back to school to become a doctor. He also said he had a beautiful Eurasian girl—half white, half Chinese—and they had lived together in Java before the war. Van asked me if I had a girl back home, but I didn't want to tell him about Lynda. I hadn't told anyone about her. She was mine. I told Van about Jhannella instead.

Since both Jhannella and Van were from Holland, the Dutchman was curious about her. Van asked about the dancing, the lovemaking.

"I bet you couldn't dance the rumba with Jhannella today," Van would say when he wanted to push me harder on my right leg. "Think of having a great time with her. Send yourself back to Belém. You're taking her out to dance. And no erections, please! Don't think too hard."

Sometimes I thought Van had hypnotized me, and other times I thought the pain was so severe that I would pass out. But when Van tried to send me back to Jhannella, my mind went straight to Lynda. Swimming with my love.

After Van would finish with the Jap guards and me, he would often work out with the dumbbells. Watching Van push around these weights was impressive. I watched his body, his breathing, how his muscles worked, how he maintained his physique in the midst of a war. Because of who he was, Van showed me who I could be.

After three months, I was walking without dragging my right foot. When Van and I went for walks around the camp at night, I always wore my POW number attached around my waist with a bamboo string. A red cross was painted on my number, signaling to the guards that I was part of the medical staff. The Jap guards waved to us, and we bowed back at them to show our respect. Van said that these guards delighted in beating POWs, and he suggested that I never go outside the hut alone.

Late one night, Van instructed me how to condition my mind to survive. "Forget about your mother," Van told me. "Forget about your father. Forget about back home. Forget about your music. Forget all about what you did before, Ralph. You'll get home someday, but don't think about that stuff now, because if you do, you'll die."

After I was able to walk, Van continued to work on my shoulder. He used light weights to increase my range of motion. Unfortunately, however, my shoulder had healed in a forward position, and it now had to be realigned.

Van talked with a Dutch doctor in camp, and they fitted me with leather straps to pull my shoulder back.

"Do I have to sleep with this fucking thing on?" I asked, uncomfortable with this new harness.

"You can take the pain, and you will get used to wearing it. Your leg is working now, and we will make that shoulder work, too. We're gonna beat them," Van insisted. I wore this harness for the next two months.

As my shoulder improved, Van introduced heavier weights, then eventually a greater challenge: the bamboo pole. Van wanted to see if I could lift my own weight by doing chin-ups. On the first day, I struggled terribly. I could barely raise myself, but Van was always there to catch me.

A week later, Van said, "Now I want to see you chin yourself at least ten times. You have the strength to do twenty. I'm only asking for ten."

Van's face would tighten when my exercises weren't up to his expectations. He became vicious. "Ralph, if you don't do better, I'll shoot you myself. I won't wait for the Japs," he would say.

Soon, I was back to my original weight in the Army Air Corps, 185 pounds.

One night, at dusk, when Van and I took a brisk walk around the camp, Van noticed me spotting some of the emaciated POWs. They looked sick—like walking death. Van sensed in my eyes that I now realized it was a different world outside his hut.

"Don't make friends, Ralph. Don't get involved," Van instructed. "Don't help them. Stay away. Just take care of yourself. I know this sounds selfish, but it's the only way to survive."

Van was now explaining that I had to condition my mind one way for rehabilitation and an altogether new way for survival.

That night, and many days and nights before it, I often wondered why the Japs had sent me to Van's hut. Why would they spend six months to rehabilitate one American? Why would they waste all the food? They could have easily taken me out and shot me, and it wouldn't have made any difference. Did they really need another worker that badly? I turned it over again and again in my mind, and all I could come up with was that the Japs wanted to take Van down a peg. They wanted to bust Van's confidence, to break his idea that he could rebuild or repair anyone.

They had a complex, the Japs did. They were small. Van was large. These small Japs were going to make a jerk out of Van. They gave him the impossible, really. I was hopeless. It was a game within a game. And Van also wasn't sure that he could do it, but the more he was unsure, the harder he worked on me.

November 15, 1942. The camp commandant notified Van and me to report to his office.

"Can you work?" the camp commandant asked me in English when Van and I met him the following morning.

"Yes, Commandant," I answered in Malayan. "I am ready to follow your orders."

Stone-faced, the commandant turned to Van and said, "You have completed a good job in giving the Japanese empire a man who can work and speak the language."

Van and I bowed and left the office.

"This war won't last more than another year," Van told me when we returned to his hut. "If they beat you, Ralph, get up as fast as you can and bow to the person doing the beating, then look at him straight in the eyes."

I looked at Van and tried to find the words. "How does a man repay his best friend for saving his life?" I asked.

Van had tears in his eyes now. He took my hand and squeezed it.

"This was my victory, putting you back together," he said.

"All I can say is thank you, Van, but I feel *thank you* is so inadequate for all you have done for me."

I understood that the Dutchman had given me my body back, but I didn't realize until later that he had also given me a shield—a mental toughness that I would carry with me the rest of my life.

Van's smile looked uneasy. "You were a real challenge, Ralph," he said. "You gave me your pain, your mind, and your total cooperation. You are my finest example, which I will never forget. Now I truly know what I can do with my hands, my mind, and my willpower."

"Me, too," I said.

* 20 *

"Nice Work If You Can Get It"

November 1942

THE JAP ESCORT BARKED, AND I GRABBED MY CLOTHES, STEPPING OUT OF THE
med hut for the first time without Van at my side. The earth was barren and
hard. Hut 6, which was just across from Van's quarters, was identical to all
the other POW huts. They were the color of dried bamboo, and the roofs
were made of coconut leaves that had turned gray from the sun.

My escort pointed to my new home, then walked off. I entered and saw
two men lying on bamboo beds. Both of them looked ill.

"Who do I report to?" I asked.

"Did you just get captured?" one of them said. He introduced himself as
Bill.

"No, I've been here. I was over at the med hut. I was just transferred
here."

Bill was thin, and his face was very red. He must have been running a
temperature or been burnt badly by the sun. A dirty sheet covered him.

Each hut held about twenty men, and from what Van told me, there were
roughly fourteen hundred POWs in Camp Malang: a hundred Americans, a
hundred Brits, and the rest Dutch.

I put my mat and belongings down in a space that was empty. A mosquito
net was draped over the bed.

Bill said he had been discharged from the hospital in Surabaja the previous April. As I nodded, the foul smell of the hut overwhelmed me. Bill
stank. So did the other poor bastard. Everything stank of fish.

"Who should I report to?" I asked Bill again.

"Everybody's out on work detail. Speak to Max. He'll check you in and
give you the lowdown."

Bill introduced me to Max that evening. Max, whom a Jap sergeant had appointed head of this hut, was six feet tall and well built, with a strong jaw. American. Max dressed like all the other POWs I'd seen walking around the camp, but somehow Max looked tougher in his sandals, tan shorts, and shirt.

"I have to clean up and get something to eat," Max said. "After that, I will spend some time with you. You look all right."

When Max told me I looked good, it was like getting a shot in the arm. The other men were thin and breaking down. I knew I had an edge from my time with Van. I was ready to go into battle.

I got my mess gear, which was stolen U.S. issue, and I walked over to the POW kitchen with Max.

"What the hell is this green stuff on top of the rice?" I asked as a POW dumped some slop onto my pan.

Max looked at me and laughed. "This crap is seaweed. We dive for it every week."

"How in the hell do you survive on this?" I asked. "It looks like a pyramid of shit."

"That's why we scrounge for food wherever we can find it," Max replied. "You're going to learn how to kill an animal and bring it back under your pants so the guards don't catch you."

I told Max that I had been eating fruits and meats from the Jap kitchen when I was recuperating in the medical hut with Van. "Tomorrow morning you'll go on detail with me," Max told me.

That night, I whispered to Max the sad tale of what I had been through from the time I got shot down to the present. I praised Van and told Max that if he ever had a chance, he should try to meet the Dutchman.

Max quickly put his fingers to his lips as the Jap guards called for lights out. I rolled over, and the buzz of the floodlights kept me awake most of the night. I had known that when I left Van's hut, I would have to work. I also knew the Japs could blow my ass out at any time for any reason. I just told myself to watch and follow. Watch and follow.

The next morning, after a breakfast of rice swill (reheated rice), we lined up in rows of ten at the parade ground in front of the Jap sergeant. "*Ichi, ni, san,*" the men counted off in Japanese.

Max then approached the Jap sergeant, spoke a few words in Malayan, and then called me to come forward. I obeyed and bowed, waiting for the next order from Max. The Jap sergeant turned to Max and said in Malayan, "Good. He will make a good worker."

I bowed again and returned to the line.

Minutes later, a few other Jap guards marched us to the camp gate, where we boarded several trucks. We traveled along a dirt road for what seemed like an hour. No one said a word. Two Jap guards rode in the truck with us. They removed the bayonets from their rifles and held the sharp blades in their hands. Suddenly, the truck stopped, and I smelled oil.

Max told me the previous evening that he had been working on this oil refinery detail for the past four weeks. The stupid Nips had accidentally bombed the refinery when they were taking over the island. Oil was a precious resource, and it was our job to rebuild the facility for them.

The guards jumped out, and we were taken to a graveyard of broken pipe that spread over two acres. We were divided into three groups and ordered to carry the pipes, which were four inches in diameter and ten feet long, to three different locations. Javanese workmen hauled it all away by truck.

Max was my POW sergeant, and ten Jap guards supervised our lot of sixty POWs. While we worked, no one spoke, no one mumbled, no one sighed, for fear of a beating. And the pieces of pipe became heavier as the morning wore on. If the men weren't working fast enough, the Jap sergeant would call Max. If it was time to eat, the guard would call Max. Everything went through Max, and no POW ever addressed a Jap guard.

During lunch, I whispered to Max that I could speak a little Malayan, offering my help to him with the Jap guards.

"You don't have the experience to handle these guards," Max said sharply. "They'll beat the piss out of you if you make one mistake."

I didn't make any more offers to Max.

After our exchange, Max had to run over to the Jap sergeant to explain what he and I had discussed. The Japs were afraid of a mutiny. They always thought we were plotting an escape. Where the hell were we going to escape to? Australia was three thousand miles away. All of us POWs were waiting, wondering when the United States would invade.

Later that afternoon, Max asked the Jap sergeant if the men could take a rest. I watched the American closely. Max ran up to the guard, bowed very low, and said in Malayan, "Your humble worker asks for the men who are very tired. They need some rest."

At first I thought this was humiliating. Max was bowing so much he looked like a horse. But then I reminded myself that Max was only playing the game. He knew how to make the little bastard feel like an emperor. Play it, Ralph. Play the game to stay alive. Little Hirohito nodded, and all the POWs sat down on a pipe and rested.

Moments later, a Jap guard approached his Jap sergeant. I tried to listen, but I couldn't hear anything. The Jap sergeant then called Max and told him we were returning to camp.

Later, while in the showers, Max informed me that the Jap sergeant had been in a good mood—you could tell because he wasn't shouting at his guards. The showers, which were built right along the canal that cut through the camp, was the only place POWs could talk with some degree of safety.

Jap guards were posted outside the showers, but the noise of the water pumping underneath the stalls made it almost impossible for them to hear us. If
they did hear someone talking, they'd come in and beat the first person they
saw, Max cautioned.

"Your men work their backs off for these bastards," I said.

Max shook his head. "There was no way to steal any food where we
worked today, which means we have to go stealing in the Jap kitchen in the
dead of night."

Max had overheard the Jap sergeant say that they were having fish
tonight, and the Japs hated the Javanese fish. They usually threw it in the
garbage, a perfect opportunity for a raid.

"Who was your partner on the last raid?" I asked, a little wary.

"He's sick, and he ain't going with me. It's too dangerous. We get the
cream, Ralph, and give the other guys what's left over."

"Why'd you ask me?"

"I need a good backup. I've watched you wrestle that pipe. You can carry
your weight. I'm going to teach you the ropes so that you can stay alive in
this godforsaken place."

Max and I waited until the middle of the night and then crawled along
the dark side of hut 6 with a large burlap potato sack in our hands. Right
above the machine gun nests in each corner of the camp were floodlights
that sprayed light at a forty-five-degree angle, covering the entire camp. I
breathed heavily as these lights shined above us and then followed Max, who
dashed toward the garbage pile behind the Jap kitchen. We crouched low,
snaking between the fifty-five-gallon drums of garbage. Max glanced quickly
toward the front gate, then nodded. We filled our sacks with duck eggshells
and the stinking fish.

"Not too much," Max whispered. "Just enough to carry back at a fast
pace."

Getting back to the hut was another challenge. We dragged the over-
stuffed bags along the ground. Our little adventure didn't alert the front
guards, who were barking in the distance. As Max and I scooped up our bags,
searching for another pocket of darkness, I heard Van in my head: *You're an
animal in the forest. Survival takes over. You have to be stronger than them.
They're running after you. They're running after you, Ralph.*

Max and I waited again for the floodlights to pass. Two Jap guards suddenly appeared. This was the worst detail for them, patrolling the camp at
night. They always walked in pairs, always talking, fearful of an attack. The
guards passed us, and, timing the floodlights again, we dragged the bags back
to our hut.

Most of the fellows were asleep, but it wasn't long before every one of them pulled out their coconut leaves and wrapped up their share of the fish before returning to bed. Max and I looked at each other. We had made it.

The next day we used an old steel helmet as a cooking pot, elevating it and heating it with a tripod made of branches. Every piece of food was cut into small pieces, then dried in the sun until dehydrated. We used markers to signify our food. Max had a purple stone. I had a white one. Most fellows engraved their names into their stones. Nobody stole from anyone else, and the Jap guards never messed with our food.

We made coconut oil from the coconuts around the camp, and we boiled duck eggs when we could get them, along with fish heads, grasshoppers, snakes, dogs, ants, and large rats. Ants were quite tasty. This was our scavenger's diet. We would also sneak carcasses into camp, tying them to the backs of our legs with bamboo string. This made people walk a little funny, and the Jap guards knew what was going on. They thought we were animals, and we thought they were animals for the way they treated us.

The camp, meanwhile, provided a daily dose of fish, seaweed, and rice. I hated rice even before I was in prison camp, but if you didn't eat it, you died. It was our staff of life.

Flies were numerous and always in our face, especially during the dry season, when our hut reeked of rotten fish and decaying meat. No one could get accustomed to the environment. The latrine was so far from our hut that guys would just piss outside anywhere, another reason the whole place stank.

We spent five more weeks on the oil refinery, and we still weren't finished. We worked six days a week, eight hours a day. The seventh day was mine. Days blended together. Food. Work. Rest. Food work rest. Foodworkrest.

Time was kept by the banging that came from the POW kitchen twice a day, signaling lunch and dinner. We received no paper or pencils and kept no records of days or months or years. Once a week, the commandant would speak to the entire camp, giving us the date before each speech. The commandant's sword was so big that it scraped along the ground when he walked. He always had four bodyguards with him.

"You're all no-good bastards," he would say through his interpreter. "Nothing's getting done. We're giving you plenty of clothing. Food. You're all going to be shot or beheaded soon." The commandant would scream, beat his chest, wave his arms. While listening to him rant, you could hear the POWs breathing.

I didn't know anything about the other fourteen hundred POWs. It was like they were in a foreign country. The only time I saw them was when we counted off three times a day. They were on their own work details—"work parties," as we called them—such as cleaning out the Jap officers' barracks, cleaning around the huts, cleaning around the camp's three electrical fences, fixing the roofs of the huts, diving for seaweed, getting firewood for both the POW and Jap kitchens, and collecting coconuts and palm leaves. I really didn't want to get too close to anyone, like Van had taught me. You never knew who would disappear tomorrow.

A POW was either on a work detail or in his hut. There was no wandering around the camp. The Japs were always changing regulations, changing rules, which kept us scared, confused, and off-balance. And this was exactly the way the Japs liked it.

＝◆＝

It was March 1943, and the dirt road leading to the oil refinery had been washed away by the heavy rainfall. Rain came down so hard that you couldn't see your hand in front of you. The ground was covered with oil, and you could easily fall on your ass, especially if you were barefoot. Fortunately, I wore sandals, but some POWs didn't have them. Everything was flooded, but the canal absorbed the runoff. The arched bridges that crossed the canal were high enough and weren't washed away. Once the rains ceased, the sun would come out.

The Japs had called in their own engineers to instruct us in reconnecting the oil pipes. We now moved the pipes inside the refinery piece by piece—more than three hundred of them. With the broiling sun beating on us for hours, we dragged these pipes with a rope. Then a Javanese workman would take them off to the refinery, where the POWs would then hold the pipe for the engineers to weld. We only stopped if somebody dropped dead or passed out. The cemetery was just two miles away.

Max told me that during the rainy season, POWs would dig holes for fresh bodies, and the graves would fill up with water. The Japs didn't care: they just ordered the POWs to throw mud on top of the dead.

Max and I spoke regularly in the showers about the other men and their health. That night, Max decided that he should meet with the Jap sergeant and explain that the Japs were much stronger than white men. Since we were weaker than they were, we needed a little more rest. After stroking the Jap sergeant this way, Max said he would ask if—to prevent fainting—the men could wear straw hats with large brims to keep the sun out of our eyes. Then we could ask for more water to keep up the pace of our demanding work detail.

Max then removed several duck eggshells from his pants and shared one with me. I watched him grind the shells into a paste with his finger. He then shoved his finger into his mouth. This is how we brushed our teeth.

"Don't tell the others," Max instructed. "Duck shells are scarce."

I nodded.

"Now remember, Ralph, when you speak to the Japs, its always 'Would you permit?' or 'Would you allow?' Never 'I would like.' Otherwise they'll beat the living shit out of you."

After Max concocted this scheme, he turned his thoughts to me. "Ralph, you better get to another detail. You're lean and strong now, but that won't last for long. You're gonna break. You've got a bad shoulder, and that leg will come back to haunt you. You should become a POW sergeant so you won't have to work—just manage like I do. Maybe I can help you."

I nodded, uncertain.

After showering, most of us would put our dirty clothes back on or drape them over our bodies. Then we would return to the hut to lie down. Some guys didn't wake up. The dead men would be carried out the next morning. When it rained at night, the hut leaked. Our bamboo beds were eighteen inches off the floor. There were puddles all around. I thought about what Max had told me in the showers. I had seen Max take a beating when some of the men were caught talking. He would step between a Jap guard and a POW. Without hesitation, Max would defend the POWs and take vicious beatings for his men, sometimes saving their lives. And Max always seemed to bounce back after these beatings. He was tough, but I wasn't ready for Max's gig because it was too much responsibility. I wasn't ready to approach the Jap guards and protect men—not yet.

On the final day at the refinery, as we were walking back about a mile to the trucks, engines were heard in the distance. Suddenly six dive-bombers came screaming out of the sky. The POWs dove into the underbrush. When the bombs landed, the ground shook, and the oil drums at the refinery exploded, belching fire with each hit. I thought the world was coming to an end.

The bombers made two runs at the refinery, and when the planes left, all the POWs came running out of the underbrush, shouting, "The Americans are coming! The Americans are coming!"

The Jap sergeant and his guards immediately lined us up in single file. Max was called out first. The Jap sergeant borrowed a rifle from one of the guards and walked behind Max, striking him in the back of knees with the weapon. Max went down, and the sergeant kicked him in the ribs. Max got up slowly, bowed, then collapsed, losing his balance.

Then the guards started in on the rest of us, using the same method of punishment. When my turn came, I tried to crumble as soon as I felt the rifle strike my knee, but the kick in the ribs really shook me up.

Bruised but hopeful after the air raid, we defied the Japs, singing all the way home, "The Americans are coming! The Americans are coming!"

For once, the Japs looked confused. Their stone expressions were replaced by fear. They now believed that the Americans were indeed coming and that the POWs would find a way to kill each and every Jap soldier.

The Jap guards didn't hit one man for singing on that joyous ride back to camp. This slavery would be over shortly, we all thought. From that day on, the prison camp was a living hell.

∗ 21 ∗

"Chattanooga Choo Choo"

April 1943

"HOW MANY YOU GONNA KILL?"

"I'm gonna line 'em up, make 'em dig their graves, then shoot 'em all."

"I'm gonna take all their swords and chop all their heads off and leave 'em for the animals."

These were some of the kinder sentiments spoken that night in hut 6. However, we found out the next day that the Japs had doubled up with more guards. They brought in Koreans, who were larger men with wider foreheads. Boisterous, cruel and eager to pick a fight with anyone, including the Jap guards, the Koreans hated the Japs almost as much as the POWs did because the Koreans were a conquered people, and they knew they would be forced to fight the Americans when they invaded.

When we lined up for counting heads the day after the air raid, the Jap and Korean guards were shoving us and pointing guns in our faces to speed up the process. The commandant also popped up more often during the next few days in full dress with his sword swinging at his side. The Jap sergeants dressed more formally for the count as well. The mood was grave. Death was in the air.

Since the oil refinery had again been destroyed by the American air raid, my work detail varied from cleaning the underbrush outside the camp to cleaning the Jap living quarters. But less than a week later, the commandant notified the entire camp that the American, Australian, and British POWs would be transferred to another camp. All Dutch prisoners would remain. The Japs were transporting us because they felt that Camp Malang was going to be invaded, and they wanted to keep us for labor. We would be moving in three days.

Once I heard the news, I went over to Van's hut and poked my head inside. He was eating dinner. "Wait here," Van said, jumping up. "I'll get you some food."

Van returned with some fresh fruit, and we spoke about the impending move. "I told you the Americans would eventually come. They will be here soon," Van said.

Van gave me his address in Holland and the address of another hospital where he thought he'd be moved. Surprisingly, Van asked me for Jhannella's address.

"Try the Belém University," I said, a little surprised.

"Thank you. I will," said the Dutchman. "I will try and get in touch with her after the war and tell her about our time together."

Then Van looked at me. "Forget about me, Ralph," he said.

"I could never forget about you, Van. You saved my life."

When I left, we both had tears in our eyes.

I don't think I would have made it without Van. I wouldn't have made it without Frerry at the hospital, either.

We were allowed to take only our clothes and a full canteen of water. At six in the morning, all the POWs lined up for count off on the parade ground. After three times, the head count was still short. The Jap guards ordered the Korean guards to search for the missing men. The guards found two Brits in the latrine with dysentery, dragged them out, and doused them with a large hose. The water pressure overpowered the men, knocking them to the ground and rolling them along the grass. The guards then stood the Brits on their feet and beat them savagely. The Brits were shitting all over themselves as they absorbed blow after blow. The commandant finally stopped it. Covered in filthy rags, their faces caked with mud, the two Brits joined the line. They could hardly stand.

I felt sorry for them, but pity had no place here. I became hardened not to feel their pain. I had my shield.

The Korean guards couldn't find anyone else, so they marched us to the front gate. Trucks were waiting. We didn't know where they were sending us. We were ordered not to talk. We were taken to the train station just outside Surabaja, where we lined up and counted off again. This time, the count was correct, and the guards seemed pleased that they hadn't lost anyone on the trip. They made us stand at attention for an hour.

The guards then marched us to the other end of the yard to a series of freight cars. All the Americans were put into the last two cars in front of the caboose, roughly fifty men to a car. There was little room to sit or lie down, so most of us stood. The Japs left the boarding doors open. We stood for another hour, and then the orders were given. The doors closed.

The only light came from the two holes overhead.

"The train will start with a jerk, so hold onto the man beside you," I heard Max call out from the other side of the boxcar. As we clung to each other, the train started to roll. Some men were mumbling prayers. I felt a slight breeze come through the holes overhead.

"Fellows, listen up," I heard Max call out again. "It's important that we stay alive in this box. We need a latrine, or we will be shitting all over each other."

Max then told half of the men to bend down to see if there was a rotted piece of wood beneath them. If there was, we would rip it out and make a commode.

"Over here," someone shouted. All the men squeezed together so Max could sneak by.

"We may be able to lift it or punch it out," Max said.

"I have a small screwdriver," said a man in the back, who surprisingly had the tool tied to his leg. The screwdriver was passed to Max at the other end of the boxcar. No one said a word, as the rickety wheels squeaked along. It seemed like an hour before Max said, "We got a good hole here. Make sure you don't lose a leg when you shit."

The temperature must have been well over a hundred degrees, but the hole in the floor provided some ventilation. Fortunately, the hole was near the side of the car, so the wall could be used to support one's back while squatting over the makeshift toilet. Unfortunately, there was a reverse draft that created an unbelievable stench. Many men rushed to use the hole at the same time, and their shit would often hit the train wheel and fly right back up at us. Those with dysentery were in a very bad way. It was as if we were trapped in someone's rectum.

In an effort to create some order, Max told half the men to stand for an hour while the others tried to sleep. Then we rotated. The floor was sloppy and wet, and I didn't dare sit down. Sitting down meant death to me. But I couldn't sleep standing up. All I could do was lean against the side of the boxcar.

As the train rolled along, the men moaned, wheezed, cried, and prayed. I couldn't see where the sounds were coming from, but they were all around me. Max found his way near me.

"If this is a long ride, half of us are going to die, Max."

"We're going to pull over to the siding very soon and get out."

"Where do you get your information?" I asked.

"From one of the guards. On top," Max said, "where the real stink is."

One of these guards then lowered a bucket of rice through the overhead hole. Max ordered one of the men to take a handful of rice and disperse it to the others. The rice was cold, so we could roll it into a ball and eat it like an apple. Water was also sent down with a small rubber hose to fill our canteens.

The train had been moving at a moderate speed the entire ride so that the guards on top of the boxcar wouldn't fall off, but suddenly the train slowed, and we veered onto a siding, as Max had predicted. The doors opened, and a gush of fresh air overwhelmed us. The Jap guards, who were now standing with bayonets attached to their guns, wore white masks to defy the acrid odor.

Prodded out of the boxcar and ordered to line up, we counted off again to make sure that no one had died along the way.

The Jap sergeant in charge then picked out a dozen POWs and ordered them to the caboose. These men pulled several hoses along the ground and connected them to the bottom of a water tower nearby. Twelve other POWs were told to wash out the boxcars. The others stood and watched.

Afterwards, all the POWs were hosed down with our clothes on. We looked like drowned rats. The Jap guards lined us up again. We refilled our canteens and received some dried fish. The Jap sergeant informed us that we would be traveling for another two days. Based on that information, we thought we had to be headed for Batavia.

As we returned to the soggy box, some wondered if we were going to be shipped out; others wondered if we would still be alive by then. During the past few months at Camp Malang, many POWs had been told that they were being sent to the hills in Batavia to build Jap fortifications. There was also a rumor that a new work camp was being constructed up there. This information came from the commandant during his weekly announcement at the parade grounds. Other rumors floated around as well. The most prominent one was that the Japs were shipping most of the POWs to China. Many POWs had different opinions about our future. At least all the rumors gave us a way to pass the time.

I looked over at Max; his jaw was still strong.

"Can I help you at all?" I asked him.

"I would appreciate a little help, Ralph. But will the men listen to you?"

No, they probably wouldn't, I thought.

"If I need you, I'll call you," Max said as he peered up at the hole above.

We traveled through the night, and the boxcar again became a putrid mess. While waiting in line for the latrine, some men wouldn't make it to the hole. We were all getting bilious and gagging.

I tried again with all my being to sleep, but I couldn't. Weary, I suddenly saw an image of Captain Montel and the other dead crewmen. They were lucky to have died rather than go through this torture, I thought.

In an effort to control my fears, I tried to remain as small as possible. If I inhaled too deeply, I was going to vomit. I didn't want to expend a single ounce of energy. My goal was absolute stillness. "I'm not here. I just disappeared," I told myself. I lowered my heart rate and closed my eyes. This way,

I wouldn't get caught up in someone else's troubles or someone else's wild rumors or have to deal with those fucking guards.

The following morning, we made another watering stop and went through the same hose-down routine as before. Meanwhile, the Jap guards, most of whom were crowded into the caboose, started to become more violent. If a POW wasn't moving to their liking, a guard would strike him across the shoulders with a four-foot bamboo pole.

That day, twenty men were down with dysentery, and the Japs weren't about to clean out our boxcar. Two men with dysentery died the following day. We informed the guards above us, but they just laughed.

"You should all die," one of them said in Malayan.

Several hours later, we rolled into the freight yards of Batavia. We lined up and counted off again. We were short by four men. The guards made us count off again, and we were still four short.

The Jap sergeant told the guards to search the boxcar. They opened the freight door, but the smell was so horrendous that the guards wouldn't stick their faces inside. Irate, the Jap sergeant rushed up to the two guards and knocked them to the ground, then ordered them to get the water hoses. We sat near the tracks, watching. After the guards finished hosing out the boxcars, they dragged out four dead bodies and tossed them on the ground.

I didn't know these POWs. I knew only a few men in the whole camp. Everyone kept to themselves. My eyes left the deceased and searched for the nearest guard. My own survival depended greatly on watching the Jap guards, not my fellow POWs.

A truck pulled up, and four Javanese workmen loaded up the dead and drove off. The rest of us were driven to a large facility. As the truck stopped, the guards at the front gates got a whiff of us and let out a scream, covering their noses. Laughing.

As we entered the gates, I noticed it was a small city of concrete structures, very different from Camp Malang. A former Dutch military camp, this facility consisted of more than a hundred buildings, and it now housed more than sixteen thousand POWs—ten thousand Brits, five thousand Aussies, one thousand Americans, and a handful of Dutch.

The POWs here also looked different than those in Camp Malang. These men weren't in bad shape. They were thin but not deathly ill. They wore clothes and sandals. Their walk didn't signify abject depression or exhaustion. After surviving the boxcar, I took this as a glimmer of hope.

American POWs were stationed at the showers and instructed us to remove all our clothes and to hold onto our canteens and numbers. My number was 20324856.

We placed our clothing into oil drums, then took cakes of soap and scrubbed our bodies until they were pink. Taking a shower and using soap reacquainted me with civilization. We hadn't had soap at Camp Malang. I felt like I was being born again.

Later, each man was issued a straw hat, sandals, shorts, and a shirt. We were then taken to the medical building, where we were interviewed by male medics who were also POWs. Food was brought in on banana leaves. We devoured it like animals.

All of us were then escorted to a building where cocoa mats were provided. These sleeping mats were made from the soft, inner bark of a coconut tree. Feeling safe for the moment, I hit the hard floor and fell asleep before I could think about what I had been through or what would come next.

IN REPLY
REFER TO AG 201 Rentz, Ralph M.
(3-14-42) EB 07302-1

March 14, 1942.

Mrs. Minnie Rentz,
38 North Wycombe Avenue,
Lansdowne, Pennsylvania.

Dear Mrs. Rentz:

It is with regret that I confirm the recent War
Department telegram informing you that your son, Ralph M.
Rentz, 20,324,856, was seriously wounded in action in
Java and that he was reported to be a prisoner of war.

The report contained information that because
of the nature of his wound it was impossible to evacuate
him from a Dutch military hospital prior to its capture
by the enemy. No further information is available at
this time, however, it is expected that the Japanese Government will ultimately report his status to this government
through neutral agencies. In that event the information
will be transmitted to you by the Prisoner of War Information Bureau, Office of the Provost Marshal General, Washington, D. C.

Your home chapter of the American Red Cross
will be glad to advise you and help you in every way possible.

Permit me to express my deep sympathy.

Very truly yours,

[signature]

Major General,
The Adjutant General.

Once my parents received this notice from the War Department, they became friendly with the Lansdowne branch of the American Red Cross. After the war, my parents informed me that they wrote me many times, but I never received a letter during my entire stay as a POW.

IN REPLY
REFER TO   AG 201 Rentz, Ralph M.
      (4-7-42) SPXBD.

April 7, 1942

Mrs. Minnie Rentz,
    38 N. Wycombe Ave.,
      Lansdowne, Pennsylvania.

Dear Madam:

    According to the records of the War Department your son, Ralph
M. Rentz, 20,324,856, has been reported as captured.

    A recent enactment of Congress (Public Act 490, 77th Congress
2nd Session) provides for the continuance, during a specified period,
of the pay and allowances of persons in the military service, and
certain civilian employees, who have been reported missing, missing
in action, interned in a neutral country or captured by an enemy.

    Under the provisions of the above mentioned Act, and within the
limitations therein contained, consideration may be given by the War
Department to the making or increasing of allotments from the pay of
any person in the status described in the second paragraph of this
letter to provide for the reasonable support of an actual dependent
within certain degrees of relationship to the missing, interned or
captured person.

    In order to file a claim for making or increasing an allotment
from the pay of the person named in the first paragraph it is necessary
to complete the attached form, which should be sent to the War Department
in the enclosed envelope, which requires no postage. However, for the
information of the Department, this form should be completed and submitted
in all cases, whether an allotment is desired at the present time or not.
It is not necessary to employ the services of an attorney or claim
agent. Your home chapter of the American Red Cross will be glad to assist
you in filling out this form.

    Upon return of the attached form it will be connected with any
prior letters you may have addressed to the War Department relative to
a claim for dependency.

Very truly yours,

J. A. Ulio
Major General,
The Adjutant, General.
By: *J.B.*

2 Incls.
  Affidavit
  Penalty Envelope

*Even though I was reported as "captured," my parents never gave up hope. As my time as a
POW passed from months to years—and my whereabouts uncertain to those back home—the
Army Air Corps offered my father a check for $10,000 (the death benefit of my AAC life in-
surance policy), but my father refused. He believed I would make it home alive.*

RE: Private Ralph M. Rentz,
Interned in Java, by Japan.

Mr. and Mrs. Rentz,
38 North Wycombe Avenue,
Lansdowne, Pennsylvania.

Dear Mr. and Mrs. Rentz:

The Provost Marshal General directs me to forward to you the inclosed short wave radio message which
was intercepted by government facilities.

The War Department is unable to verify this
message and it is not to be construed as an official
notification.

If additional information concerning the above
named person is received from any source, you will be advised.

Sincerely yours,

Howard F Bresee

Howard F. Bresee,
Colonel, C.M.P.,
Chief, Information Bureau.

1 Incl.
Radio Message.

FCCF E2

BATAVIA IN ENGLISH AT 1:30 AM TO UNITED STATES

(AMERICAN PRISONERS)

1. RALPH M. RENTZ, PRIVATE UNITED STATES ARMY AIR CORPS, JAVA, TO
HIS MOTHER AND FATHER, MR. AND MRS. RENTZ, 38 NORTH WYCOMBE AVENUE,
LANSDOWNE, PENNSYLVANIA, UNITED STATES.

"DEAR PARENTS: I AM A PRISONER OF WAR IN JAVA. MY HEALTH IS GOOD
AND THINGS N GENERAL ARE FINE. I HOPE TO BE HOME SOON, SO DON'T WORRY
CONCERNING MY WELL-BEING. SEND MY REGARDS TO ALL. LOVE."

As a boy, I used to play around with a ham radio at a friend's house after school. I became fascinated with the idea of sending and receiving messages. In order to send this message from Batavia, I only had about 15 seconds. I didn't know if this short-wave radio message would reach my parents, I just sent it east and hoped it got there.

Here's Jojean and me while I was recovering in Denver after the war. That's Zip Zummo with Carlita and another POW, Fred Willow, with his gal. It was good to feel wanted again.

My Father, Izzy Rentz, and my mother, Minnie Rentz. Next to my parents are my older sister, Sylvia, and my youngest brother, Zeldon. I really wanted my parents to be proud of me. I had disappointed them so much, especially because they wanted me to be a professional man and I wanted to be a professional musician.

11 December 1943

RE: R. M. Rentz.

Mr. and Mrs. I. Rentz.
   38 N. Wycombe Avenue,
      Lansdowne, Pennsylvania.

Dear Mr. and Mrs. Rentz:

The Provost Marshal General directs me to reply to your recent inquiry in regard to the above.

No further packages may be sent to American civilians and prisoners of war of Japan. When negotiations have been completed for the sailing of relief ships at some future date, the next of kin will be notified and parcel labels will be forwarded without request.

It will be of interest to you to learn that in addition to personal parcels, selected medical supplies and clothing, the MS Gripsholm carried over 80,000 specially prepared American Red Cross gift parcels. These extra parcels are intended for periodic distribution to American nationals now interned in Japan and Japanese occupied areas.

They will also be given to all prisoners of war and civilian internees who are as yet not reported or were reported too late to permit the next of kin to ship a personal package via the MS Gripsholm which left New York on 2 September 1943.

Sincerely yours,

Howard F. Bresee,
Colonel, C.M.P,
Assistant Director,
Prisoner of War Division.

FOR VICTORY
BUY
UNITED STATES
WAR
BONDS
AND
STAMPS

Supplies from the American Red Cross only reached us once while I was a POW in Java, and the Japanese kept the entire load for themselves.

Rentz's Market at 38 N. Wycombe Ave, Lansdowne, Pennsylvania. Our whole family—the seven of us—lived upstairs.

Even though I am smiling here, I never felt comfortable in my uniform. I felt like a stranger in it. I always preferred a tuxedo.

Together again. Zip Zummo and me at Fitzsimons General Hospital in Denver just before they released me from Ward 26, the special ward for POWs who contracted tuberculosis in the Pacific.

My mother took this picture of *The Three Bandits*—Zip, a fellow named David, and me. Zip and I met David when we first arrived in Denver. He passed away in the hospital.

✴ 22 ✴

"Saturday Night Is the Loneliest Night of the Week"

May 1943

WE WERE AWAKENED THE FOLLOWING MORNING BY A JAP BUGLER WHO sounded like a wounded monkey. After we lined up and counted off, a Jap sergeant asked if anyone spoke Malayan. I hesitated. Max raised his hand, and the sergeant told him to step forward. Max bowed, then stood at attention. The sergeant barked instructions at him.

"We are going to be interviewed separately for the next two days by a Jap officer who speaks English," Max translated after the sergeant left. "We will have to stay around these quarters until our numbers are called. Keep a low profile if you want to stay out of trouble."

My interview was on the second day. The previous night I had learned from the others that the Japs had information on us from the time we landed on Java. They were just updating their files.

I was escorted to a back room. A Jap officer sat behind a desk in a white ruffled shirt. He spoke to me in Malayan, asking me to sit down. I was caught off guard because Max had told us that he would speak English.

The Jap officer smiled, as if he enjoyed my awkwardness, then said, "Mr. Van Doren taught you the language when you were recovering in Malang," said the officer.

I nodded.

Then the officer spoke in English. "I have your records from the hospital. I also know that you were left in the hospital when your commanding officer, a Colonel Eubank, flew to Australia."

Frerry? I wondered. Who else could have told the man? How else could this Jap officer know this? They had all our military files. Everything.

I turned my face into stone, just like them. The officer studied me, then continued. "I also know you didn't come down from the Philippines."

He watched my eyes. I didn't blink. He continued, "I know you're a sergeant and a radio operator. The only hole that I have is—where did you come from before Malang?"

I thought a few seconds, edgy. Did he know about the secret mission? The gold? How could he?

"Darwin, Australia, Sir," I said firmly.

The officer smiled. "That is what your copilot told us. All I wanted from you was to confirm the information we already had."

The interview was over, but as I was escorted back to my quarters, I kept wondering if the officer knew more than what I gave him. Was Frerry here? Was he still alive?

I discovered later that the Japs would be separating POWs by country, then placing them into different buildings. The next morning, an American POW who introduced himself as Zip Zummo of the 131st Field Artillery called my number.

"How do you like the bicycle camp?" said Zip. Rugged and slender, Zip was a middleweight boxing champ from Texas. He was twenty years old.

Zip led me through a building that looked identical to all the others and mentioned that he had been taken prisoner about a year earlier. I was immediately impressed with Zip because he seemed to be holding up well. His attitude was positive in comparison to the average POW, and he had all his teeth, which was commendable for a boxer and a prisoner of war.

"You're just going to be here a short while until you're shipped up north to another camp in Sumatra, where some of the Aussies have been sent," Zip told me.

"Where do you get your information?" I asked him.

"Huh?" Zip said, flashing me his winning smile. "I make myself useful to the camp and the Nips, whom I hate with a vengeance."

"Why do they call it the bicycle camp?" I finally asked him.

"Oh, because of the Javanese. The locals bike up to the wire fence and do business with the POWs and guards. They sell and trade anything, from food to cigarettes. Come on. I'm here to educate you on all procedures."

Zip then introduced me to the other POWs in his quarters. They were housed in a one-floor building with indoor plumbing, showers, and utilities. My new roommates were also members of Zip's artillery unit, which had been sent over to Java with just two guns. They were captured on their first day. This was the only camp they had been in. I told the fellows about the nightmare train ride, mentioning the four POWs who died on the way.

"If those bastards have a reason for killing you, they put down 'died of dysentery' on the record," Zip said. "Listen, Ralph, you better go on sick call tomorrow morning, huh?"

I nodded and told Zip I didn't have a mess kit. All I had were the clothes on my back and the four-inch piece of shrapnel in my pants pocket.

"Don't worry," said Zip. "I'll take care of you."

Zip checked me in with an officer of these quarters, then gave me a tour of the camp, pointing out who the Jap bosses were inside and outside of the wire. The bicycle camp had a single fence, not an electric one like Camp Malang, and the fence had many small holes, but there was really nowhere to escape to. Zip told me that five Dutchmen had escaped and had even gotten as far as the Pacific in a rowboat. They thought they were going to make it to Australia or hoping a U.S. ship would save them. Instead, a Jap destroyer found them. The commandant brought the men back to the camp, and during an evening ceremony, Jap guards dressed in black and white robes beheaded the five POWs in front of everyone.

Zip also mentioned which Jap guards enjoyed beating the POWs and which ones looked the other way. "Be careful about bringing anything into the camp," cautioned Zip. "If it's edible, eat it outside the wire; if it has to be cooked and it's not too big, strap it on your body where it won't be detected. The gate guards sometimes check for something unusual as you walk through. Also, a POW officer and a POW noncom will be in charge of every work detail. Of course, a Jap topkick and his guards will be herding the group all the time."

The next day, I was told to report to the interrogating Jap officer again. Was Frerry indeed here? I was nervous.

"Do you know how to swim and dive?" the Jap interrogator said.

"Yes," I replied, a bit confused.

The officer smiled and continued in Malayan. "You will receive more rice and fruit, and you will go to work tomorrow morning. Exercise is good while you work."

That evening, a POW detail officer, Lieutenant Jones, entered my quarters and told me when and where to fall in tomorrow morning.

There were thirty-six men in my new detail. After the count off and visual inspection, we marched through the front gate. One truck was loaded with empty oil barrels and supplies; the other four were for the Jap guards and POWs.

We rode along the beach until the Jap sergeant located a patch of seaweed floating on the ocean surface. Everyone climbed out of the trucks, and Lieutenant Jones lined us up in three groups of twelve. The first group would swim, dive, and cut the seaweed. The second group would drag the seaweed to shore. The third group would then squeeze the seaweed dry and then cut it and pack it into the oil barrels. This seaweed would be our dinner four days from now, after the salt had been removed.

The Jap guards distributed knives to the POWs in the first group, who also received flat rubber glasses to help in seeing underwater. Although these glasses were useful, they also limited one's peripheral vision, like horse blinders. A diver had to keep turning his head continuously to follow the flow of the seaweed that was moving all around him, which made the work both stressful and dangerous. If you got tangled in the seaweed, it was like a giant had gotten hold of you. You thought you could wiggle out of it, but the second arm would get you.

After one hour of this routine, the groups switched duties; later, we stopped for lunch—rice, fruit, and monkey meat, which was considered a delicacy. This was our only chance to rest, and unlike Camp Malang, we were allowed to talk among ourselves.

I was on this seaweeding detail four days a week, eight hours a day, for three weeks. During the fourth week, Lieutenant Jones took ill, and a new officer named Walker replaced him. When POWs were told that an officer had taken ill, it meant that he was being shipped off to China or Japan on the hell ships. Officers didn't get any special treatment. Frerry had probably been shipped out, I figured. It was impossible to find out, useless to ask. And Frerry was a cripple. He wasn't here. He was dead or gone or both.

Since Walker didn't speak Malayan and knew nothing of seaweeding, I was named noncom in charge of the detail, probably because the guards knew I spoke Malayan. On my first day in charge of the detail, there were moderately rough seas. I swam out with the men in the first group and noticed that the current had a heavy undertow.

The seaweed was moving with the undertow, and its branches were pushing down under the rush of the current. We had to dive deep to cut the seaweed because the undertow pulled it down. Trying to avoid an extremely dangerous situation, I ordered the divers to stop cutting. I wanted to speak with the Jap sergeant. As I approached him, I thought about Max. I hadn't seen him since we arrived at the bicycle camp.

I employed Max's technique of bowing and being humble when I informed the Jap sergeant that the ocean was churning with an undertow, but he called me some name in his native tongue, scrunched his face, and pointed to the water. I swam back out there in a hurry, telling the men to use the buddy system to keep a close watch on the tails of the seaweed, which could ensnare limbs.

We had to dive down about twenty feet, holding our breath, to cut the green shit. Less than half an hour later, one of the men screamed, "My buddy's down." His partner was caught in the seaweed.

POWs from the first and second groups went under, starting the search. They ripped the man out of the water, cutting and tearing the seaweed from around his neck and arms. When the POWs dragged the victim to shore, one fellow revived him while the Jap sergeant and guards remained stone-faced. The victim, a kid named Gabriel, coughed water and started breathing again. "It's suicide!" he gasped, "Don't send the men back out there." He was looking at me.

I told Walker that the seaweed couldn't be cut in this undertow. It was uncontrollable. Walker then told the Jap sergeant, who surprised me by agreeing.

When we arrived back at camp, Walker and I were escorted into the commandant's office. The commandant and a Jap intelligence officer were both seated behind a large desk. The intelligence officer looked at Walker and spoke to him in English. "You will have an additional day of work this week to catch up."

Walker nodded.

Then the intelligence officer addressed me in Malayan. "I understand you are the new sergeant for this detail," he said. "You did a good job by supporting the honor of the Imperial Japanese Army."

Walker and I bowed, saluted, and exited.

"I hope that undertow slows down by tomorrow or we are going to be in trouble with the Imperial Japanese Army," joked Walker once we got outside.

"Yes. We'll work at night."

"Shit," Walker sighed.

"I'd rather take a beating than swim in that washing machine," I said.

If the water was uncooperative tomorrow, we'd probably take a beating for it, I thought, savoring the absurdity of it all.

But the next day, there was only a mild undertow. The men were happy, and so was the Jap sergeant. However, after lunch, one of the men noticed a floating batch of seaweed that hadn't been pulled to shore from the last cutting. It was swirling. Then I spotted a fin.

The men became frightened. No one stepped into the water. A school of sharks appeared, splashing near the seaweed. Suddenly, one of them clamped down on the tail of a large fish and leaped over the seaweed to avoid getting tangled. This was quite a spectacle.

With the blood of the dead fish bumping along the surface, bound to attract more sharks, the Jap sergeant called off work for the rest of the day. He was angry, swinging his bamboo stick against the oil drums as we loaded them onto the truck.

For the next two weeks, we worked on the seaweeding detail every day, and the Japs made sure our quota nearly doubled. The conditions, however, were becoming even more treacherous because of the trade winds and changing seasons. The tides were rough, the currents were stronger, and the sharks were fishing closer to shore. Every POW was near collapse. Walker and I tried to speak to the commandant but were denied permission.

Some POWs were going on sick call with bronchitis and breathing problems, and training their replacements wasn't easy. An accident was waiting to happen.

Seaweeding was similar to the way I felt about my fellow POWs: I didn't want to get too close. I didn't want to get wrapped up in anybody who would pull me down. I learned to distance myself from the men as I trained them. I couldn't feel sorry for them, because I couldn't feel sorry for myself. *"Don't get involved."* Van was still in my head.

One of the new fellows asked me, "Do they have section 8s here, or do they just kill you?"

"What do you think?" I replied.

Late at night, I often discussed my day's work with Zip, who had a much cushier job sweeping out the Jap barracks.

"You know, I'm only twenty-five, Zip," I said, "and already I've been under the control of the U.S. Army, the Army Air Corps, and now the fucking Japs. When I get out of this mess, I'm going to be my own boss with my own set of rules."

"Easy, boy," Zip said as he laughed. "The U.S. Army and Air Corps are fighting on the eastern islands as we speak. It'll be only a matter of time before they reach us."

"Where do you get your information?" I asked him.

"Ralph, quit asking me that! Trust me, will ya?"

"I can't trust anyone, Zip."

∗ 23 ∗

"Between the Devil and the Deep Blue Sea"

July 1946

WE STOPPED AT A MOTEL NEAR THE COLORADO BORDER FOR THE NIGHT. BOB was up early the following morning. He had already showered and shaved when he came out of the bathroom.

We mumbled a greeting to each other as I passed him on the way to the sink, and Bob said, "Who's Zip?"

I looked at him strangely, as if he had known something that he shouldn't have.

"Last night, you were talking in your sleep, Ralph. You said, 'I can't trust anyone, Zip.' Who's Zip?" Bob asked again.

I turned on the faucet and started to brush my teeth. "A pal of mine," I replied.

"Oh yeah?" Bob said, leaning against the doorway.

"I was in the hospital with him. In Denver. Before I came home."

"Really?"

"Yeah."

I spit in the sink, then shut the door.

That day, we were heading toward the Grand Canyon, but I asked my father to stop at Pikes Peak in Colorado Springs, where I had spent time with Zip and some friends when I was recovering in the hospital before I returned to Lansdowne. This place was a good memory, one of the few I had had in weeks.

"If we drive too high, will you be short of breath, Ralph?" my mother said as she turned around in the front seat.

"I'm okay," I said.

My parents had brought along an oxygen mask with a control valve, just in case. They kept it in the trunk, though, so I wouldn't see it.

My right lung was still weak, but the sight of the glorious mountains rejuvenated me. I decided to call Zip at the hospital.

"Hey, Ralph!" Zip shouted into the receiver.

"Hey!"

"Hey!"

"Hey, how are you, Zip?" I said.

"It's dead around ward 26 since you left," Zip said with a laugh.

Zip told me Dr. Gibson wouldn't release him because of the large infection he had developed in his lung from tuberculosis.

"But I'm trying to get transferred to Houston, Ralph, because I'm going to marry Carlita. We're engaged now, you know."

"Congratulations," I said. "That's wonderful, Zip."

Zip asked me to come up and visit him, but I didn't want to go back to the hospital. I was happy for him, but Zip's engagement to Carlita only reinforced my concerns about my own future. What the hell was I going to do with my life? Who could I ever be comfortable enough with to marry? These questions didn't seem to stop Zip. Nothing stopped that crazy bastard.

As we continued west, I thought more and more about my conversation with Zip. I became increasingly depressed. The trip became agonizing. I lost my patience with riding in a car and seeing things that didn't interest me. My mother was pampering me, my father was staring at me, and Bob wouldn't shut up. He was talking about his war stories, still trying to prompt me to open up.

When we stopped at a steak house for dinner, I mentioned to my parents that I felt too confined. "I think I'd like to go back home," I said.

Just then, my steak and potatoes arrived. My parents had prime rib with rice. Every time I saw rice, it sent me back to prison camp. Bob had filet mignon and a side dish of spinach. I saw a barrel of seaweed.

☆ 24 ☆

"The Nearness of You"

June 1943

WE WERE USING THE BUDDY SYSTEM AGAIN THAT MORNING WHEN I NOTICED two men were missing in the water.

"There!" shouted Gabriel, pointing to a leg caught in the seaweed, swaying with the current.

The undertow was quite heavy. Two divers who were trying to rescue each other were now both entangled in the seaweed. All the men in the group rushed to help. Some grabbed the seaweed's main branch, while others cut and slashed. But this was all in vain. The two new divers had already died from strangulation. The seaweed's flexible branches had hugged the men around the necks in a killer embrace.

These two dead POWs were first-timers. They were supposed to be paired up with experienced partners. I found out later that they were friends in camp and had asked to swim the detail together. Fortunately, the Jap sergeant never discovered that bit of information, or the whole detail would have taken the beating of their lives.

The two dead bodies were taken off the truck just before we reached the camp. A meeting was held that evening in the POW officers' quarters. Walker had spoken with the commandant and was told that another group of POWs would be taking over our detail. We were too weak, and the current was too strong. All of us would be reassigned shortly. More importantly, we also learned that most of the POWs were going to be moved out to different camps within the next two months.

The rain came down with a vengeance the next few days. Half the work details were canceled. The sun would occasionally come out, but then another tropical downpour would last for an hour. Men would wear stuff over their heads to protect themselves from the rain—banana leaves, coconut leaves, even their mats. Drizzling rain mixed with fog followed. Sometimes the fog was so thick that you could get lost within the camp. Heads bowed and arms across their chests, the men shuffled along as if they were going to a funeral.

We just tried to keep warm and dry, but this inclement weather produced much sickness. Many men were fighting pneumonia, and their incessant coughing could be heard throughout the night. All the POWs were deprived of medication.

Much of this ill health resulted from our clothes. They were always wet or filthy. When the sun decided to show itself, everyone would hang their soggy clothes on a bamboo rope tied between palm trees. If a POW had one shirt and two pairs of shorts, he was rich.

The rainy weather, however, didn't stop the Javanese locals from coming out to do business at the fence. The Japs were paying the POWs with something called invasion money—currency that was as thin as tissue paper that we received each week in an envelope with our POW number on it. The Japs were very serious about invasion money. They said, "You are not a slave. The Imperial Army is paying you for your labor."

Bartering at the bicycle camp was not unlike a swap meet. The Javanese would set up shop around the camp's perimeter, with sometimes as many as a hundred vendors selling things like toothbrushes, toothpaste, and monkey meat. Cigarettes were sold, too, but were expensive because they were difficult to obtain. The Jap guards would watch the proceedings but never said a word. They were pleased that the invasion money was changing hands. Anyone caught with Dutch guilders would be shot on the spot.

My number was called for a new detail, and I met with a POW officer named Kraft. He told me that I would be working on the Batavia docks, rolling oil drums onboard Chinese junks—the same junks that my B-17 crew had been bombing more than a year earlier. Fucking Eubank. When I imagined him now, I saw him stuffed with cotton. A dummy. He didn't send anybody to Bali to check on the Japs. I hated Eubank for being stupid. He shouldn't have been in charge of something he didn't understand. He was an army man, not Army Air Corps. His judgment was wrongheaded. He shouldn't have been an officer. Bastard.

There were seventy-two POWs on my new dock detail, and we were separated into six groups. Rolling oil drums onto the Chinese junks was mindless, backbreaking work. And we couldn't talk unless the Jap sergeant got drunk and passed out, which was often. The Jap sergeant would bring out two bottles of sake, and by lunch he was finished. He would lie down and sleep while the guards gambled and played cards and we stole food from the ship's kitchen. The Chinese cooks would bitch, but we threatened to kill them if they ratted. We took bananas, mangos, papayas, tomatoes, peppers, and string beans. Anything.

During our lunch breaks, we would eat with the Chinese sailors who worked beside us. They spoke a little Malayan, but most POWs did not. They didn't want to learn any part of the language. The POWs instead used sign language as best they could, and I became their interpreter. The Javanese dock workers, who were also slaving with us, ate by themselves, never wanting to associate with either race.

At the end of the first week, I was appointed the POW in charge, probably because I spoke Malayan. Van was right: this language gave me a greater chance to stay alive—and to eavesdrop.

When the Jap sergeant would wake from his daily stupor, I would overhear him talking to his guards, celebrating that they were winning the war. I was skeptical about this information because the Japs had a terrific propaganda department in the commandant's quarters. The guards were told brilliant lies such as that the U.S. Navy had been completely decimated. Another dandy was that when the war was over, all Japanese citizens would be wealthy, owning plots of land all over the east. I told these rumors to one of the Chinese sailors, and he laughed. The Chinese, who had traveled by water from China, also mentioned that they hadn't seen any U.S. ships along the coast. They said the U.S. ships were on the outer islands—Borneo, Iwo Jima, and the Philippines. Since the Chinese hated the Japs, I believed that they wanted to share the truth with a fellow captive. And after I spoke with them, I believed the Americans weren't coming. We were forgotten men. Abandoned. What kept me going here was my next meal. Food. Food and hate.

A few days later, the British and Australian POWs were given notice to move out within twenty-four hours. No one knew where they were being shipped. All their work details were canceled. Since my dock detail was comprised of two Brits and three Aussies, our Jap sergeant picked five more Americans to round out the crew.

When we went down to the harbor the next day, I saw three more rusty Jap merchant marine ships in the water. Hungry for some answers, I spoke to the Jap sergeant, and he told me that many of the Jap guards were going with the British and Aussie POWs. He didn't know the final destination, but the bastard made sure to tell me that everyone would be moving to wherever for the good of the Imperial Japanese Empire.

When we returned to camp later that afternoon, trucks were lined up for at least a mile around the perimeter. All the Jap guards were dressed in full battle regalia, and the British and Australian POWs were counting off as the searchlights criss-crossed the camp. At three or four o'clock in the morning, they were still counting, loading, and moving out. Depressed, I decided to go back to my hut. I remembered the hellish train ride from Camp Malang to the bicycle camp, and I figured better them than me. I went to sleep.

The following day, fifteen thousand men were gone, and the place was a dump. Living minute to minute, meal to meal, there was little time for a POW to reminisce with others. However, as the remaining Dutch and American POWs cleaned up the camp, Zip and I worked side by side, talking freely. The Jap guards allowed the POWs to converse because our captors were now frightened. They didn't want to be here when the Americans invaded. They were chattering away themselves, pissed off, wanting to go home and claim the land they had been promised.

I didn't know much about Zip because normally we had only twenty minutes to talk at night before lights went out, and with four other POWs in the room, Zip and I didn't share much except news about our work details.

Italian and Catholic, Zip was a churchgoer. He enjoyed talking about his boxing days in the service and how he had trained every day in Houston. Zip struck a boxing pose and threw a few jabs in the air.

"That's a hard way to get a guy down—boxing," I said, remembering what John Foreman had taught me. "Why don't you kick him behind the knee? That'll bring him down. Then you can beat his brains out."

Zip laughed. "That's no way to box, Ralph. I don't want to box with you, Pal."

Zip wasn't very articulate, though, and I started to do most of the talking as we bent down and picked up dirty woven mats and dried banana leaves.

I didn't tell Zip about my parents or growing up in Lansdowne; rather, I talked about my music days with Charlie Spivak and all the other bands. Zip was curious about all the traveling I did with the big bands. Since Zip was Italian, I mentioned one incident in particular. At a nightclub in West Virginia, each table had been dressed with expensive glassware, silverware, and linen, and these tables were set away from the stage, creating a wide-open dance floor. As the band was setting up, I noticed that our audience was mostly miners, blue-collar workers who were rough and loud—big shots for a night, then back to the mines.

Our band would get many requests, and the bandleader would write them down, playing every number in the order it was requested. However, people in this crowd became annoyed if their tunes were not played immediately. It was nine o'clock, and they were already drunk. They hollered out their requests or marched up to the singer, badgering her with song titles. As the night wore on, it became a circus. One couple was asked to leave because they were hogging the dance floor, shoving other dancers out of the way. It took two bouncers to escort this couple out the door. Men were pawing women, and then three fights broke out at the same time and blood started to scatter.

The bandleader quickly rolled into "The Way You Look Tonight" as two guys were arguing at a table near the stage. They started throwing punches. A bouncer saw the elbows flying and interceded. Suddenly, the two men grabbed him and tossed him on to the stage, just missing our music stands. Three more bouncers came to the rescue, and a brawl ensued. Wine bottles were sailing. Fists were flying. Women were hiding under the tables. Almost everyone was drunk. But Mr. Scarlozi, the club manager, signaled for us to keep playing.

"Oh, Madonn!" Zip said in Italian.

"Wait. Wait," I said. "It gets good."

As we ducked the flying beer bottles and water glasses, we grabbed our instruments and music books and jumped through the back curtain. Four bouncers were now lying unconscious on the dance floor, and the patrons were still fighting among themselves.

Still in our tuxes, we quickly checked out of our hotel and made our getaway. But as the bus driver motored down the highway, we noticed a car gaining on us. When we reached the state line, the chasing car stopped about three hundred yards behind us.

"Mafia, right?" Zip guessed.

"Right," I said. "The bus driver pulled off into the highway patrol station, and we waited to see what the car would do."

"What'd it do?" Zip interjected.

"It made a U-turn and disappeared into the night. I thought we were going to get gunned down, Zip."

Zip was laughing along with me now.

"But the windup is that the bandleader was hiding in the toilet throughout the whole chase. He had a bad case of the shits."

Zip kicked over an old steel helmet that had some rotten food in it.

"Did ya get a lotta broads on the road, Ralph?"

I told Zip about Karen in Revere Beach and then about a steamship gig where I met a girl named Susan.

"You would have liked her, Zip." I said.

"Pretty?"

"Oh yeah. A doll. A nice Catholic girl. She was traveling with her grandparents through South America as part of her high school graduation gift. After I played a clarinet solo of—I think it was 'In the Mood,' no, 'Blue Skies,'—we fell in love."

I told Zip that Susan and I were having sex and hiding from her grandparents the whole trip, through Venezuela and Brazil, all over the continent.

"But the best part of that trip," I continued, "was when my buddy Harry and I—"

"Who's Harry?"

"Harry?" I said with a smile. "Trumpet player and ladies' man extraordinaire. Harry and I split off from the band and hopped over to Havana for a week."

Havana was my finale before I had to return home and finish high school. I was only sixteen, but I will never forget the time I spent there. Harry and I got an apartment on the Prado, which was the main boulevard in Havana where all the hotels and nightclubs were. A third of the people there were tourists; they loved Americans down there. We'd sleep all day and jam all night.

"Jam and jelly, we used to call it, Zip. Eight-hour jam sessions," I said, getting excited just thinking about it again.

"Jeez, Ralph. You really lived it up."

"Yeah, we would jump from one nightclub to the other, taking our horns with us. They'd have two or three bands going in one place at the same time. Harry and I loved the Cuban rhythms, all the new sounds, the samba. It was spontaneous. Guys would cut loose, nothing was written down, nothing was rehearsed, like we did it on the ship. It was primal, raw. It got into your blood, Zip—the smoke, the booze, the women dancing in our laps."

"Holy shit!" Zip exclaimed. He stopped working and waited until I finished my story.

"Harry and I had two girls who were waitresses in the nightclubs. He picked them up—a young one for me, and he took the older one."

"What was her name, Ralph?"

"Names weren't important. We drank a little, smoked a little, then jammed and fucked a lot. I named mine Siesta. It was fantastic. It was the life," I said.

"Damn, Ralph," Zip said, looking hypnotized. "You've been all over the place. I haven't even been to New York."

"Great town," I replied. "I was there in '36 working for the CBS orchestra."

"Bullshit."

"No bullshit. My Aunt Katie helped me get the job. I think she had something going with this fella who did the hiring, if you know what I mean."

"Hey, it's all who you know in that business, right?"

"Right."

"Who'd ya know to get this prime gig, Ralph?"

"Don't ask." I said, as we started cleaning up again.

"You goin' back on the road when you get home?"

"I'd love to, but—I got a girl," I said.

I had never told anyone about Lynda before. I don't know if it was because Zip and I were close in age, or if it was because of the way he showed me around when I first arrived, but I trusted Zip. It felt wonderful inside his attention. As a POW, no one really cared who you had been before. Zip was different. He thought I was the most sophisticated guy he had ever met. Over the five days it took to clean up the camp, there was something about Zip—he felt more like a brother to me than Zeldan or Joe.

"I'd give it all up, though, to be with Lynda," I told Zip.

"Oh yeah?

"Yeah."

"I wish I had one waiting for me."

"I'm pretty serious about the whole deal, Zip. I want to marry her, I think."

∗ 25 ∗

"I Don't Want to Set the World on Fire"

June 1943

A DAY AFTER WE FINISHED CLEANING THE BICYCLE CAMP, THE SAME INTELLIgence officer who had interrogated me six weeks earlier called me into the camp commandant's office. I bowed and sat down, wondering what in the hell I had done to deserve this attention.

"The Imperial Japanese War Office has asked me to reestablish a shortwave radio station that has been damaged in Batavia," he said. "From your records, we know that you are a radio operator. You must know certain things about a radio and how it works. There are four other POWs that we have picked who will join you in this effort. You will always be guarded, and there will be a Japanese sergeant in command. If there is anything that is needed, you will tell him. You will not discuss this with anyone when you leave this office. This is an order."

Two Americans and two Dutch POWs were already waiting in the truck. I didn't have time to say good-bye to Zip, and I wondered if I'd ever see him again. "Why don't they just fix the damn thing themselves?" I thought. A Jap sergeant named Satu dropped the canvas over the back, ordering us not to talk. It was dark.

After twisting and turning down a road for what seemed like an hour, the truck finally came to a stop. I heard an iron gate creaking. Satu rolled up the back canvas and told us to jump out. We followed Satu into a medium-sized house. I hadn't been in a house since Jhannella's parents' place in Brazil, and that seemed like ages ago.

Satu lead us through an immaculate kitchen that was gleaming with appliances, then up a flight of stairs and down a long hallway into two large rooms. There were five beds, lamps, a chest of drawers, and a mirror. Two pairs of tan shorts and shirts lay on each bedspread, and a pair of sandals sat at the foot of each bed. The five of us looked at each other. We thought we were in a first-class hotel. Satu laughed at our bewildered faces.

There were bathrooms, showers, toilets, washbowls, and fresh towels in each of the two rooms. We showered, tossed our old rags into the trash can, and put on our new duds. I felt almost human again.

Satu then took us back downstairs to a room littered with shortwave radio equipment and then led us out into the backyard, where two generators sat. A radio tower was rigged up between several palm trees. All the equipment was old and ratty. We didn't say anything because Satu was with us, but it seemed like an impossible job.

A Chinese cook named Charlie was also at our service, and he told us that our food was ready. We were ushered into a large dining room with seating for twelve. We sat down, and Satu pulled up a chair, too. Two Javanese houseboys arrived with rice, cooked monkey meat, and plenty of fruit. Knowing that our stomachs had become smaller from eating such small portions at the camp, the five of us ate the meat and fruit slowly, leaving the rice untouched. Coffee was also served, which was a real treat. Even the aroma was enticing. I couldn't remember the last time I had had a cup—yes, I could: with Stuart, the morning we left the base at Sangosari before that fateful flight. Stuart was still so alive in my mind that I found myself saying his name in my head. Why had the kid been killed? And if Stuart had been killed, why hadn't I died, too? Eubank should be lined up and shot wherever he was.

Suddenly, a door flew open and a Jap in uniform entered. We all got up, saluted, and bowed. Satu introduced us to Major Tukamato, a tiny, tense man who told us in English to be seated and finish our coffee. Satu debriefed the major on our communication backgrounds, then called out our names. He pointed first to the two Dutchmen, Jacobson and VanWrotten, and then to the Americans, Steve, Roy, and me.

"I think you men know what you are doing here and what the Imperial Japanese Forces expect of you," the major said, never once looking us in the eyes. "We have given you the best living quarters and food in exchange for your help. If there is anything you need to fix the equipment, you will let the sergeant know, and he will obtain it for you. We expect to have this station up and operating within six days."

The taller Dutchman, Jacobson, spoke up: "Major Tukamato, how can we fix the equipment in six days if we don't know what needs to be replaced? How long will it take to get the new parts?"

The major smiled and said, "My orders are to have this station operating in less than a week. I don't care how you fix the equipment, but make it work. We will start counting the days tomorrow morning."

The five of us began our inspection of the radio equipment and the two generators that afternoon. The two Dutchmen pulled off the lids on the sending and receiving equipment, and Steve and Roy examined the two generators. The generator for the house was relatively new and was connected only to the indoor facilities; the second generator was corroded, and this one had once powered the shortwave radio station. From the looks of it, this second generator hadn't worked for months: all the wiring had been ripped out.

Meanwhile, I climbed up a ladder leading to the steel radio tower. "Garbage," I said, indicating that all the wires up here had been pulled away as well. It was apparent that all this equipment had been damaged by hand.

The five of us went back to the equipment room and made a list of parts that we thought were necessary, including a new generator.

"This equipment is shit," said Jacobson. "Some of the parts are completely destroyed and others can be rewired—maybe." Just then, Satu stumbled in and told us to get ready for dinner. His legs were loose; he had liquor on his breath.

When the coffee was being served after dinner, Satu was still pounding sake until he finally passed out at the table. Steve and I dragged him to a nearby couch as the cook came in. Charlie began to laugh, watching us lift the lifeless sergeant. After we finished with Satu, we went upstairs, and I got something off my chest that had been eating at me.

"Are you sure you guys want to fix this damn equipment?" I said. "I mean, we're all enjoying the food, the clean clothes, the whole deal, but I don't want to be a part of the Jap propaganda machine, do you, Steve?"

"Boy, I don't know, Ralph," Steve answered, uneasy.

"Well, we either fix it or get our heads cut off, right?" Roy said. "What's your pick?"

"I don't know," I said. "I've been thinking. . . . Maybe we rig the equipment."

"What do you mean?" asked Jacobson.

"We rig it—sabotage, like—so it blows up in their Jap faces," I said.

I asked the men to sleep on the idea. No one said another word that night.

The following morning, the five of us reviewed our lists of replacement parts. Satu finally turned up at lunch, and he was in a sour mood. We left him alone until he had eaten and then gave him our list.

After dinner that night, our crew was told to wait for the major in the living room. The major entered, and he wasn't smiling. He paced around the room with his hand on his sword, tapping it lightly. Then he stopped and stared at us. "What the hell kind of communication experts are you men?" he shouted. "You think that we can get all those parts to repair this station? I told you to make this work. There isn't a new generator on this island, and half of the parts you asked for can't be located for months. Now you go to work, and you better fix this station so it will work. I will get you as many items we have in the city, and they will be delivered tomorrow night."

As we still debated how to proceed with our assignment, I was thinking about how to stretch this detail as long as we could and enjoy this vacation from prison camp. If the major thought we were working hard and everyone was busy, he might give us more time.

After dinner, the major and sergeant arrived with tools, different sizes of wire, and about twenty spare parts.

Later that evening, Jacobson spoke up. "You know, Ralph, I was thinking about your idea. I think I might be able to clean up that old generator by rewiring it."

"Where are you going to get the power to test it if you ever get it going?" asked Steve.

"Maybe we can change the wires and connect the house generator to the radio equipment," Jacobson said.

"Yes," followed VanWrotten. "If we channel higher voltage into the radio equipment, we could blow it up good!"

"That's it! That's it!" I exclaimed.

The next morning, we told Satu our plans to use the house generator. Satu got approval from the major, and we connected some heavy cables to the tower and ran them to the house generator. This was hot and heavy work under the midday sun, with the temperature pushing 120 degrees, but at least we could take breaks when we saw fit. We could talk freely without Jap guards always watching. We would go into the equipment room every forty-five minutes or so to cool down.

"Do you think this is going to work, Jake, or are we kidding ourselves?" I asked the Dutchman.

"Yes, it will work, but how do we explain the uncontrolled power surge when it all blows?" replied Jacobson. "Remember, there is a regulator on the main line. The Japs will know we rigged it."

That evening, the major paid us a visit. We had candles on our workbenches and used flashlights for specialty work, giving him the impression that we were making progress. He asked us how long it would take to have the station ready for testing. Jacobson did most of the talking and really gave the major the run-around. He was perplexed by all the technical jargon and left in a huff, taking Satu with him. When the Japs went back inside, we could hear the major screaming at the top of his lungs at the sergeant. The five of us looked at each other, very concerned. The pressure of our scheme was starting to weigh on us, and we all had symptoms of dengue fever: high temperature, dizziness, sweatiness, the shakes, and headaches.

Later that evening, we hooked up the house generator to the radio equipment for testing and controlled the current with the voltage regulator. Our control board lit up.

It was about one o'clock in the morning, just before we quit testing the sending and receiving units, when I suggested sending a message. The others agreed, and I took over the electric key. My ear for music was helpful for mastering both Morse code and the electric key because each message had a rhythm of its own, similar to a fox-trot, waltz, or rumba.

I sent a message to my mother and father in Lansdowne, Pennsylvania, informing them of my health and location. I just sent it east, not having the slightest idea if it would be picked up, and then shut off the equipment immediately so that the location could not be picked up by Jap surveillance. The five of us then raced upstairs like kids and gathered in one of the rooms. The conversation bubbled over. Jacobson had another idea.

"Why don't we take the voltage regulator off the main line to the equipment so that when the higher voltage comes in, it will—"

"Shazam!" I said.

"Right. Like the place was hit by lightning," followed Roy.

"The whole station will go up in smoke," Steve said, now beginning to see the light.

The Dutchmen now turned to each other and spoke in their native tongue. Jacobson then came up with a slight alteration.

"Wait," he said. "Let's not remove it from the main line. Let the higher power surge through and fault the regulator, but the regulator dial will indicate a low voltage reading. This can be our excuse."

"Bad parts," finished VanWrotten.

We looked at each other happily, pleased with this brainstorm. The short-wave radio station would be tested tomorrow before a live Jap audience of two.

"This will be a good day for the Japanese Imperial Army," Major Tukamato said as we all assembled in the equipment room the next morning. "These communications will aid our cause by telling the outside world that the Japanese people are a great nation that controls Asia with a good heart. The world will know that we are a civilized nation, a strong nation, with intelligent people ready to be peaceful to all who join our imperial government."

After this little speech, the major gave me the signal to turn on the station. I bowed deeply and said, "No. The honor is all yours, Major."

Steve and Roy looked at me like I was insane. The major accepted my offer, bowed, and walked toward the black box as I took a step backward, looking for a place to hide. As the major flicked the switch, it was as if God had plunged a thunderbolt through the room. Electrical currents danced from one piece of equipment to another, crackling, sizzling, cooking the metal. Everyone hit the deck.

Suddenly, the door flew open. The Chinese cook and one of the Javanese houseboys came running in, throwing pails of water over the burning equipment. The major, meanwhile, was screaming as he crawled through the smoke into the kitchen hallway. Just then, the other Javanese houseboy tripped over the major, spilling water all over him.

I jumped up and shut off the power from the generator when I heard a roar.

"*Kiwotsuke!*" Satu yelled, which means "attention" in Japanese.

We all stood up.

No one was hurt, except the pride of the Japanese. The major reappeared, soaking wet. He looked like a wet marionette as he waved his arms, shook his head, and ordered Satu to send us to our rooms. It was the first time I had ever seen a Jap completely lose his composure.

An hour later, the sergeant ordered us to the large living room, where the major was waiting. The five of us bowed and waited at attention for the major to order us to sit down. The command never came. The major just continued pacing, the way he did when he was aggravated, tapping his sword lightly, knowing this terrified us to no end.

"You men think that you can make fools out of your conqueror?" he screamed. "I want to know what happened! I want an answer before you are all shot."

Jacobson was brave. He spoke up. "Let's go back to the equipment room, Major. Half of the equipment was old. We need to see where the power surge came from, so we can tell you what happened."

Major Tukamato approached Jacobson and slapped him across the face and then kicked him. Suddenly, the major pivoted around and slapped Satu across the face as well, barking an order in Japanese.

Satu directed the five of us to the equipment room. The major trailed us back to the scene, demanding answers. "I want the problem found in the next hour, because we are going to make this station work," he insisted.

The Japs left the room as we studied the charred equipment. We knew what the problem was, of course. We removed the metal covers from the equipment and saw nothing but black tubes and wiring burnt to a crisp. Our defense—our only reasonable defense—was to explain to the major that the parts he had brought us were defective. Since the regulator dial displayed the wrong voltage reading, there was no way of accurately testing the power of the house generator.

Jacobson came up with the wise idea to make another list of necessary equipment that we knew was not available on the island. Major Tukamato and Satu returned, and Jacobson spoke for the group. When the major realized that Jacobson was politely stating that the shortwave radio station would never operate without new equipment, his face became grotesque. He turned and screamed, ordering us to our rooms. We waited there nervously for the thrashing that would surely follow.

Jacobson suggested we should all put on as much clothing as possible. He reasoned that if we were going to take a beating, more padding would help with the scarring and blood loss. Minutes later, Satu came in and took the two Dutchmen with him. A truck pulled up to the gate, and we heard Satu tell them to get in the back. That was the last I ever saw of Jacobson and VanWrotten.

Then Charlie came into our room. "The major went with them," he said. "The sergeant will be back. Sorry, fellows."

No one said a word. We were just hoping another truck would take us back to camp. Sometime later, Satu returned and marched us to the backyard, where three bare-chested Jap guards held bamboo poles in their hands. Satu shoved Steve against the house, threw Roy at the palm trees, and pushed me toward the tower.

"*Kiwotsuke!*" Satu shouted. I straightened up, knowing I was going down. Quickly, I repeated to myself, "Just roll with the stick."

Satu bowed, and I bowed in return, but as I lifted up to face him, I saw the stick out of the corner of my left eye. I could hear the guard's breath. He took a deep one just before he swung. When I heard him exhale, I anticipated the stick across my shoulders, which decreased the shock.

"*Kiwotsuke!*" Satu called again. As I stood up, I still heard heavy breathing and then the *whoosh* before the stick hit the back of my knees. Bang. I crumbled backward. Dazed, I saw my torturer grinning at me. I tried to catch my breath.

"*Kiwotsuke!*" Satu shouted for the third time. I couldn't stand up. As I struggled to get to my knees, *whack*, I took another wallop across the back. I didn't hear that one coming. The guard now started to boot me in the ribs, countless kicks, many of them nearly lifting me off the ground.

"*Kiwotsuke!*" Satu called yet again, and the guards stopped kicking. Woozy and weak, I couldn't see Roy and Steve, but their moaning indicated that they were still alive. Satu waited for the three of us to get to our feet and then approached me. I was seeing double at this point, but I still didn't see the punch coming. Satu blasted me in the left eye, then countered with a left to the nose. I went down again.

Satu then went after the other two men, while my bare-chested victimizer threw a pail of water in my face. Both Roy and Steve were on the ground now, getting another dose of it. I tried to stand, but I couldn't. Down and broken, I collapsed and passed out.

September 1943
Ralph M. Rentz
Batavia, Java
POW Camp-Japanese

Honey,

I hope this letter reaches you somehow or somewhere in the Far East. The Army Air Corps informed me and your dad that the Red Cross services may be able to deliver this letter. Dad and I were told on 3/14/42 by the Adjutant General that you were seriously wounded and were most likely a prisoner of war. Then on 6/24/43, the War Department informed us that they had received a radio message stating you were in Batavia, Java. It read:

"Batavia in English at 1:30 A.M. To United States (American Prisoners)

Ralph M. Rentz, United States Army Air Corps, health is good and things in general are fine. Hope to see you soon."

This message was unable to be construed as true even if it was an official notification.

It is now over 15 months since we know whether you are still alive. The entire family is keeping the faith that you have survived your injuries. The Armed Services offered your father the $10,000 insurance policy to be cashed in, but dad turned it down and said, "I will talk to my son after the war, then I will decide, or my son will decide, if he is dead or alive."

Lynda has called me every week since you have been missing, and she has cried while speaking with me. I keep telling her that you will come home. You are a fighter.

Your brother, Joseph, is in the Army Air Corps and sends me a letter or we receive a phone call every week. Zeldan is now old enough to work in the store along side Sylvia. The store is very busy, and we can't get too much help because everyone is in one or the other services or working at the shipyards in Philadelphia and Chester. All the cousins and aunts are calling here just to support our feelings of helplessness. Some of the customers just come in the store to visit us and want to know if we have heard any word from the U.S. Services about you. Nana is praying night and day and still believes the war will be over soon and you will be marching home.

I'm going to give this letter to the Red Cross who already know Dad and I after many conversations with them. Take care of yourself and remember you have an angel on your shoulder.

Much love,
Your mother and dad

✳ 26 ✳

"June Is Bustin' Out All Over"

June 1943

I DON'T KNOW HOW LONG I LAY THERE IN THE BACKYARD. I REMEMBER BEING carried inside by the two Javanese houseboys. Blood covered my sheets, my clothing, my face. The Chinese cook arrived with cold Turkish towels to stop the bleeding from my nose.

"My fucking ribs," I heard Steve cry from the other bed. I didn't know if my ribs had been injured as well, but my breathing was labored. I was wheezing, spitting blood, wondering what was coming next.

Hot tea and rice were brought in. No more coffee for us. No more fine cuisine. We weren't in the mood for eating, anyway. We just wanted to disappear.

Later in the afternoon, Satu told us we were being moved back to the bicycle camp. I heard the iron gate creak open, and a truck pulled up near the house. Satu, Charlie, and the houseboys helped us outside. We could hardly walk.

When the three of us got into the truck, I lifted my hand and jiggled it at Charlie and the houseboys, trying to say good-bye. The two houseboys were crying, and Charlie had a look on his face as if to say, "Good-bye, Friend."

I felt every bump, every stone that went under the tires. My nose started to bleed again, and I tried to use one of my shirts to stop it, but it wouldn't stop—it just kept coming. Like these Japs. They just kept coming. There was no stopping them.

We arrived at the camp. The gate guards ordered us to stand for inspection, and then I was rushed to the med center. A Dutch doctor set my nose and placed cold compresses on my face and cold towels around my back and ribs. He wrapped my knees with cool bandages. I couldn't move.

Steve and Roy were carried in a little later, and we had a three-day re-union. On the fourth day, we reported back to our buildings.

Zip woke me up in the evening, and I told him all the sordid details.

"Ralph, you're just as crazy as I am. To pull off a stunt like that is just terrific," Zip said, laughing.

I told Zip never to repeat a word of it to anyone. "If that story gets back to the Japs, I'm a dead man, and so are the other fellows."

Zip put his hand to his mouth and made the sign of the cross with his thumb.

"Listen," Zip leaned in. "Some of the Americans are going to be shipped to Singapore. There is another rumor that the Japs are preparing for an invasion by the Americans and Australians. They're moving all of their heavy guns up into the hills near Bandung."

Bandung was a small town about ten miles southeast of Batavia, just a short distance from a Jap air base.

"Where do you get your information?" I asked.

Zip laughed. "From the Nip guards, where else?"

"When?" I grunted, my sides still hurting.

"The announcement could come tomorrow, or it could be weeks away. I don't know," Zip said. "When the Japs tell us the work details are stopped, we'll know we're moving either to Singapore or Bandung."

I nodded my head, accepting what Zip told me. My hatred for the Japs was like a syndrome now. Hate kept me going. "They are not going to kill me," I told myself as I lay there. "I can last as long as they can, worrying about the American invasion. Then those bastards will die."

＊ 27 ＊

"I Get a Kick Out of You"

October 1943

"Women's work" was what the Japs called my next detail. A dozen men, working in pairs, made beds, washed toilets, cleaned showers, and mopped up the wooden floors in the Jap officers' barracks. And by the time we finished a day's work, I had stolen enough soap for two months. I was now called the Soap Man.

I began selling and bartering soap with the Javanese vendors for fruit, cucumbers, snake meat, and peppers, and business was thriving. The Javanese stole all their stuff in town and then sold it. The swap meet was open from nine in the morning until six in the evening, and we shopped during our breaks. We had to wait in line.

When I did business, I wrapped the soap in dried banana leaves before I'd make exchanges at the fence. Duck eggs went for two bars of soap. I used the shells as Max had taught me: my teeth were important to me.

I also traded soap for onions, mangos, and tomatoes with the dirt still on them with the POWs who worked on the farm detail. Farming, however, was rapidly becoming a serious concern to the Japs because the Javanese locals were not cooperating in selling fruits and vegetables to their captors. Instead, the Javanese had become bold after two and a half years of Japanese rule and adherence to their "Asia for Asiatics" economic slogan. The Javanese planted only for their own use and hid rice and vegetables in their kampongs. The Japs quickly discovered this and started to behead or shoot any Javanese hiding reserves of rice, chickens, pigs, and especially young girls, whom the Japs abducted for their "comfort houses." The Javanese now realized that they had been better off under the Dutch-controlled democratic government. Food eventually became scarce, and the Javanese finally learned that they were doing all the work for the cheap invasion money and getting nowhere. The Japs were paying debts with the invasion money, and inflation was skyrocketing.

The economics of war eventually trickled down to the POWs in our daily food rations. Java shipped its long, first-grade rice to the rest of the Axis countries and then bought third-grade rice for pigs, chickens, and POWs. The rice was shipped from China and left in storage on the housing docks. The rice we were now eating was at least four or five years old. Because the white rice had turned brown and was now infested with maggots, both the Japs and the Javanese wouldn't eat it. We would pick over this rice until one day a Dutch doctor told us to eat the maggots but get rid of the small stones that were also found inside our bowls. At least the maggots had protein.

Roughly 850 of the 1,000 American POWs at the bicycle camp received notice that they would be leaving for Singapore within three days. My friend, Zip Zummo, was one of those being shipped out. Before the shortwave radio incident, I had thought I'd never see Zip again, and now when I said good-bye to him I figured this was probably our last good-bye. Both of us had seen so much death that we knew we'd be lucky to make it home alive.

"See you in the States, and that's for sure," Zip said when we parted. "Keep your cool and see this thing through, Ralph. We'll be seeing each other up there or down here. Have a little faith, Pal." Zip and I shook hands, and he was gone.

A month later, the remaining American and Dutch POWs were moved to Bandung. The bicycle camp would be used exclusively as a Dutch women's camp from now on.

The Japs told us that when the Americans invaded and the fighting started, we would be in a safe zone in Bandung. Of course, these bastards were lying through their teeth as usual. The Japs had another reason for moving us; they brought the American and Dutch POWs further south to build a new prison camp, which we called the jungle retreat. The site had previously been a prison for Javanese convicts, who would now be working alongside us.

As construction began, we used coco mats for walls and heavy bamboo beams for our sleeping units, which packed in twenty POWs per hut. Latrines were built over a small creek that carried running water from the hills. A bamboo floor was installed over the running water with a twelve-inch-wide slit so the prisoners could defecate. Since there was no toilet paper, a Dutch POW showed us how to use a long-necked bottle filled with water to wipe ourselves.

Sleeping conditions were also a logistical nightmare during the first six weeks, when we were building the camp. Either we slept at the camp in bamboo huts, or the Japs shuttled us eight miles back to the bicycle camp to sleep in our old quarters.

After the huts, showers, and kitchens were constructed, it took several days to clean up the mess. Scraps of bamboo, coconut rope, wire, and palm leaves covered the grounds. We asked the camp commandant for a two-day rest, but we were denied. However, the next morning during count off, the commandant was lifted onto a stand to address us. "The Imperial Japanese Army has decided to give you two days rest before you start on the next project," he said through his interpreter.

All of us nearly fell over laughing. The Japs would first reject almost all our requests and then the next day they would give some bizarre excuse and change their minds. They were becoming irrational about how to handle the POWs and our daily work.

During our two-day layoff, most of us washed our shirts and shorts in the stream. The sound of the water reminded me of when my mother taught me how to swim as a child at a place called Union Grove in New Jersey. *"You'll get home someday, but don't think about that stuff now, because if you do, you'll die."* Van's words seemed to be burned into me. I tossed my wet clothes on the roof of our hut to dry and went to sleep.

The next morning, the commandant announced the true reason we had been brought to Bandung: the rail bed.

A mammoth hill stood several miles from Bandung, above the camp. The Japs wanted to prepare themselves for the U.S. invasion by transporting guns and munitions from the camp to a cavern that was being cut deep into the side of the hill about four thousand feet up. However, jungle lay between the camp and this cavern, and it was now our job to clear that jungle and create a pathway to this strategic location. Since the Japs were sure that an invasion would take place within the next year, they wanted this facility up and running as soon as possible.

My work detail was picked, listed, and given to one POW officer in charge of all the American work details. Each work detail comprised twenty POWs, one American sergeant, ten Javanese convicts, one Jap sergeant, and twelve Jap guards. I was one of the American sergeants, and my detail was made up of men from my hut.

We awoke at five o'clock in the morning to the sounds of the Jap national anthem, with the fog rolling in off the ocean. In the trucks by six, we traveled along a bumpy road for about an hour until we reached a Jap army truck that was parked on the edge of the heavy growth. No trucks could get beyond this terrain. As the POWs unloaded, I noticed a table set up. It was glimmering in the hot sun. There must have been thirty broad-bladed, twelve-inch, pirate-sized knives on the table. The Japs had engraved our POW numbers on our knives to inventory them all. We were told that after each detail our knives were to be hung from bamboo in our huts. If you lost your knife, you lost your ass.

The Jap sergeant in charge of the rail bed, Tomucka, who had an erect posture and strutted like a peacock, pulled me over to his surveyor's map to indicate where we would start the clearing. However, the path from the camp to the cavern wasn't straight. It zigzagged up the hill to avoid larger trees and very heavy growth.

Tomucka subsequently pulled a few of the Javanese aside so that they could show the American POWs how to handle the knives before we started cutting. During the demonstration, Tomucka noticed the long scar on my right shoulder.

"Japanese got you?" Tomucka asked. He was smiling.

"Yeah, Japanese got me," I said, removing the shrapnel from my pocket and showing it to him.

"You should be dead," Tomucka said, examining the jagged steel.

"I wish I was."

Like the seaweeding detail, this jungle-clearing detail was broken down into three groups: cutters, pullers, and loaders. Chain saws and axes were used to remove larger trees. After an area had been cleared, POWs would level the area and begin digging the rail bed. Construction of the tracks was to follow, using lumber and stone to scale up the steep hill. A half-mile down from us, another group of POWs and Javanese convicts were doing the same thing, and so on and so on, right down the line. It reminded me of black prisoners working on country roads in the American South. The Dutch and Americans cleared the jungle, while the Javanese did most of the construction.

Since this land was virgin forest, the trees sheltered us while we worked—until we cut them down, of course. Then the tropical sun would really beat down on us. After fifteen minutes of cutting, a POW was dripping wet in the hundred-degree heat, and the men needed as much water as possible, which kept Red, the POW waterman, hopping. My job as a POW sergeant was to make sure all my men were working and had enough drinking water so that they didn't pass out from the heat. Red was always right behind me, lugging a bucket to give a man a drink.

Red was a massive man, built like an upside-down pyramid, and his job was dangerous. Carrying a bucket of water with a dipper, Red had to be nimble enough to dodge between the knives to reach a thirsty POW. Otherwise, Red would get slashed to pieces. If a POW needed water, he would raise his hand. The other men around him would halt until Red filled the canteen, which each man carried around his hip, strapped down by bamboo string.

Every thirty seconds, Red would be running. Running and dipping. Running and dipping. No words were spoken. The guards would inch closer to make sure of that.

Patrolling in their undershirts, the Jap or Korean guards had heavy rifles on their shoulders and cigarettes in their mouths. These bastards were miserable about being put on this detail, and they took their frustration out on us. Bored or drunk—or both—a guard would scream, and all the POWs would turn their heads. Bizarre words fired out of their mouths in small bursts, almost cutting us.

The guards would make chopping gestures with their hands, demanding that we cut faster. They would always try to spot a POW who was working too slowly—who had stopped to catch his breath, to straighten up his back, to wipe his brow—and then the guard would strike. Guards generally would club POWs with the butts of guns or with bamboo poles, and then the injured POWs would run to POW sergeants, like me, for help. Meanwhile, the victimizing guards or one of their fellow thugs would yell at the POWs to get back to work. At this point, I would step in and attempt to pacify the guards, so that the medics, each of whom carried a chair and sat under a tree, would come running to treat the injured POWs. If Tomucka was in a good frame of mind, he would usually step in to stop a vicious guard. Such an environment was conducive to violence, and some beatings could lead to death.

My role was a difficult one. There were six men on each of the three details, plus a waterman, and crews were changing continuously. Supervising the POWs kept me roving all over the place. Sometimes a guard would leave his post to take a leak, and I would watch him out of the corner of my eye so that he wouldn't sneak up on one of my men. Some men passed out because of the heat. They needed more water. During breaks we had a bucket of water on wheels, and each man refilled his canteen. Still, the men were in a state of exhaustion. They must have had twenty servings of water a day.

The heat was one thing, but the bugs were another. Working in the jungle, we shaved our heads and wore straw hats to keep the vermin out of our hair. We'd pass around a shaving razor and do each other's heads so we wouldn't cut ourselves to pieces. You couldn't have let your hair grow long, anyway, because the Japs didn't like it.

During the winter of 1943, our progress on the rail bed was way behind schedule. The Japs did not celebrate Christmas, Hanukkah, or New Year's. The holidays made some of the men more depressed; many POWs would cry, pound the ground, or just lie in bed not talking to anyone. These guys weren't weak. They were sick in the head. But I wasn't going to get that way. The moment you started to give in to self-pity, you were a dead duck. I had to turn my self-pity into hate. I always felt that if I could hate long enough, the war would end someday. But if I stopped hating, I'd break down. And I'd seen men break down. When men started hallucinating—talking to their sisters, mothers, and brothers—I knew they were on their way out. Others who traded food for smokes had at most three or four more days to live. And anyone who really wanted to die could do so easily by refusing to drink water. Seventy-two hours without water in that heat, and you were finished.

Many POWs tried prayer as a remedy. I gave those men this advice: "If you think you're losing it, talk to me. But I'm not going to pray for you. God helps those who help themselves."

I mostly kept to myself, though. After my time with Van, I had become heartless. My love for companionship was gone. I didn't believe in anybody—not in God or man. Not even in myself, really, because I didn't know if after what I'd seen so far, I was sick in the head or if I was still in my right mind. "Just listen to Van," I told myself over and over again. *"Send your mind to Belém,"* he would say. And to reproduce this mind conditioning he had taught me, I would put myself under. I would send myself back to a place I had been before, to a place I had had enjoyment. I could have been screaming at the same time I was doing this, and I wouldn't have known it. I was practicing self-hypnosis.

During the twenty minutes before lights out, I would fiddle with something. I would tear at my toenails or repair my pants with a needle I had stolen from the med hut. I needed something in my hands to get into a rhythm. I never knew where I was going to send myself before I started. I just closed my eyes and sat back against the bamboo wall. "I wonder when I'll get back there?" I asked myself, and the next thing I knew, I had my subject.

Jhannella.

I was in her car. She kissed me on the cheek.

"I'm going back there after the war," I told myself, furthering the memory along. Now Jhannella and I were dancing. Then we were having sex. It was like a song I had memorized. I knew it by heart—every movement. I tuned out the others in my hut while I conducted my own little number. I was in control. I had my shield.

By January 1944 we were deep into the jungle, and we weren't alone—rats, snakes, wild pigs, and monkeys were prevalent, and the monkeys were becoming impossible. Their screaming was getting closer every day, and we couldn't hear a command. Four feet tall with sprawling arms, the monkeys would jump from tree to tree, shrieking, as if our presence was an invasion of their home.

One day, a monkey dropped onto a Jap guard and tore his throat wide open. Blood spurted everywhere. The wounded guard fell to his knees, and other guards began firing, but the monkey had already escaped up a tree. Everyone was in shock, especially us POWs, who were on the ground, unarmed. The guard was dead within minutes.

The Jap guards continued spraying the trees with bullets, but the monkeys had made their getaway. They were screaming in the distance now; they seemed to be laughing at us.

Tomucka called everyone back to the truck because of the dead man. The Jap guards, normally loud and boisterous like the monkeys, didn't say a word the entire way back to camp.

Later that afternoon, all work details scheduled for the rail bed were assembled before the commandant. He spoke through his interpreter, telling us always to carry our knives with us when we were in the jungle. If any POW harmed a guard with a knife, the prisoner would lose his head. The monkeys had spoken.

When we reached our work site the following day, the Jap guards immediately sprayed the trees with bullets, and the monkeys got the message in a hurry. They fled the area, but we could still hear them, shrieking and rattling tree limbs, taunting us from afar. We knew we hadn't seen the last of them.

During the lunch period, Tomucka had one of his guards give us a demonstration on how to deal with an attacking monkey. The guard instructed us to wave our knives in the air and scream at the top of our lungs if the monkeys got too close. "Monkey see, monkey do," I thought. After this unimpressive display, one of my men asked me if he could show the fellows how to throw a knife. Curious, I spoke to Tomucka in Malayan, and he laughed.

"Bring him over to me, and I will pick his target," the Jap sergeant said, amused.

I brought out John, who had a walk of a cowboy, and he bowed to Tomucka, who pointed to a tree about thirty feet away. John, who was a tall, lanky man, squinted at the tree and then backed up two or three feet. Without a moment's hesitation, John flung the knife at the target. The blade moved faster than the eye could follow, and it stuck directly in the center of the tree trunk, about five feet above the ground.

I looked over at Tomucka, and his mouth was hanging wide open. All the POWs were equally dumbfounded.

"Where the hell did you learn to do that?" I asked John once we got back to our hut.

"I was raised in the circus," he said. John told me that his parents had worked in the business for years, and one of the performers had taught him to wield a knife.

"Would you teach me how to throw like you, Circus John?" I asked.

"Of course, Sergeant," he said. "We can start tonight before it gets too dark."

Circus John gave me my first lesson behind our hut, which was just out of sight of the tower guards. He set up a target and showed me how to balance the knife by gripping it lightly so that it would fly straight as an arrow. On my first throw, I was concerned that I would crack the handle against the tree, but John was a fine teacher.

"It's all in the wrist," Circus John said. "Try to gauge the spin of the knife in yards, then estimate the distance to your target."

I practiced with Circus John every day for an hour after our detail. Our sessions helped me stop dwelling on our plight as prisoners, allowing me instead to concentrate on the spot on the coconut tree. Circus John gave me confidence, and after a few days, I put the blade on target. My knife soon became my friend and confidant. My new instrument. I would often pat my knife when I was wearing it on my thigh and talk to it as well.

"There will come a day when you will kill a yellow terrorist," I would say to my new partner. "Then you will get a medal from me."

I felt so much safer with my knife strapped to my right thigh now. We had snakes, rats, monkeys, and all kind of ground animals in the jungle, and my knife became part of me. Without it, I was bare. I started talking to my knife more and more. "When will I throw you next?" I used to say. You are my defense. My life." I think the hatred in me was finally spilling over. I became distant from all human companionship. I felt better talking to my knife than to another POW. I called my knife John.

Construction remained six weeks behind schedule. The guards were still shooting at the monkeys but seldom hit one. Because of the monkeys and the extreme heat, we were working at a very slow pace, and the commandant wasn't pleased. At count off one evening, he got up on his wooden box and said he was disgusted with the way this camp was operating, and then he started banging his sword. Every POW would now work six days a week until we finished the rail bed. Many of us were already exhausted and overworked, and we knew this change meant dehydration, fainting, and even death. A POW officer asked for a hearing with the commandant, and two Jap sergeants beat him in front of all of us. I had a feeling that this was the beginning of the end.

After instituting the six-day workweek, the commandant lengthened our workday, which meant we had to get up at four in the morning. There was also another change as well, a changing of the guards. Northern Koreans—large, no-brained animals who would just as soon kill you as talk—replaced most of the Jap guards. These Koreans did not speak Malayan, and every bit of communication was performed in rude gestures. I hated to admit it, but it was a good thing we still had Tomucka.

When we arrived at the work site the following morning, we noticed that the cavern detail had doubled. They were dynamiting the mountainside to build the munitions storage location, and the constant explosions made the monkeys even crazier.

Later that afternoon, one of my men ran over to inform me that a POW had passed out. I sprinted over to the unconscious man, and so did a Korean guard. Before I reached the POW, the Korean guard kicked the man twice in the ribs. I quickly jumped between the guard and the defenseless man. I pointed to the POW and then ran my hand across my throat, trying to indicate that the man was dying. The Korean guard screamed at me in Japanese. He was ready to hit me with the butt of his gun. Just then, Tomucka appeared, and he whacked the Korean guard across the back with his bamboo pole. Tomucka ordered the guard back to his post and instructed me to give the POW some water and a fifteen-minute rest.

"These guards are going to kill my men, and the rail bed will never get finished on time," I said to Tomucka in Malayan, my eyes red with anger.

Tomucka just smiled at me, as if impressed by my rage. Then he said in English, "Okay."

Five men were taken to the med hut with dehydration that first six-day workweek. I spoke with Tomucka about the sick men, and I got a slap across the ear that knocked me to the floor.

"Find another five men, or you will take a real beating for not following orders," he said.

I was furious when I got up. "You no good son of a bitch!" I told him with my eyes. "You are just like the fucking Koreans." Although I wanted to slit his throat, I restrained myself, bowing deeply instead.

"Where in the hell can I find five more men?" I thought. My search led me to one place only: the med hut. I told the Dutch doctor that if I didn't get five more men, I would be in the med hut myself sometime tomorrow.

"Fine," said the doctor, "I will fill your guys up with fluid and tell them to report to their work detail tomorrow morning."

I thanked the doctor and went back to my hut, thinking of the lightest job for the five sick men to perform.

The detail lined up the next morning, and I had my twenty men. We worked for a few hours before Tomucka approached me.

"Why so many watermen?" he asked.

"These men have been dehydrated. This was the only way I could use them."

The Jap sergeant stiffened and then called me to attention. Tomucka walked behind me slowly and belted me behind the knees with his bamboo pole. I was on my back in seconds, staring up at him in a cold sweat. I studied his eyeballs: "I must show no pity," they said to me, "or my guards will show me no respect."

As I got to my knees, Tomucka struck me again across the back. I pitched forward onto my chest.

"*Kiwotsuke!*" he ordered.

I finally got up and faced him. Tomucka rushed me, almost chewing my face.

"I am the sergeant!" Tomucka shouted. "Any changes in work detail must be approved by me!"

Tomucka walked behind me again and blasted me behind the knees a second time. I fell, and the sergeant left me there as an example for the others.

It felt like both knees had been broken. I tried to stand, but my legs wouldn't hold my weight. I sat there alone, rubbing the back of my legs. It took me two hours until I could walk with little discomfort.

When work ended that day, several POWs helped me to the med hut.

"I warned you I'd be back, Doc," I said, trying to find humor in all this. One of the medical assistants massaged the back of my legs, and a few hours later, I could walk without help. Before the doctor released me, I said to myself, "From now on, I will bother that Jap sergeant about the smallest decision. I will drive him crazy with the bowing and asking."

When I returned to my hut, the men had saved my wormy rice, cucumbers, and tea. I spoke to the five men that I had appointed to carry water, informing them that they would have to go back to clearing the jungle. They all agreed and were grateful that I had taken a beating for them.

"I should have known better," I said. "I should have asked the sergeant before I made any changes."

The five disagreed with me. "Sergeant, you were due either way for that beating," one of them said.

Maybe he was right.

My self-hypnosis sessions, meanwhile, were becoming a regular thing at night. This is where I derived my peace.

"I wonder when I'll get back there?" I would say to myself as I tore at a toenail. I would close my eyes, and then she would appear.

Lynda.

I was there again with her at Steel Pier. In the water, swimming with Lynda. Her wet hair tangled across her face. Then we were talking on the beach.

Other nights my mind would call up Ruthie on the swing. Or Juanita. Another night it could be Van talking to me, reinforcing his words. It always seemed to be women or Van. My mind wouldn't go to Stuart—just wouldn't go there. I had conditioned it not to go there.

It was hate by day, hypnosis by night. I was somehow able to control my memories, to orchestrate them. I let my mind wander, but I never let it wander out of bounds—never did I see Stuart or Yasha or my mother or father. I controlled everything, and I couldn't let it go out of balance because then I'd lose it, and I wouldn't know what I was thinking about. Then I'd hear the other men crying, cussing, screaming, or praying at night, and I didn't want to hear them. Maybe I was going crazy. After a while, I didn't know if these little sessions were a good thing or if was I cracking up. But I got deeper and deeper into it until the squeaky bugle blew in the morning.

"Do you know you have a smile on your face?" Circus John said when I woke up the next morning.

"Why?" I said. I didn't know I had a smile on my face.

"Yeah, you do. What are you, sadistic or something?"

"I have to think of something nice every once in a while," I said.

February 15, 1944. We were finally on schedule. Approximately fifty men had died in the process. The med hut could not handle the number of sick men. Medications were nearly depleted, and the Japs told the Dutch doctor not to give us anymore. POWs were losing weight and barely hanging on as a result of the grueling workweek. Even the monkeys were challenging us now, creeping closer to camp and stealing any food they could find. They were spending more time now on the ground, losing their fear of humans as well. The Jap and Korean guards were growing increasingly violent, driving us to finish the rail bed on time. The beatings were becoming more regular, more severe. They flowed from the top down: the camp commandant would beat up the sergeant, who beat up the guard, who beat up us—"The plague's on," we would say.

A few days later, a POW on my detail struck a rock or root as he was cutting the heavy growth, and his knife went flying. It landed some distance away from the nearest guard, but another guard, a Korean, saw the knife in the air, and he thought the POW was attempting to kill the guard. This suspicious Korean guard rushed the POW and punched him in the face. I immediately jumped between the two, having witnessed the whole incident from the start. But when I interceded, I lost my cool and said *"Teta ba goose"* to the Korean guard's face.

The Korean guard released the POW, marched over to a tree, and laid down his gun. While the other POWs kept working, the Korean guard starting clubbing me with his bamboo pole. Tomucka let him do it.

I tried to defend myself, but the Korean guard just kept swinging away. Blows landed across my back, my shoulders.

My head.

My arms. My neck. My ribs. My thighs.

My head again.

And just as the beating started to acquire a rhythm, I blacked out.

∗ 28 ∗

"Someone to Watch over Me"

March 1944

After this beating by the Korean guard, American POW Sergeant Ralph Rentz no longer responded to his name. He now answered to *Louie*, after an American boxer, Louie the Lug, who bounced back up every time he got knocked down in the ring.

"Careful," the guards would say to each other about Louie, "He doesn't care if he dies."

Where Ralph would bow, scrape, or pacify the Japanese or Korean guards as Max had instructed, Louie now went nose to nose with them.

"You can't beat him! He's my man," Louie would scream at a guard, defending a POW. "If you want to beat my men, go and get permission." Louie then pointed at Tomucka.

Tomucka immediately noticed the transformation in the American sergeant. "Do you feel all right, Sergeant?" Tomucka asked.

"No," Louie said in Malayan. "Maybe I've got a little dengue fever."

Nevertheless, the Japanese sergeant admired the way Louie defended his men and allowed Louie to talk to his captor a little bit more each day. Tomucka let Louie get a little closer. Louie would be disrespectful toward the guards, but he always put Tomucka on the throne. Louie always bowed deeply to the Japanese sergeant and always asked for permission before making a move. In short, Tomucka now preferred Louie to Ralph, and the Japanese sergeant was going to exploit the change in the American's personality.

"You are in charge, Sergeant," Tomucka instructed Louie. "We have only so many days to finish this."

Tomucka was in a delicate position, however. He didn't want the other guards to think he was too friendly with an American, but the Japanese sergeant knew that if he wanted his rail bed finished, he needed a wild, hard-driving POW sergeant like Louie to complete that task on schedule.

And once Tomucka gave Louie this assignment, Louie pushed the POWs relentlessly—so hard that many of the men thought Louie was working for the Japanese. The men wondered why any POW would push a fellow prisoner to near death.

Louie's behavior, of course, confused all parties. His voice was guttural. His jaw jutted, his head swiveled, his eyes darted. Louie prowled around the jungle like he was in complete control. He didn't shuffle like the other POWs. This was his element. He had a swagger.

"You're pushing too hard. You're gonna kill us," many POWs complained. Yet these same men knew if they were about to take a beating, Louie would be standing right in the middle of it. There were times, of course, when, to avoid showing favoritism toward the American sergeant, Tomucka allowed the guards to go after Louie. And when the Japanese and Korean guards beat Louie to the ground, he reared up on all fours and barked like a dog until the guards walked away, shaking their heads, laughing.

Circus John was concerned about his friend. He tried to talk to Louie but couldn't reach him. Circus John tried calling the sergeant Ralph, but Louie shrugged off all questions. During breaks in the work detail, Louie would eat his rice, seaweed, and anything else he had caught off by himself. Circus John and the other POWs often observed Louie talking to his knife. And at night before lights out, no one spoke to Louie. No one wanted to speak to him.

One day, Louie discovered from one of the Javanese laborers that a kampong close to the camp traded food supplies for invasion money. The laborer spoke to the head Javanese workman, Sandu, who agreed to introduce Louie to the leader of the kampong.

Sandu had been trading at the kampong for more than six months, having designed a way to get out and back into the camp. Louie demanded that the men in his hut pool their invasion money to buy more food to survive. The men didn't argue with Louie. Some of the men thought about killing him, but they wouldn't argue with him.

Two nights later, Sandu showed up with two burlap sacks. The hut was quiet, then the POWs whispered, "Good luck, Louie." They didn't know where he was going or if he'd ever return. Some would have been glad to be rid of him.

Louie followed Sandu to the eight-foot canal. They both slipped into the water. It tasted like lime. The sky was clear, and they could see despite the darkness. The sound of the rushing water drowned out any noise they made, and Louie and Sandu swam side by side until they reached a hole in the fence that Sandu had cut months earlier. Sandu employed the breaststroke as he passed through the broken wire, and Louie was right behind him. They rode the current together for about a quarter of a mile until they reached the kampong.

Sandu had instructed Louie not to wear sandals and taught the American how to avoid every twig along the way. Sandu seemed to know this path blindfolded. They didn't make a sound.

An elderly Javanese man named Nuvack, the leader of the kampong, greeted Sandu and Louie. Louie shook hands with Nuvack and followed him inside a small thatched hut. Bamboo tables overflowing with fruits, vegetables, and dried monkey and snake meat immediately surrounded Louie. The old man spoke Malayan, and Louie bargained with him, purchasing some fruit and a larger amount of dried meat. Louie paid three times more than the Japanese would have for this food, and he would have bought more if he had had the money. Louie went through his entire stack of invasion money. The whole transaction took fifteen minutes.

When Sandu and Louie returned to the canal, Sandu decided that they should head north on foot rather than fighting the current. When they got north of the broken fence, Sandu and Louie hopped into the water and let the current carry them to where they had originally slipped in. As the two of them neared the camp, the searchlights spilled around them. Sandu and Louie split up.

It must have been two o'clock in the morning when Louie crawled into his hut. Everyone was up waiting for him. When the men saw the food, they were surprised.

"He's a spy," someone whispered.

"Bullshit," Louie growled. "You go next time, Fucker."

The men quietly divided up the food.

"How'd you get out of the camp?" one man asked.

"How did you get back in?" whispered another.

"My secret," he told them. "Go out and get money, even if you have to steal it from the fuckin' Japs. They think it's worthless. They laugh at us every time they pay us." From that night on, the men in Louie's hut became money hungry.

The Japanese enjoyed playing cards, and they loved to gamble. Louie's hut had a POW, Tex, who was a professional gambler. During breaks, Tex would pull out a deck of cards and shuffle them. A group of POWs would join Tex and flash their invasion money. Tex would then deal to each man as if they were playing a game. This show enticed the Japanese guards, who would come over and watch for a while, break up the game, and detain Tex. The guards would then sit down and order Tex to deal the cards. Tex made sure to remove his wad of invasion money, motioning for the guards to do the same. The guards didn't care how much invasion money they lost: most of their wages were paid in yen and were sent back to Japan for their families. Tex soon became the largest contributor to Louie's small business.

Louie continued to sneak out of camp every third night for about a month, and he always went alone. Fearing for his friend's life, one night Circus John asked to accompany Louie. The sergeant gave in when Circus John pointed out that two men could bring back more food than one could.

When Circus John returned with Louie, soaking wet and carrying a second bag of food, the rumors that Louie was a Japanese spy ended. However, one excursion was enough for Circus John; he feared for his life even though it seemed that Louie had no such fears. Circus John never slipped out of camp again with Louie, but he often wondered why Louie risked his life like this. Was it guilt? Did guilt push Louie the same way Louie pushed his men? It certainly wasn't love or compassion. Perhaps Louie got a thrill out of pulling one over on the Japanese. Who the hell knew what was going in Louie's mind? Maybe Louie was just plain crazy, like everyone said.

Louie and Nuvack eventually became friends. Nuvack now had his young wife fix Louie a hot meal when he arrived, and Louie purchased food at cut rates. While Louie gulped down his meal, Nuvack packed the burlap bag.

Everyone in Louie's hut of course appreciated the food, but then someone blabbed to a POW outside Louie's hut. A new rumor swirled around the camp: someone in Louie's hut had made a deal with the Japanese for food. Like wildfire, the news spread that there was a secret way out of camp, and food could be bought from the natives. Louie demanded answers, but the men were silent.

Consequently, Louie didn't sneak out of the camp for another three weeks, and the hungry POWs wanted to know why. The men had become spoiled. Louie told them there were POWs now working as spies for the Japanese, trading camp information for food. The men didn't know who or what to believe.

Tomucka told Louie that someone was breaking out at night. The rumor reached the commandant. Security was tightened.

When Louie asked for the invasion money the next day in the hut, the POWs said they would rather starve than risk their hut being caught. The men feared that if Louie was apprehended, they too would be shot or beheaded. But Louie wanted to alert Nuvack about the rumor. The old man's life and family were in danger.

There was a quarter moon that night when Louie crawled out of his hut. He slipped by the patrolling guards without a problem, then dipped into the water, holding his breath for as long as he could. He then tiptoed to Nuvack's kampong. Louie devoured a warm meal as he told the old man about the spy trouble back at the camp.

"Thank you for telling me. I will leave in the morning," said Nuvack. "You can have anything you want for nothing. Please get back to camp before the Japanese wake up to our dealings."

Louie stuffed his burlap bag and gave Nuvack a hug. "Get out before daylight," Louie advised.

Sensing that he was being followed, Louie decided to take a different route back to the camp. He dropped into the canal about one hundred yards north of his usual spot. Louie swam as quietly as possible, but all the old man's food weighed him down. He was having trouble staying above water. Louie coughed, and the sound echoed through the night. Afraid that he had attracted attention, Louie quickly got out of the water to rest. Wet, ragged, and shivering, he looked like some absurd Santa Claus with his bag beside him. He coughed again. Too much water. He gagged. When Louie looked up, a bayonet was in his face, and flashlights blinded him. Four guards were now on top of him. Louie froze. He knew he was a dead man.

The Japanese guards dragged Louie to the guardhouse, shouting, "We caught him! We caught him!" The camp lights kicked on, and Louie was still coughing up water. The commandant appeared, and the guards showed him the burlap bag.

"The crazy sergeant," the commandant said, shaking his head.

"I'm trying to save the lives of my men," Louie exclaimed, defending his actions. "They're starving."

The commandant was unmoved and ordered the guards to throw Louie into a bamboo jail. Trapped inside this four-by-five-foot box, Louie coughed himself to sleep.

At dawn, two Japanese guards took Louie to the commandant's office. Tomucka was also present. The Japanese sergeant glared at Louie, then bashed him in the left side of the head, knocking him across the floor. Just then, the commandant walked in with an intelligence officer.

"*Kitwotsuke!*" Tomucka called, and Louie got up slowly, then fell to his knees and bowed from there. Tomucka yanked Louie up while the commandant addressed him in Malayan. "Why did you go out of camp to steal food from the natives?"

"My men are dying," Louie answered. "They need more food to work or they will all die."

"Who did you buy the food from?" the intelligence officer asked. "What is his name?"

"I called him Old Man," Louie said. "I did not know his name. I used the money from all the men to buy food. The men can work faster if they have more food."

After the intelligence officer conversed with the commandant in Japanese, the commandant locked his eyes on Louie, disgusted. Louie stared back, concentrating on how he was going to kill them all.

A Japanese guard then dragged Louie to another room. The guard pointed his bayonet in Louie's face, and then Tomucka entered.

"You were very good to your men, but you broke the commandant's rules," Tomucka told Louie. "I will try to help you if I can, because you are a good sergeant."

Tomucka dismissed the guard and left the room, closing and locking the door. Louie collapsed in the corner. Exhaustion and torment had finally caught up with him.

✶ 29 ✶

"Let's Face the Music"

August 1944

SOMEONE KICKED LOUIE'S FOOT THE FOLLOWING MORNING. TWO JAPANESE guards loomed over him. One of them motioned for Louie to get up. The guards then walked Louie to his hut and ordered him to put on more clothes and grab his straw hat. A few men in the hut who were sick that day thought that the crazy, fearless, POW sergeant who used to bark now looked like a whipped dog.

The two Japanese guards took Louie to the far end of the camp. About thirty yards from the nearest hut lay a freshly dug hole. A pile of dirt sat nearby. The Japanese guards pointed at the hole. Louie didn't move. Each guard then gripped one of Louie's arms and shoved him into the eight-foot pit.

Louie's legs gave way when he hit bottom. He fell on his side and lay there in a fetal position. Hours passed, and Louie changed positions. He sat. He stood. He started to panic. There was no food or water in the pit. Darkness moved in.

As Louie tried to sleep, some dirt fell on him from above. Louie looked up and saw a shadow of a head.

"Sergeant, here's some food," said a voice in English.

Louie knew that voice.

"It's tied on a rope," the man whispered. "Eat and drink fast, then bury anything that's left so the guards don't notice."

The man lowered the food and canteen. Louie untied it and then jiggled the rope. "I'll be back in ten minutes," the man said softly before he fled.

Louie quickly pushed the food into his mouth.

Minutes later, the rope hit Louie's shoulder. Louie tied the empty canteen and banana leaves around the rope, then jerked it to get the man's attention.

Louie slept little that night because his mind was racing, wondering how they were going to kill him. Would he be tortured with a long bamboo poles with sharp points and bled to death? Would they drown him by filling the hole with water? Would Tomucka help him? Or would Tomucka cut his throat and tie him to a wagon, then parade him around the camp?

When dawn came, Louie was groggy and weak. Two Japanese guards strolled by the pit. They stared at Louie and then one of them kicked some dirt at him, laughing. Louie flashed a demented smile.

"Crazy," one of them said. The guards shook their heads and walked away.

Louie dug a hole with his hands in a corner so he could defecate and urinate, then covered the hole up with dirt. He pulled his straw hat down over his forehead and closed his eyes. He clutched his elbows, trying to rock himself to sleep. Awakened by the hot sun, Louie was now in a cold sweat. Harsh sunlight was beaming down directly onto his makeshift toilet, making it hard to breathe. Louie dug a second hole and piled the dirt on top of the first hole, trying to quell the intolerable stench.

When the sun went down the second night, Louie was lying on his side, trying to sleep. His head was pounding. He was ravenous. Would someone again bring him something to eat? Under the moonlight, Louie suddenly heard a voice.

"How do you like being on the road, Kid?"

Louie quickly turned his head and realized he wasn't alone. He saw Harry.

Harry was now sitting across from Louie at a table. There were some other musicians with the trumpet player as well. All of them were dressed in tuxedos. They wore friendly smiles.

Louie sat up and pulled his legs close to his chest. He didn't reach out to touch Harry, afraid that he would disappear if touched.

"I'm never home," one of the other musicians said. "I'm divorced. I love my kids, but they don't recognize me when I come home."

Louie stared, squinted.

"Sergeant," came a whisper from above the pit.

It was the man again with food and water. He lowered the stuff to Louie, then left.

Louie pushed the food into his mouth again, then stopped in a gesture to offer food to Harry and the others. But the musicians were eating eggs, bacon, and sweet rolls.

"Where have you been, Harry?" Louie said in his head. Then Harry and the boys vanished.

Louie quickly got up and went to the wall, but they were indeed gone.

"Where'd you learn to do that?" Lynda said softly.

Louie snapped around now and saw an image of Lynda projected on the wall behind him. She was wearing gorgeous baby blue dress with a pearl necklace and earrings.

"We'll have to do it again," Lynda continued. "Because I think I missed a few things."

"You're still very pretty," Louie said in his head. "And I know you are waiting for me. I will have to tell my mother and father that we are getting married."

The rope hit Louie's shoulder. He quickly tied up the leaves and canteen, and when he looked up again, Lynda had vanished.

Louie was now trembling. He trembled until he passed out.

On the third day, the odor was so bad that Louie was gagging. With the scorching sun beating down on him, Louie just lay there, passing in and out of consciousness. When he awoke that night, Louie saw a mound of red ants and steaming oxen shit. He heard the screams of wild animals. Then another voice spoke to him: *"You're an animal in the forest. . . . Survival takes over. . . . You have to be stronger than them. They're running after you. . . ."*

Louie covered his ears and closed his eyes, shaking, trembling again. Then suddenly everything went silent. Raising his head, Louie then saw three faces: Izzy, Minnie, and Sylvia.

"Dad, I'm falling in love with Lynda," Louie heard himself saying in his head.

Minnie turned to Izzy and said, "He has been going out with Lynda for a couple years now. You know her parents. I think it's a good thing."

"I haven't gotten married yet," Sylvia chimed in. "I should be the first to get married in the family!"

The parents started to laugh. They wiggled their noses, scratched their ears, and winked as if they were communicating in some unknown language. Louie just stared at their images. He didn't move.

"Well, Ralph will be home soon," Minnie said. "And he will get married—after they finish school."

"Where is it going to take place?" Louie said in his head.

"At the temple," Minnie replied. Then the three of them vanished.

Louie continued to stare, even though they were gone. It was as if everything the Dutch physical therapist, Van Doren, had told the American sergeant to forget—music, family, home—all of it was now leaking out of him.

Four days later, when the Japanese guards lifted Louie from the hole, he was babbling about a monkey.

When Louie finally came to, he found himself in the med hut, sprawled out on a table. He was kicking and screaming, "It's my turn now! It's my turn!"

Two medics struggled to pour water down Louie's throat. "Ralph! Stop!" yelled one of the medics. "You're dehydrated and running a fever. You must drink water or you will die."

The medics called him Ralph because they matched his POW number with his medical records. Louie, however, thought the two medics were Japanese guards trying to drown him. The two medics then washed Louie's body with cool water, trying to bring the fever down.

That night, as cold towels were applied to his head and body, Louie was fighting a war with the monkeys. "Die, you fucking bastards! Die!" he screamed as he imagined himself slicing off their heads and arms with a huge sword. Exhausted and dehydrated, Louie passed out again.

Louie remained in the med hut for three days, until he was strong enough to walk. He had lost ten pounds.

Arriving back at his hut, the men gave him a great welcome.

"Louie, you made it!" they shouted. "We were afraid you had died in that stinking hole!" Some wished he had died.

That evening, Tomucka surprised Louie with a visit.

"I am sorry this happened to you, but you broke the rules," Tomucka said. "The commandant was about to have you beheaded, but he asked for my opinion of your worth to the Imperial Japanese Army. I told him you were the best POW sergeant on the work detail."

"Thank you," said Louie, but he didn't mean it.

"The commandant wanted to see if you would live through the ordeal," Tomucka continued. "I think he thought you were going to die."

Louie noticed that the Japanese sergeant had something in his hand.

"Japanese cookies," Tomucka said, as he presented Louie with the bag. "When do you think you'll be ready to go to work?"

"I hate cookies," Louie replied.

"I will bring you fruit and meat tomorrow evening."

When the Japanese sergeant left the hut, Louie said he would be ready for work soon. The men thought this was very funny, because Louie could barely walk a straight line.

Tomucka visited Louie every night for the next two weeks, bearing gifts. The men in Louie's hut, however, viewed Tomucka's visits, his cookies, his gifts, as very strange indeed. Notions of Louie working for the other side resurfaced. Circus John, Red, Tex, and the other POWs kept their distance.

Louie was soon getting his strength back, hobbling around the camp. It had been a month since the pit. Now, Louie was ordered back on the rail bed detail.

The monkeys were still swinging and screaming in the trees, and the guards had sore necks from constantly searching for the animals. Occasionally, monkeys would drop from the trees and run across the rail bed, diving into the underbrush. The guards would fire in their direction, but the monkeys escaped. Nothing much had changed really, except that the rail bed was about half completed.

While Louie and his men were walking up the rail bed one morning, a dozen monkeys were waiting for them. Two of the larger monkeys started to shriek and wave their arms. Tomucka instructed Circus John to throw his knife.

"Sergeant," Circus John said to Louie. "You take the one on the right, and I'll kill the other one." The monkeys were jumping now, screeching, almost inviting an attack.

The two men crept closer, and so did the monkeys. Circus John and Louie glanced at each other, then, like two gunslingers, they drew their knives and threw at the same time. The screaming was silenced in seconds. Ten monkeys fled the scene, while their leaders now lay dead, with knives stuck in the middle of their chests.

Several Japanese guards with wide grins rushed up to Circus John and Louie, pumping their hands. The next evening Louie's men ate one of the monkeys for dinner; the Japanese guards had the other. Tomucka strutted around the camp as if he himself had killed the monkeys.

☆ 30 ☆

"I've Got You under My Skin"

September 1944

THE MONKEYS DISAPPEARED FOR A WHILE, BUT THE RAIL BED DETAIL WAS behind schedule again, so the men had to work extra hours. Because of Louie's intense pace, many men collapsed from exhaustion. Many more suffered from skin ulcers, malaria, beriberi, dysentery, and tuberculosis.

Skin ulcers developed when a virus attacked broken, exposed skin that had come into contact with certain plants in the jungle and when the area was exposed to the hot sun. The typical skin ulcer would start with a pimple, become a pus pocket, and then grow red all over, with pus building up in the middle. If the pus got into the bloodstream, it could kill. To deal with the skin ulcers, rashes, and irritations, the Dutch doctor would go to the Japanese kitchen and get ice packs to place near the wound and then apply tourniquets to stop the bleeding. Since the Dutch doctor had no scalpel, he would sharpen the end of a teaspoon and use it to scoop the pus and crust from a POW's arm, leg, or back. The doctor would then immediately cover the hole with a Red Cross bandage. As many as five men had to hold down an afflicted POW when the doctor performed this procedure. There was no sulfur, no anesthetic.

Malaria developed from mosquito bites, which no one could escape. Bugs were everywhere—in the jungle, the kitchen, the latrine, even the food.

There were two types of beriberi, wet and dry. Both were caused by a lack of vitamin B, which caused a person's immune system to shut down. Wet beriberi originates at the feet, where it causes swelling. The fluid works its way up to the testicles, enlarging them to the size of melons. Eventually, the liquid constricts the heart, resulting in death. Dry beriberi, which Louie contracted, attacks the muscles in the legs, but this condition is not fatal and can be remedied over time by a protein-enriched diet.

176

There were also two types of dysentery, amebic and viral. Amebic dysentery is fatal. Bugs invade the lining of the stomach and eat away at the innards, causing excrement to turn white. Viral dysentery, however, is treatable. With viral dysentery, excrement is normal but somewhat runny and white. Similar to dry beriberi, viral dysentery can be remedied with an improved diet of meats and fresh fruits.

POW deaths doubled, mostly as a result of amebic dysentery and tuberculosis, which developed because of malnourishment and the wet weather conditions. Coughing up blood was a telltale sign of TB. When a Japanese guard saw a POW do this, he would be ordered back to camp and was never seen again.

Most of the POWs knew what diseases they had contracted, but the Dutch doctors lacked the medications needed to treat these illnesses. The Japanese made sure of that. The POWs needed another med hut to accommodate the sick men, but the commandant denied the request.

* 31 *

"Bewitched, Bothered, and Bewildered"

October 1944

WHEN THE POWs WERE SETTING THE STEEL TRACK WITH LARGE CROWBARS, the men were nothing but skin and bones. The Japanese gave the men double rations of rice and seaweed, knowing that if the POWs died, the project would never be completed on time.

When Louie needed twenty men for his detail, he could only find ten. Fifty percent of the POWs were either sick or dying. Every day, Louie would march into his hut and order each sick man to walk out. If a POW didn't get up, Tomucka ordered a guard to beat the man without asking why he was sick. The Japanese always thought that the POWs were faking illness to avoid work, a concept the POWs referred to as goldbricking.

Tomucka was growing more concerned that the construction of the rail bed would fall further behind schedule, for which the Japanese sergeant would take a beating. Tomucka was becoming a real monster, even striking his guards for taking time off for lunch. The Japanese sergeant also scaled back the POWs' rest periods, making them work faster, longer, and harder. Louie attempted to speak with Tomucka, but all the American received was a beating behind the knees because the Japanese sergeant thought the POWs were lazy.

Since the Japanese guards were becoming more fearful of Tomucka beating them, they now started to beat the POWs more frequently and more brutally. One time, when a couple of POWs were being beaten, Louie intervened and was jabbed in the ribs with a bamboo pole. An electric shock raced up his arm. From that day on, Louie had spasms in his scarred right shoulder.

Soon afterward, Louie began noticing that his stomach and back were giving him considerable pain. One evening, Louie spoke with Tomucka, who observed that Louie's upper leg was yellowish-green. Tomucka gave Louie permission to visit the med hut.

"Sergeant, you have gall bladder problems," said the Dutch doctor after examining Louie's skin. "You had better check in here before you collapse."

Louie informed Tomucka of the doctor's prognosis and spent the night in the med hut. Later, when the doctor placed Louie on a bamboo table and pressed firmly under Louie's ribs, the pain was excruciating.

"You must have an operation, Sergeant. I think you have gallstones," the doctor said.

The Dutch doctor gave Louie a laxative to clean out his system, then tried to convince the commandant to approve Louie's operation. The doctor told the commandant that Louie would die if the operation wasn't performed. The commandant didn't care. The doctor then tried to entice the commandant by telling him that this gallbladder operation could be an educational experiment for Japanese medical research.

"Your Japanese sergeant really gave a great pitch," the doctor said the following morning as he greeted Louie, smiling. "He told the commandant that this operation would save thousands of wounded soldiers. He also told him that you were a good manager for your men and that you took many beatings for them."

There was another small matter to be considered as well. The POW med hut was full, and the Japanese of course wouldn't let the American sergeant into a Japanese hospital. Tomucka convinced the commandant to erect a surgical hut. It took fifteen Javanese laborers three days to build the site. Tomucka also ordered medical supplies, which were shipped in from the hospital in Batavia.

In the meantime, Louie was running a fever, and anything he ate would come up fifteen minutes later. He was living on water, and sometimes even that wouldn't stay down. He was dying, little by little.

Shaved and washed down, Louie saw the Dutch doctor enter with five Japanese doctors on the day of the operation. They gathered around the table. The smell of ether filled the air, and then Louie felt like he was being smothered. He was out.

Fifteen hours later, Louie awoke, throwing up bile.

"Don't pull that tube out of your stomach," said a medic. "If you pull it out, we'll have to open you up again. The commandant has ordered that you must get well."

"Who the fuck does he think he is?" Louie shouted. "If I want to die here, I'm gonna die here. He won't be able to stop me."

The medic tried to calm Louie. "We all have a lot of confidence that you will pull through, but if you don't, the commandant will shut down this surgical hut."

The next four days, Louie suffered the devil's wrath. He was strapped to his bed. No drugs were available, so there was little the Dutch doctor could do. Louie drifted in and out of consciousness as the medic tried to soothe him with cold rags.

On his next visit, the Dutch doctor explained to Louie that the five Japanese doctors had lost their patience after a few hours of the operation and kicked him in the shins to make him work faster. The Dutch doctor also mentioned that Louie had a gallstone caught in the gall duct. The doctor had removed Louie's entire gall bladder and inserted a tube to drain the bile and stomach fluid.

"Sorry about the lack of painkillers, Sergeant," the doctor said. "The Japanese wouldn't give us any because they needed the drugs for their own soldiers."

A few days later, the tube was removed from Louie's stomach, and it looked like he had two navels. The doctor had made an eight-inch vertical incision along Louie's abdomen, slashing the stomach muscles and nerves rather than making a smaller, horizontal cut. The Dutch doctor, the commandant, and the five Japanese doctors soon visited Louie in the med hut.

"He's too thin," the Dutch doctor said. "He must have lots of food or he will die." These words seemed to surprise the commandant, who conferred with his five doctors and then said, "This soldier will be receiving food from the Japanese kitchen."

When the Japanese exited the hut, the Dutch doctor said, "The commandant must keep you alive because he will become a hero when your case is written up in the Japanese papers. He will take credit for the whole operation of saving a POW's life. This will ignite a big propaganda show so all the world will see how well the Japanese are treating the American POWs. Enjoy yourself, Sergeant," advised the doctor. "You are a privileged POW at the present time."

<hr />

Two days before Christmas, the commandant announced to the camp that the International Red Cross was sending the POWs clothes and foodstuffs.

Five army trucks drove onto the assembly field. Fifty men were ordered to unpack the Red Cross trucks. Two other trucks followed, carrying Japanese guards, who quickly surrounded the five trucks and set up machine guns.

"Did they come to feed us or kill us?" whispered one of the POWs.

After the trucks were unloaded, the commandant led three Red Cross representatives to a podium. The commandant spoke first: "The Japanese people are very kind to allow the Red Cross to bring Christmas gifts to all you prisoners of war." He sat down and folded his arms.

One of the Red Cross representatives, who spoke in broken English, began by telling the POWs how kind and humane the Japanese were and then mentioned that most of the gifts had come from the United States.

When the commandant heard this, he jumped up and immediately stopped the show. The podium was cleared, but the POWs remained on the parade grounds to receive their gifts. The commandant's adjutant announced to the POWs that the Red Cross boxes would be repacked onto the trucks.

"The commandant will decide how the distribution will be made in a few days," the adjutant said in Malayan. It was an uneasy moment. All the POWs were near-skeletons, with pointy elbows and brown teeth, and they wanted their Red Cross packages. But the Japanese kept the packages for themselves. The food went to the Japanese kitchen, the new khakis to the officers.

Louie, meanwhile, walked slowly around the camp and regained some weight. Tomucka told the American that he would be back on the rail bed detail the following day. However, Louie was still sweating profusely and battling agonizing headaches in the surgical hut. He received permission to go to the showers.

The cold water felt good on the back of Louie's neck and shoulders. Louie then slowly raised his head and saw an image against the flat, bamboo wall: his father. And his mother. They were working at the store. His father in his apron. His mother with her white hair. They were talking. Faceless customers passed to and fro.

Was this a vision? Or was it a memory?

"My God. I'm dead," I said to myself. "But I can feel the water on my head.

"Are they dead?" I wondered, still seeing Izzy and Minnie on the wall.

I started shaking because I thought I had died. I began to cry.

Now sobbing, I lowered my head and noticed a fresh scar on my chest.

"What happened to me?"

Completely terrified, I raised my head and the pictures disappeared.

☆ 32 ☆

"Don't Sit under the Apple Tree (With Anyone Else but Me)"

December 1944

STILL SHAKING, I WALKED OUT OF THE SHOWERS WITH MY HEAD DOWN AS AN-other POW walked in.

"Merry Christmas, Louie," said the POW. "I see you're up and around."

"Louie who?" I answered.

"What, Sergeant?"

"Louie who?" I repeated. "You said—"

The POW stopped, and I didn't finish my sentence. He studied my eyes deeply, curiously. "You've been out of it for a long while, haven't you, Sarge?" he said. "You've had a real bad time of it."

"What do you mean?" I asked.

"You're a real son of a bitch. We all thought you were gonna kill those Jap guards. They must have given you one helluva beating."

I nodded, totally confused.

I dried myself off again with several old rags and started to move slowly. My feet just seemed to know where to go, as if I had never left. Had I left? I wasn't lost in the camp, but I did feel a profound sense of loss. I felt a unique sense of instability. I thought I was going insane, but I didn't want to say anything.

Somehow, I knew my way back to the hut, and when I entered, I passed under the four little lights strung across the place. I didn't recognize any of the faces. Nobody said a word. I walked over to my rack, and I saw Circus John. I remembered him. He and everyone else in the hut were skin and bones. Circus John saw the look on my face but didn't say anything.

I hung up my rags on the bamboo pole behind my bed. I was very dis-placed. All I did was stand there and wonder, "How did I get this scar on my chest? Am I alive? Is this all a dream?" "Just keep your mouth shut," I told myself. I sat down on my bed, thinking: if I asked one of the other men, "Hey, what's this on my chest?" they would think I was nuts.

Christmas? Did that fella outside the showers say "Merry Christmas?" Was he kidding me? Who the hell is Louie? Why have I lost so much weight? Why does my chest hurt? What's happened? Am I dying? Or am I dead? Is this up in heaven or down in hell?

Things were going so fast in my mind—questions, flashes of my father, my mother—that my head hurt. It all seemed disconnected. "Ralph, you were never like this before," I told myself. What had happened? It was like being inside a huge rubber ball that was rolling down a hill, and I didn't know when or where it would stop.

I would scare everyone by asking all these questions. "Keep your mouth shut, Ralph," I told myself.

Just then, the Japs rolled out the hot wagon of rice and seaweed. I followed the others out of the hut. This routine didn't feel strange to me.

I sat beside Circus John, who seemed to be watching me. While he was eating, he said, "Well, we've got about five thousand yards to go."

The last I had heard, we had about ten thousand yards to go on the rail bed. I couldn't say anything to Circus John because I didn't know what to say. I sensed that he was updating me, but as he was updating me, he was confusing me even further.

I got up and washed out my tins. Eating and washing didn't feel foreign to me. It grew dark.

Before lights out, I still didn't want to ask Circus John anything because I really thought I was going out of my mind. As I lay in my rack, I kept thinking, "Who in the hell is Louie? Where in the hell have I been for five thousand yards?" I couldn't remember anything. I couldn't remember a thing. Had everything gotten to me? Was I going completely nuts? The last thing I remembered was working on the rail bed. I didn't sleep much that night.

I heard the bugle sound the next morning. I sat up and looked at my chest. My scar was as red as a beet. It looked like somebody had slashed me. Every time I lifted my arms, it was excruciating. I didn't feel like I was in a stranger's body, but I knew something had happened to me. I didn't know what. After seeing my father and mother on that bamboo shower wall, I still didn't know if I was alive or dead. Maybe this was all a dream.

"You gonna work today?" Circus John asked me.

"Of course, I'm gonna work," I said. "I just hurt."

"I would hurt too with that goddamn gash down the middle of my stomach. You went through hell, Louie."

"What are you talking about?" I asked. "What Louie? Who's Louie?"

"You're Louie," he said.

"I'm not Louie. I'm Ralph. Where did you get the Louie bit?"

Circus John started to laugh and then studied me closely as he slipped on his wooden sandals.

"Did you say your name was Ralph?" Circus John whispered.

"Yeah, my name is Ralph," I said. "When was it something else?"

Circus John didn't answer me.

I reached for my knife, which was hanging from the bamboo rack with all the others, strapped it to my right thigh, and went outside.

I ate my 140 grams of rice and seaweed. Circus John sat next to me, but he didn't say a word. I was thinking, "I don't know what happened to me, but I'm afraid to ask. Did someone stick me with a knife, and I'm still here?" I decided to leave it alone. Got to work, I told myself. See how the whole fucking thing evolves.

When the men lined up on the parade grounds, I saw more faces that I didn't recognize. Faces I had never seen before—or maybe I had. I couldn't remember. It was all very bizarre because of the new faces, yet somehow the routine was familiar.

"Count off," I yelled, and the men obeyed.

When I returned to the rail bed detail, three groups of twenty were working, the same as before; however, Aussies and Brits were now on my crew.

"Sergeant, those men could hardly walk," Circus John told me when I asked where all the others had gone. "They were mere skeletons when they were taken away."

These new men called me Louie. I didn't answer them. I did notice that we were deeper into the jungle than I remembered. But the men were looking at me strangely all morning.

"You should be over about fifteen feet," I said to one of the men who was working. I didn't know his name. The man looked surprised. So did a few of the others. I didn't scream the order. I didn't holler it. The Jap and Korean guards also seemed confused.

Tomucka, whom I did remember, took notice. "How do you feel after the operation, Sergeant?" he asked me.

"It hurts a little, but I can do my job," I said in Malayan. "What operation?" I wondered. I just nodded my head. What the hell had happened to me?

I didn't push my men very hard that morning, but they were working very fast nonetheless. During our morning break, I went under a tree to sit down. Circus John joined me.

"How do you feel, Sergeant?" he asked politely.

"I'm hurting," I said. "I'm weak."

"You've been working like a dog for months. See if you can get time off again."

The look on Circus John's face concerned me. I wasn't paranoid about him and the others staring at me, because I was too busy trying to sort things out in my head. Was this my head? I was out in no-man's-land.

"The fellas all call me Louie," I said to Circus John. "Who was Louie? Was he another guy working on the detail? Was I sick? I don't understand."

"Let's just leave it that way for now," Circus John said. "I'll call you Ralph, but the rest of the guys will call you Louie."

"What? I don't understand?"

Circus John looked deep into my eyes. "Ralph and Louie are the same person," he said.

I couldn't open my mouth. This man was crazy, I thought—until he started giving me specifics.

Circus John then told me about a beating I had taken seven or eight months earlier from a Korean guard. Apparently, I had passed out and was lying unconscious on the dirt. Circus John picked me up and pulled me under a tree. He had used cold water to wash the blood from my head, my arms, and my legs and then asked, "Ralph, you okay?"

Circus John said I replied, "Ralph? Who's Ralph? My name's Louie."

I didn't remember this beating or being pulled under a tree.

According to Circus John, after that beating I was sent to the med hut for the night. The next day, I was back on the detail, but my behavior, my personality, was completely different.

Circus John explained that as Louie, I ran the detail like a slave operation. He said that when the bugle went off, Louie made sure he had twenty men lined up and ready to go even if they had dengue fever, malaria, or dysentery. And on the job, Louie pushed the POWs mercilessly, driving some of them close to death to finish the rail bed.

"Louie had no fear, Ralph," Circus John continued. "He was a very difficult person to get along with. He was a son of a bitch."

"That's what that fella outside the showers called me, too," I thought. A son of a bitch.

"The guards think you're crazy," Circus John continued, sipping from his canteen. "You would go eyeball to eyeball with those fuckers, Ralph, screaming and calling them whatever the hell came into your head."

I couldn't believe what I was hearing. I knew for sure that anyone who behaved the way Circus John was telling me would have been shot on the spot. What in the world was this man saying to me?

Circus John continued. "Sometimes you'd take a beating and go down. Then you'd bark at the guards like a dog, bite at their heels. Then you'd call the guard a bastard, which he never understood."

I smiled, embarrassed, humiliated, ashamed. I couldn't form a word, let alone a question.

Circus John smiled. "I'm glad that Ralph is back," he said.

I was in a state of confusion, and Circus John knew it.

Circus John now spoke in a soft tone. "Don't let the men take advantage of you by slowing down, or Tomucka will have the guards beat the shit out you. Don't help the waterman like you did this morning. You're taking power away from Tomucka, who sets the rules. That's not your job. Don't get involved with the work; just manage the men, Ralph."

Tomucka called us back onto the detail, but my mind was still on what Circus John had told me. How could it not be? I realized now that everyone thought I had lost my mind or broken down. No wonder they were looking at me like that. All of them.

I was trying to find a comfortable pace for the men to do their work. I was just doing it as I used to do it. I didn't know how Louie did it, even though Circus John said I was him for a while. No POWs were hit that afternoon. No beatings.

During our ten-minute afternoon break, I met Circus John again under a tree. I told him that my chest was hurting badly. I was sick to my stomach. The heat bothered me. I was constantly drinking water.

"Do you know you were operated on?" Circus John asked. "You were gonna die. Tomucka had them operate on your gall bladder."

"They took my gall bladder out?" I said to myself. "How am I gonna eat? How is my liver gonna work? I got nothing in reserve. I'm gonna die! Can you live without your gall bladder?"

I looked down again at the scar on my chest, then up at Circus John. I suddenly became deeply afraid of him—not afraid of *him*, really, but afraid of what he was going to tell me next.

After the detail, when we returned to the camp, Circus John pointed out the special surgical hut that had been constructed for my gall bladder operation. They never used it again for surgery, Circus John told me. It was now a garbage bin. I didn't want to go near it. Maybe I should have died in there. I thought, "Why can't I die? Why can't I get out of this pain?"

When we got back to the hut, I saw a little bag under my rack. I didn't remember it. I opened the bag and found a piece of shrapnel and something that looked like paper money.

"I have a piece a metal in my hand," I said to Circus John. I had no idea where it had come from.

"You were shot down, Ralph," he said. "Your shoulder."

Circus John pointed to my right shoulder. I hadn't realized that there was an eight-inch scar back there. I couldn't see it. I reached over and touched the scar. I didn't remember getting hit. What the hell had happened to me? Now shaking, I was afraid I was passing through to the other side.

Circus John said he had saved the shrapnel for me. Then he sat me down on my rack and reminded me that I had told him about my days at the hospital in Surabaja and at the two other prison camps I had been at before this one.

"Remember Malang, Ralph? The bicycle camp? Remember?" Circus John asked, trying to jump-start my memory. "Your pal, Zip, remember?"

I didn't remember a thing.

"Get some rest, Ralph. Get some rest." Circus John put me to bed. I put the shrapnel into my pants pocket, thinking that maybe it would help remind me of who I was.

I was scared to death that night. All I thought about was whether I would wake up as Louie again. I tried to stay awake to prevent that from happening. How had I gotten to the bicycle camp, I asked myself. Did we walk? That was five hundred miles from Malang. Jesus Christ, you couldn't walk five hundred miles. That's ridiculous. I didn't remember Malang. I didn't remember how long I had been in this camp. I didn't remember how I had gotten here. And Zip. I didn't remember anyone named Zip. I wondered how he got to the bicycle camp? How had I met Zip? Slowly, logically, I told myself that the only way I could have gotten to the bicycle camp was by train. It must have been by train.

As I was reasoning all this out that night, an image of a young girl suddenly popped into my head. She was introducing her parents. I didn't recognize her. I didn't know who I was seeing in my mind's eye. I didn't know her name. She had her hair pulled up. Was this a memory? My own invention?

Who was I looking at? I was infuriated, thoroughly confused. The girl wasn't moving or speaking. It was a like a black-and-white still photograph.

Who am I looking at?

I concentrated on the image:

A girl introducing her parents.

A girl introducing her parents.

A girl introducing her parents.

A girl introducing her parents.

A girl introducing her parents.

Her hair pulled up.

A girl introducing her parents.

A girl introducing her parents.

A girl introducing her parents.

She's smiling.

A girl introducing her parents.

A girl introducing her parents.

Her hair pulled up.

A girl introducing her parents.

A girl introducing her parents.

A girl introducing her parents.

I couldn't identify the girl. I cried myself to sleep.

The next day was wash day, which meant we didn't have to work. We had the day to ourselves. Most of the POWs were smoking, talking or complaining about their work details, or trying to trade for another detail. I couldn't account for many faces. Lack of food, TB, and other diseases must have killed off many men, I thought. Maybe men had been shifted to other details. New faces replaced the dead every day. I didn't want to think I had pushed a fellow POW to his death. I tried to put all this out of my mind. But the thing I noticed was that no one except Circus John came near me.

"Why don't the guys want to talk to me?" I asked Circus John as we scrubbed our torn pants in our hut. We were alone.

"Most of the men hated you, Ralph," Circus John said quietly. "They thought Louie was a Jap spy."

My stomach was churning. I had a headache. Circus John continued. "Some of the men were plotting to kill you after Red died. I heard some of the guards wanted to kill you themselves because of the way you got in their faces."

Red was dead. I remembered Red. Had I pushed that waterman to his death? How many other deaths had I been responsible for? I didn't want to believe it. What had happened to me? I must have lost my mind. But I didn't know I had lost my mind because I was doing the same job as I had done before, ordering men around. I didn't know I had been acting crazy, but somehow this Louie was in me. I was using what was in me, but I didn't realize I was using it. I didn't know I had broken down. It wasn't a weakness, I told myself, because it was out of my control. It just happened.

I now had tears in my eyes, thinking about how I could apologize to each man and inform him that I had been sick. My gut hurt. Circus John tried to be polite with me, as if he didn't want to tell me, but he knew that I needed to know. I wanted to know everything that I did as Louie. The worst things.

"If a Jap or Korean guard would come too close to you, Ralph, you would growl at them," Circus John continued. "If you had to walk by a guard, you would walk around him so you wouldn't have to bow. But you treated Tomucka differently. You bowed only to him. The Japs thought you were a sideshow, but they were afraid of you, too. We all were."

"I must have looked like a crazy man," I sobbed.

Circus John smiled and said, "I'm glad it's over with, Ralph. I knew you were crazy, but when you would walk around talking to that knife as if it were a friend of yours—shit. Nobody else would talk to you, and that knife ain't gonna talk back. Or did it?"

"John don't give me that bullshit," I said.

"I'm telling you the truth. You used to keep your hand on your knife all the time, poised, ready to strike. It kept the Jap guards on their toes," Circus John said. "I told you they wanted to kill you, but Tomucka wouldn't let them."

I kept wondering how I could explain this situation to my men. I couldn't explain it to myself. I started to work myself into a panic again.

I bet that the other men were thinking, "One day he's barking like a dog on all fours, the next day he's walking slow and not pushing us like a crazy man. . . ."

I couldn't tell the men anything. It wouldn't do any good to try to explain, anyway. They didn't believe anybody, including other POWs. We all were constantly told lies. We all distrusted everyone and everything.

But I had to trust Circus John to be my memory, even though I felt I was going out of my mind.

"I don't want to hear any more," I told Circus John. "I was sick. I couldn't help it."

I was completely ashamed of myself, as if the men all had a right to call me a son of a bitch. But didn't Louie save some men by taking beatings for them? My conscience was starting to bother me. I didn't feel comfortable with my surroundings. I felt that one day—someday—these POWs were gonna stick me.

Circus John touched my shoulder and shook me gently. "I'm still your friend," he said.

✻ 33 ✻

"I Got It Bad (And That Ain't Good)"

December 1944

THAT NIGHT, I STILL WONDERED HOW I COULD APOLOGIZE TO THE MEN. How could I be trusted again? How could I turn this situation around before I had become Louie? I was also terrified that if I got beaten hard again, I might turn back into Louie. I knew the Japs felt that beatings only made you stronger. Hopefully, the guards were still confused. Maybe they were still afraid of me. Would Tomucka continue to tell them to lay off me? I didn't know.

Circus John impressed on me that I still had a job to do whether I was Ralph or Louie, and if it didn't get done, I was gonna get shot. If the men didn't walk quickly enough or work quickly enough, I'd be pushed in the middle. And I didn't want to get my ass caught in the pliers, but that was my job. All I could think about was whether Louie would come back again.

As I lay down on my rack that night, I closed my eyes and breathed deeply. Suddenly, the young girl appeared again in my mind, the same girl introducing her parents. She was a welcomed distraction. I concentrated on her.

The girl introducing her parents.

The girl introducing her parents.

The girl introducing her parents.

Who are you?

The girl introducing her parents.

Hair pulled up.

Smiling.

Hair pulled up.

Lynda.

The name popped into my head. It was Lynda. She was smiling at me. I remembered her. Lynda. That girl was Lynda. I could feel that I was smiling. Now crying. I was in love with that girl. Would I ever see her again? Then Lynda faded out, and another girl faded in slowly.

She was dancing. In a nightclub. It was a frozen image in black and white, just like the one of Lynda. I concentrated on the new girl.

Dancing girl.

Dancing girl.

Dancing girl.

Chiseled cheekbones.

Dancing girl.

Nightclub.

Dancing girl.

Dancing girl.

Rumba.

Chiseled cheekbones.

Jhannella.

Her name popped into my head. I had danced with her; I had had sex with her. I smiled. I remembered Jhannella.

This is how my mind started to work those first few days back. The past came back to me slowly. I had to focus on what I was seeing and work to have it make sense.

I would have one thought and dwell on that thought, sometimes for hours, and finally that would lead to a name. Some memories took days to identify, others two days. My two brothers, Zeldan and Joe, came back to me instantly.

Eventually, I started to remember more: my sister, Sylvia; Nana; even Mr. Stein, the haberdasher. I recalled working at the cash register, my four tuxedos, Father Marque. Harry had a trumpet in his mouth when I remembered him. Zip was posing like a boxer.

But then my mind started to work a little differently, sort of like word association: When I remembered Max, a flash of the men starving on the train followed. When I remembered Yasha playing his clarinet, a flash of my black instrument case followed. Images started to fade in and out more frequently, and my mind made the connections. I remembered I was a musician, but I didn't know what instrument I played. It was confusing. Then something very peculiar started to occur. The more I had recurring thoughts of home, the more I started to hear a voice in my head. A voice that contrasted thoughts of love and family. "*Forget about everybody,*" the voice said. "*Your friends. Forget them all.*"

I couldn't recognize the voice. It was just a voice at first. I thought it might even be my conscience talking to me.

I didn't have time during the work detail to sort out the voice. I had to be alert at work or I would take a beating. But as soon as I got into my bed, I didn't sleep much because I was trying to remember everything. But the voice in my head was telling me to forget. It was quite a battle, a tug-of-war in my mind.

However, I started to concentrate more on the voice. It now began to flood all my thoughts. Was it the voice of Captain Martin? McCarthy? Max? As I heard the voice, I started to feel pain in my shoulder, in my back. And that pain took me back to the hospital in Surabaja and then to Frerry, who would call the nurses for me. Then I discovered the owner of the voice.

I had a flash of a hospital floor . . .

"You'll fall into a depression first. You won't hear the guards giving you orders," the voice said.

. . . then Frerry was lying in the bed . . .

. . . then a hand holding a piece of shrapnel . . .

"The Japs aren't going to give up. Shut it down, Ralph."

. . . glass jars filled with colored oils . . .

"Shut it off. Don't remember."

. . . jungle ropes hanging from a hut . . .

"Don't remember, because you'll die doing so."

. . . then his close-cropped hair.

"Hold that shield up. Hold that shield up. Hold that shield up."

I was trying to figure out what the voice was talking about. I thought I had been in the crusades or something. What shield? I didn't see any shield.

. . . then Van's face popped up.

Van was talking to me in my head. Van. I now recalled that Van had re-conditioned my body and mind. Van had given me my shield, my edge. But now, as I lay there, remembering my shield, I wondered if that shield had cracked when I became Louie. No, I told myself. My shield didn't crack. I dropped it. When I took the beating from that Korean guard, I dropped my shield. I was weak. Completely weak. Bare to the elements. Exposed. Vulnerable. That's when Louie took over—when I was weak.

I was now looking for my shield again.

When I strapped on the knife after Circus John told me I had been talking to it, it felt all right. But it was just a knife. I didn't converse with the fucking thing like Circus John had said I did. I don't ever remember talking to my knife. Still, nobody except Circus John wanted to talk with me. I was obsessed because the rest of the men didn't realize what I had gone through.

Those who did talk to me were standoffish. I'm sure they were still confused, thinking, "This sergeant drove us like a madman as Louie; now he wants to be friends."

Strangely, even when I was trying to talk civilly to the men, I was getting pieces of what Van had told me at Camp Malang: "*Don't make friends. Live by your wits. Watch your back. Watch your back.*"

Nonetheless, after a few days, most of the men on my detail knew me as Ralph. I never got down on my knees and barked like a dog. *I* didn't do that. It took a while for them to know *I* was back.

Tomucka heard some of the men call me Ralph, and I went up to him.

"Fellas decided to call me Ralph again," I said in Malayan. "They called me Louie because they were playing games."

Tomucka laughed and said, "As long as you do your job."

Tomucka was uptight. He walked away, and I noticed two Korean guards watching me closely, laughing, pointing at my shoulder scar. Fuckers.

Fortunately, through all this I had Circus John to rely on. He was the only one who sat with me during our breaks. He was a mentor to me. He would sometimes think for me or tell me how to think. I would ask him what I should do with a kid who wasn't working, wasn't pulling his share.

"What would you do?" I asked Circus John.

"Get him to the side during a break. Sit him down and talk to him," Circus John replied.

I followed through on that, and it seemed to work.

Circus John though never asked me about my memory coming back to me, and I didn't tell him what I was going through at night. I think Circus John didn't want to confuse me any further by asking me all kinds of questions. But even though I was stitching it all together slowly, there were many nights when the thoughts didn't make sense to me. Things simply fell apart.

I was in the water . . .

. . . Sharks were chasing me. . . .

. . . My only way out was to swim into seaweed. . . .

. . . I got tangled in seaweed; I was drowning. . . .

. . . I was cutting my way out, slashing the seaweed. . . .

The sharks were getting closer.

Then I woke up, drenched in sweat. Had this really happened to me? Or was it a nightmare?

I saw Father Marque . . .

. . . then a priest and a nun having sex on a kitchen floor . . .

. . . then a gang of priests chasing me, waving their arms.

"Was God going to kill me?" I wondered when I woke up in another cold sweat, trying to explain this to myself. These had to be nightmares. They had to be.

It was very disturbing, however, because I never saw myself—at any stage of my life—in any of my memories. I classified the shark and priest episodes as nightmares only because I was present in them, and I was in danger.

All the POWs on the detail were pointing at me . . .

. . . Tomucka took me by the arm over to a tree stump . . .

. . . then he raised his sword and was about to cut my head off.

I never died in these nightmares; I always woke up soaking wet. With the nightmares, night sweats, memories, and Van's voice whispering in my head, I was still in a fog. I wanted to sort out my past, to reclaim my identity, but the nightmares thwarted my progress. They threw me off. Things still weren't holding together in my mind.

There was no mental doctor in the camp to see about my condition, and I wouldn't have talked to one, anyway. I felt that talking about what was going on in my head would only bring on more nightmares, more sweats.

I just tried not to think about it. I focused on the work. We worked twelve-hour days the last two weeks on the rail bed, and the men were dropping like flies from exhaustion before the afternoon break. The fucking Jap and Korean guards would kick the men when they fell. I interceded. Fortunately, the beatings I received were light. I took a few blows to my neck and head, and thankfully Louie didn't return. I viewed this as a positive sign that I had become a little more stable. Perhaps Louie would never come back again.

At night, though, I couldn't help calling up thoughts of my parents, my brothers, Yasha. But I would hear Van tell me, *"You shouldn't be doing this. You should get some sleep so you'll be ready for tomorrow. Why are you doing this?"*

Finally, I gave in to the voice. I stopped trying to remember who I was. I didn't see my parents or Harry or Yasha anymore. Van's voice now overruled these thoughts somehow. And so I reconditioned my mind again. I put myself under hypnosis, as Van had taught, and I saw myself for the first time in my memories rather than just in my nightmares.

Again, I pushed out the sounds of the other POWs in the hut while I concentrated on the women I had been with: Lynda, Jhannella, Juanita, Karen, Ruthie. I saw them over and over again. I was swimming, dancing, making love. After about a month, I felt I had regained my shield. But I was still afraid I was going to drop it again. "Just be Ralph," I told myself.

Even though I was still very confused about what had happened to me, hate came back quickly. I was still a slave. I was still in hell, working for Satan.

But I knew I could take the pain because of my time with Van. If I could just hate a little longer, I told myself, I knew I could make it.

Most of the teenage POWs, however, had a lower tolerance for pain, and had a higher death rate than those in their mid-twenties and thirties. I spoke with Tomucka about my beleaguered men, but he had an insane desire to finish the rail bed on time. Every time I asked Tomucka for a little relief of any kind, he would give me a piercing stare. He looked vicious and was ready to pounce.

"The dog's gone a little crazy because his head is on the table," I told the men.

After all the six-day workweeks, the twelve-hour days, the beatings and death, we finally finished the rail bed, tracks and all, only one week behind schedule. The following day, the commandant inspected our work, nodded in approval, then told all the POWs there would be a ribbon-cutting ceremony the following week. We were all "invited" to attend—or else.

⋆ 34 ⋆

"Give Me the Simple Life"

April 1945

THE CAVERN IN THE MOUNTAINSIDE WAS NOW READY TO RECEIVE THE SHIP-
ments of munitions and guns from Batavia. However, there were many problems with transporting the munitions along the rail bed. When the trucks
were unloaded at the base of the hill, the POWs had to carry the artillery
shells to the flatcars. A group of twelve POWs—six on each side of the car—
then used ropes to pull the car up the curving rails to the cavern and stored
the munitions. This process took hours, and it was a Sisyphean feat. If it
rained during the night, the ground would become slippery, making it impossible to get a foothold. Men would dig their toes into the earth for some
leverage. We rolled in the cold mud for nearly six weeks.

When the mud became too much of a challenge, the Japs moved all of us
into the cavern to transfer munitions from one end of the storage facility to
the other. The Japs would move the munitions around whenever a new artillery officer would visit. Those artillery shells weighed almost forty pounds
each, and after weeks of labor, the med hut couldn't handle the flow of
POWs who herniated themselves.

The men just seemed to melt away. Of the sixty POWs who had made up
the three details on my section of the rail bed, only twenty remained. We
lost a man a day. We were so exhausted when we went back to the camp that
we could hardly bathe ourselves. We showered with our shorts on, scraped
the mud off, then let the clothes dry on our bodies. Of the twenty men in my
hut, only twelve were left. Circus John overheard that most of the sick men
supposedly had been transferred to the rehab hospital in Batavia, but many
POWs thought the sick were buried alive, used for medical experiments, or
put onto boats to be torpedoed.

With death all around me, I was remembering more and more details of my life. I recalled my aunts and uncles, Yasha resting his chin in his hand as I told him about my road trips, jamming with Harry in Havana. I was seeing myself more often in my memories, not just in my nightmares and my night sessions.

However, my high school days remained a huge gap. They were almost a complete blank.

Things came into my head out of order, out of sequence. I did remember more about the bicycle camp and Zip, and I wondered how he was doing. Was he still alive? I recalled *Dolly*, our plane; Betsy, the elephant; the short-wave radio incident; the entire crew, not just Frerry; the gold rib; the secret mission; and Stuart.

I couldn't forget Stuart. I could never forget him. I saw a young man's face . . .

. . . I saw a young man's build . . .   . . . then a plane flying in the air . . .

. . . then the ham radio I played with as a child.

"*Forget*," said Van in my head.

. . . then my radio equipment on the B-17 . . .

. . . then a needle being pulled from my chest . . .

. . . there was a plane crash . . .

"*Forget everything*," Van said in my head.

. . . then I saw Stuart's bloody head . . .

. . . his bloody shoulder . . .

. . . then Stuart's face.

It was the same face that started off the sequence, except now it was drenched in blood. I remembered Stuart the split second after I saw all that blood on his head. But I had to banish that thought from my mind.

Whenever a flash of Stuart wedged itself into my thoughts, I immediately distracted myself. For some reason, this often happened on the detail rather than at night. When I saw the blood, I would go talk to someone, even though no one wanted to talk to me. Or I would just move around, agitate myself, trying to walk away from the thought.

As if the Japs and my shaky mental state weren't enough at this time, our sleeping conditions were also starting to become a real hazard. Rats the size of small cats crawled into our hut at night, searching for food. Since there had been a crop shortage the prior year, packs of ten to fifteen rats were scouring our neighborhood to find meals. Rats thrived on rice, but if they were starving, they would attack any animal—including human beings. To protect ourselves from the rodents, we wrapped our feet in burlap sacks. This merely made the rats work hard for their dinner. The rats would rear up on their hind legs and nibble away, eating around our toes, sucking our blood. A few men had their toes gnawed before they woke up one morning. Blood was all over the dirt hut.

Because we were not getting enough sleep, our hut decided to put two POWs on rat patrol every night. Each man carried a bamboo pole with a sharpened tip to spear the intruders.

One night I was awakened when I felt something moving along my left leg. I looked down into the darkness and saw a tail hanging over my bamboo bed. It was a small cobra trying to wrap itself around me to stay warm. I lay there virtually motionless for almost an hour, sweating. Finally, the snake circled itself around the bedpost and slid down to the damp floor. By now I was having the shakes, and I shouted, "Cobra!"

The lights went on, and the other POWs jumped up, searching the floor. A Jap guard who was just outside the hut charged in, spotted the snake, and sliced it in half with his bayonet. I was soaking wet.

Shortly afterward, I knew I was coming down with something vicious, because I could hardly get up when the camp radio speaker blasted the Jap anthem at dawn. Fortunately, our job on the cavern detail had been taken over by the Javanese. The men in our hut were told to rest for a week. I could hardly believe it. I spoke with Tomucka, hunting for information about the war, but he said he didn't know what was going on. He did, however, offer me a job in the Jap kitchen, which was a really cushy deal. Tomucka also mentioned that the radios in the Jap barracks had been taken away at the beginning of the year. This was exciting news to me for two reasons: first, I no longer had to listen to the annoying Jap music, and second, and more important, the news hinted that the U.S. invasion was close at hand.

Tomucka also told me he couldn't contact anyone from his homeland. His family was lost to him. I was surprised when he showed me pictures of his children similar to the way the older musicians did at Steel Pier. Tomucka looked confused. His cocky strut disappeared. His fire was gone. He often walked with his head down, as if wandering around without a future. He hadn't been home in five years, he said, fighting in China before coming to Java. Every Jap was confined to the camp. They were prisoners now, just like us.

The head cook in the Jap kitchen had me scrubbing pots and pans, skinning and cutting papaya, washing and draining coconuts. There were no beatings on this detail, and we were able to eat two good meals a day and to shove as much extra food into our mouths as we dared. I knew I had the symptoms of tuberculosis—labored breathing, high temperature, exhaustion—and if I did cough a little blood, I made a point to do it in the latrine, where no one else could see me. The heat from the iron stove was further aggravating my lungs, though, and I was starting to suck air. I was experiencing extreme pain in my back and chest. Finally, I collapsed.

"Sergeant, you have wet pleurisy with pneumonia and a collapsed lung," said the Dutch doctor, who by this time was getting sick of seeing my sorry ass.

I knew I was a mess, but I didn't think things were that bad. I asked for a cold washrag for my head and then started to shake. I thought my luck had finally run out. The medics threw a blanket over me. I couldn't breathe anymore. I couldn't exist as a POW anymore. I was on my way down the path that so many fellow POWs had traveled—death. "I can make it, I can make it," I kept repeating. I was talking to my shield.

✶ 35 ✶

"Let's Call the Whole Thing Off"

July 1945

" . . . NAME?" I HEARD A VOICE SAY.

"Whuh?" I responded.

I could barely speak. I was seeing clouds now. Then I saw Lynda. We were getting married in a temple. My parents were there. Nana. And Harry, too. He was the best man. Lynda was standing by my side, looking exquisite and stately.

"I love you so much," Lynda murmured in my ear. A chill overwhelmed me when I heard her say this.

"What is your name?" asked the Javanese nurse, louder this time. Her little black face was looking down over me.

"Ralph. Ralph Rentz," I gasped. At first I did not realize that my mouth and nose were covered with an oxygen mask. I tried to speak again, but the appliance stopped me.

The Javanese nurse told me I had been moved to this hospital in Batavia three days earlier. I noticed the intravenous tube in my arm. The nurse called in a Dutch doctor, who removed the oxygen mask.

"Ralph, you are a lucky man," said the doctor. "We had to remove the liquid from your right lung to get control of the pneumonia and lower your fever."

There was a tiny tube inserted into my right side to drain fluid into a large glass jar.

"I took the oxygen off your face to see if you could breathe with one lung," the Dutch doctor continued.

"Oh, great," I thought, "he's experimenting now. One lung? Did he say one lung? I'm gonna die!"

200

"Everything went well," the doctor continued. Then he paused and looked at me dead in the eyes. "I hope you can get along on the one lung temporarily."

I took a breath, and it felt like somebody had stabbed me. My music. No. If I can't breathe, I can't play. I can't live on one lung! I'm gonna die! "Wait until you get back to the States," I told myself. "Maybe they'll make it work when you get back there." The nurse gave me a shot, and I was out.

They kept giving me shots so I could sleep. Bedpans. Drugs. I was stuck in bed, weaving in and out of consciousness. A druggie again.

Because I knew I was going to die, I started to make plans: Where are they going to send my body? Are they going to bury me on Java? I want to be sent back home. Yeah, ship me home. Bury me with the rest of my family in Larchmont cemetery. The whole family will be gathered around me at the tombstone. Crying. Praying.

I couldn't focus on my burial plans anymore. I wasn't angry. I was too doped up to be angry. Who could I be angry at when I felt like this? It was the end of my life, and I wasn't making peace with anybody because I was an atheist. I just lay there, motionless, and then I told myself, "The doctor thinks I can make it. Dammit, I'll make my body listen to my mind."

I woke up later, and it was dark. The night nurse came in and gave me another injection in my arm.

"You still have liquid in that right lung. Take it slow," the nurse said before leaving. I passed out again. I remained in bed for the next month and a half, doped to the gills.

August 1945. There had been just one other POW in the room with me. I didn't recognize him. He had labored breathing. His tongue had swelled so much that it choked him. I didn't know what the hell was wrong with him. Neither did the doctors. His whole mouth was full. He died.

Now the only POW in the room, I recovered slowly, walking around the ward. My hobbled gait reminded me of when I had been at Surabaja hospital. Those days became vivid in my mind. That was the only time I thought of killing myself. The pain then was immense, much more than now, I told myself. Back then I feared that if I couldn't work, I wouldn't live long. Even though I believed I didn't have long to live, my mind still returned to Van and how he prepared me to be a POW. Whenever I thought of Van, I got stronger.

Just then, the double doors flew open, and twenty-seven American POWs from Camp Bandung were rushed in. Japs wearing white masks carried several more prisoners in on stretchers.

"The camp has been burned to the ground, Sergeant," Circus John said as he approached my bed. "The Nips found out from the doctor that we all had TB. He said it was very contagious, so here we are. Quarantined."

I didn't know what I looked like. I hadn't seen a mirror in ages, but I knew what Circus John looked like. You could see right through him. He pointed at me and shouted, "Hey, guys! Get a load of him with a bed, sheets, and pillows."

"Find a bed next to me so we can talk," I said to him.

Circus John told me that only 54 Americans remained from the approximately 150 who had arrived in Bandung in December 1943.

After both wards of twenty-seven POWs were settled in, the Dutch medical staff arrived. "You all look like skeletal displays," said one of the doctors who spoke English. We didn't need to be told this. Our hearts were still beating. The doctor then mentioned that he had never heard of our camp, which meant no POWs from Bandung had ever been admitted to this hospital. The survivors now looked at each other quietly. This news only confirmed what we had thought all along—the sick men from our rail bed detail were resting, just as Tomucka had said—resting in their graves. Many more from this ward would be joining them very shortly, I thought.

Circus John was coughing up blood constantly, and his eyes were set back deep in his head. He could barely raise his hand. "Could we talk about Louie, Ralph?" he asked me. I was surprised.

"I don't think I can take a second beating about what crazy Louie did," I said.

I didn't want to hear any more about Louie. Once I had gotten some of my memory back, I thought Louie reminded me of McCarthy, the leather-faced marine at Camp Shelby. He was an animal to me. McCarthy taught us to be animals. Killers. Maybe Louie was part marine and part animal. Maybe Louie had a little Max in him, too. Or a little of my mother when she got angry. Or maybe a little of my father when he sent me to see John Foreman. How far did it go back? I didn't know. I didn't want to know. I didn't want think about it, really.

"There are only a few more dramatics that went on, and I think you should know, Ralph," Circus John said.

Like a dying man who wanted to get something off his chest, Circus John now told me about how Louie snuck out at night to buy food from Nuvack. Circus John spoke in a low, monotone, hacking between words, speaking in fragments. What he was telling me, I think, was that Louie had had a good side. Louie might have pushed some men to death, but he also risked his life to keep the same men alive.

"Where did you get the guts?" Circus John asked me. "They beat the shit out of you, and all you did was smile."

How could I give him an answer? It was all news to me. I wondered how I had jumped into that canal, how I had carried food on my back, how I had swum with a water-soaked bag. Where had I gotten the strength? Where had Louie gotten the strength?

Suddenly, I started to realize that Louie wasn't all bad. And I felt a little better about that. About Louie—about myself, I mean. A little less shame. I certainly wouldn't have escaped from camp and risked my life to feed the men, but I did do that! I just didn't remember it!

What had possessed me to do it? I didn't have a clue. Louie was becoming more and more of a mystery to me, a riddle I couldn't figure out, and one I didn't know if I wanted to or ever could unravel.

Circus John starting hacking again and then said he had joined Louie one night before I was caught with a bag of food by the Japs who threw me into hole and left me there to die. Circus John said I was down there for a week.

"How did—how did I survive?" I asked in disbelief.

"I brought you food and water one or two nights," Circus John said, coughing. Then he steadied himself and said, "You just had it in you, I guess."

During the next few days, there was a complete change of attitude in the Jap doctors and nurses. I saw strained smiles. The doctors would sit at our bed-sides and actually try to help us. The stone faces were gone. All the POWs were wondering what the hell was going on. The enemy was now helping us. Was the war coming to an end? Something was happening, but we would be the last to know. Then the food changed, and they started giving us monkey to eat. That was my first sign that the war might be over.

A Dutch doctor finally appeared one afternoon, and he walked into the middle of our ward. "Fellows, the war has been over for ten days," he said, "but the Japanese are still in control of the island. A British cruiser is outside the harbor. They are going to pick up all the American POWs in a few days."

The doctor also suggested that we shouldn't show any exuberance in front of the Japs until we were safely onboard the vessel. I didn't agree with him on principle, but I didn't give a shit because I was in no condition for a long boat trip anyway. Most of the men who had TB like me didn't give a shit about raising hell in front of the Japs. We were all more concerned about not going directly home just yet. We wanted to buy time to get a little healthier. Half of the POWs had tears streaming down their faces when the doctor left the ward; the rest of us were angry. For more than forty-two months, I had wanted to get the hell off this island, but now, after all that I had seen and endured, the last thing I wanted was for my family to see me in this condition.

"If the war's over, Ralph, when they pick us up, what are they gonna do with us?" Circus John asked me, pausing to spit. "What am I gonna do at home? We're dead men now. What can we do?"

"I don't know," I said. Everyone was depressed.

The next morning at dawn, one of the POWs who had posted himself at the window all night noticed something.

"I don't believe it," he said. "I don't believe it. I don't believe it." The British cruiser was leaving the harbor.

Leaning over toward Circus John, I said, "Something must have gone wrong with the communications between the Brits and the Americans."

Circus John nodded. He knew he was dying. He now looked like he had mascara under his eyes.

"Boy, do I have a headache, Ralph," Circus John told me. His voice was hoarse, his breathing heavy.

"Call a nurse. Get some pills."

"Jeez, I feel like hell, and I really don't want to go home, Ralph."

"You've got to go home, John," I said. "You can't stay on this island because the Japs will still be here until the Dutch tell them to leave."

"I think I'm more excited about not going home, Ralph. I think I've lost my mind."

Circus John laughed, and I laughed with him. Every once in a while he would extend his hand, and I would squeeze it. This man had saved my life; the least I could do was hold his hand.

Later in the afternoon, the same Dutch doctor returned and addressed all of us again. "When the British cruiser arrived on August 25, it was carrying one hundred Gurkha marines,"—Indian soldiers with the British marine corps who were highly trained at infiltrating and destroying enemy units.

The doctor continued. "Apparently, the captain of the British cruiser was informed that three years ago, five Gurkhas died of malaria in a Japanese prison camp. However, the truth was that these five Gurkhas were forced to dig their own graves and then were shot. Seeking revenge last night, fifty Gurkhas left the British cruiser and raided a motor pool, where they killed twenty Japanese guards. Then they slipped into the main barracks and knifed approximately three hundred Japanese soldiers and officers. After each kill, the Gurkhas sliced an ear off each victim and carried it in a little leather bag. After these murders, the Gurkhas returned to the British cruiser. Once the captain learned of their night of terror, he deemed it too dangerous to re-trieve you American POWs, and he decided to flee the harbor immediately."

All the POWs were thrilled by this Gurkha raid because so many Japs had been killed. We really didn't want to go back home with the Brits, anyway. What had happened to the U.S. Army Air Corps? And why weren't they here the day the war had ended?

A week went by until the Jap hospital administrator informed us that the Army Air Corps would be picking us up within forty-eight hours. We all got dressed at four in the morning of the day we were to leave. I gathered my be-longings: my short knife, one cent in invasion money, and my four-inch piece of shrapnel, all of which I tied together in a little bag.

When I looked at the shrapnel, I thought that the piece of metal could have gone straight through me if it hadn't hit the bone. But this was the one that had killed me. If that shrapnel hadn't hit me, I'd have been in Australia. I'd have been with Eubank and the rest of the groups that escaped. This lit-tle piece of metal changed my life—what life I had left. I didn't know if I had one left.

That piece of metal became sort of an enemy to me. But I was going to hold onto it to remind me that it made me a POW.

Dressed in new beige shorts and shirt, I hobbled out of the hospital. The Japs hadn't issued any shoes, so we were all barefoot. There was no scream-ing. No celebration. First, those POWs who couldn't walk were taken away by stretcher. The rest of us followed. They were now taking us out of our en-vironment. We were used to the hot weather. I didn't know how I was going to make it in the cold weather. At this stage, I had no thoughts of Louie, or Tomucka, or the work detail, or the pressure—the pressure now seemed greater because we didn't know what to expect. Who was going to under-stand us? Did the doctors know how to treat us?

"Are we all sure we are going to the airport?" one of the men said on the way out, "because I don't trust those damned Japs."

This comment frightened me until I saw the tremendous American plane in the middle of the runway. "Where in the hell did they build a plane this big?" I thought. It looked like it could never get off the ground.

Some men were crying now, many were sobbing. Others were in disbelief. They thought that this was a captured plane and that the Japs were toying with us like they did with the Red Cross supplies. But when I saw the U.S. insignia on the side of the plane, I knew we had been freed at last. I was shaking. Three years and seven months of my life were gone, taken from me. I was twenty-seven. What lay ahead for me? I did not know. I was going back home, but to what? I was a crippled POW. Who would want me? The only thing I had left was my tongue to communicate, and I didn't want to talk about anything. My dad's brother, Uncle Fred, had come back from World War I in a wheelchair. He died young.

The medical assistants placed us all on stretchers, like human cargo, and hooked all fifty-five men onto the side of the fuselage, three tiers high. It was odd to hear doctors and nurses speaking my native tongue.

"We've got a load of dying men back here," I heard one of the assistants say. "I hope they all make it to Singapore."

We were all covered with heavy blankets and given a cool drink as soon as we settled in. I heard each engine start up, and I got the chills, even with the blankets on top of me. The nurses thought I had malaria, but my temperature was normal.

The plane made its turn for the runway, but the Jap tower held us there for close to an hour. Thinking that the Japs were pulling one of their little games of terror, I asked a male attendant what was going on.

"Permission to take off needs to come from the Japanese commandant," he said. I shook my head. That little bastard. Finally, though, word came from the tower.

With the constant crying and praying, the mood before takeoff seemed like a funeral. I began to think of my parents visiting me in the hospital. There would be questions. Lots of questions.

As we reached flying altitude, the sounds bouncing around the fuselage seemed to hypnotize me. It sounded like a drummer moving his wire fans over the drums. I fell asleep.

The medical staff gave each POW an injection. About fifteen minutes later, we were all knocked out, and three hours later, we landed in Singapore. Once we touched down, I was allowed to remove my rubber oxygen mask and the restraints that held me in place on the air hammock. I noticed ten stretchers were being taken off the plane. While we were refueling, I asked one of the attendants where those men were being taken.

"Sergeant, they passed away on the trip," he said.

Circus John was one of them. I recalled the day when he first taught me how to throw a knife. "I'm still your friend," I said to myself as a tear rolled from my eye.

Once the dead had been removed from the plane, we were served rice, vegetables, and tea. I ate fast, like I did in the camps, wondering if Circus John and the other recently dead would have lived if they hadn't gotten on this plane. Perhaps they lost their will to live, knowing that they were heading home.

After our meal, twenty more American POWs were carried onboard and strapped in like we were. Every medic and POW on the plane was wearing a cloth mask to protect against the constant coughing.

Because all the POWs were so weak and frail, we were informed that we'd stop in Calcutta, India. The doctors told us they wanted us to rest a few more days before we arrived home. It was a long and tiring flight, but there were no rats. No Japs. We landed the following day, and we were carried to a host of ambulances.

Several Indian medical personnel wearing white clothes and nothing on their feet greeted us. Taken inside a small building, we were split into groups of ten and ushered into separate quarters. This place was not a hospital; it was more like an old Quonset hut with dirt floors. It smelled like cow shit. Cleanliness was what I wanted. And oxygen. As long as I could breathe, I knew I could make it.

Breathing with only one lung, however, was debilitating. I lay down on a smelly mattress, sunken from overuse. The place was a hothouse. I felt like I was being roasted.

Finally, some white coats arrived, and an Indian doctor spoke to the man next to me. "How do you feel today?" asked the little brown man in a clipped British accent.

"I'm dying. How are you doing?" replied the POW.

The little brown man, who couldn't have been more than twenty-five, looked stunned.

"You're a horse doctor to work here and let us die!" shouted another POW from across the room. The men were becoming rowdy.

The Indian now approached my bed and stood a considerable distance away from me as he asked what diseases I had. As I spoke, he shook his head and said, "I am very sorry. I am very sorry. I am very sorry."

The Indian doctor then called an attendant to bring in some drinking water and fresh towels. The doctor helped me stand up, and a scale was shoved near my bed.

"How much do I weigh, Doc?"

The doctor paused then said, "Not too many stones."

"What stones?" I replied. I had never seen a scale like this. I didn't know what the hell was going on. "When do I get something to eat?" I shouted.

The doctor mumbled something while I lay down again on the bed, weak as a kitten. I was contemplating how long I could stay alive in this boiler factory as the doctor took my temperature.

"You must drink as much water as you can hold," he said. "You have a temperature."

"No shit! What are you going to do about it?" I raised my voice again.

"You call yourself a doctor!" screamed another POW nearby. "You don't have any conscience."

The Indian doctor didn't respond.

Rice, dried fish, and tea were served later. The fish looked inedible. Everything was cold. The room was on fire, but the food was cold. I thought, "I'm not going to survive on this diet, and I'm nearly dead now." Weak and weary, I fell into a deep sleep and had a nightmare:

I was clothed in piss and shit, and I was standing in a deep hole—a pit. Above me were five beardless Japanese doctors. They were laughing at me. They were chanting, "He will die. He will die. He will die." I woke up screaming in a puddle of sweat. My shirt and shorts were soaked.

One of the medical attendants helped me to the men's room and then ran for a doctor. Minutes later, a stretcher arrived, and I was loaded into an ambulance. Two British nurses stripped off my wet clothes and wrapped me in a large blanket. I had the chills as the ambulance was racing.

After we arrived somewhere, an English doctor put an IV in my left arm, and two Indian attendants started washing my entire body. The attendants dressed me in hospital attire, then moved me to a bed in a ward. I still didn't know where I was. With the oxygen mask covering my mouth, I was about to scream for a nurse when a British doctor stopped at my bedside.

"Sergeant, this is a British hospital, and we are at full capacity," he said. "I have read your medical records, and I will give you the best attention you have had in three years and seven months, but you will only be here a short while."

The doctor then threw his head back and laughed. "It's a good thing the English won this damned war or you would still be in that prison camp," he said.

"I don't give a damn who won the war," I answered. "But I want to thank you for giving a Yank a chance to survive."

"I know you have been through hell down there in Java," said the doctor as he headed for the door. "You will make it, Yank. You have guts."

⋆ 36 ⋆

"Seems Like Old Times"

September 1945

SINCE I WAS HAVING A DIFFICULT TIME DIGESTING MY FOOD, THE BRITISH doctor changed my diet to mashed vegetables and mashed rice for every meal, and I started to gain a little weight. During the next few days, Indian medical attendants held me as I used a walker. After living in dirt huts—practically on the ground—and working in the jungle, I was happy when I saw tile or linoleum or whatever the hell it was. It felt cold under my feet—cold but clean. So much safer than the warm earth.

A week later, after some massages and breathing exercises, I was walking by myself. However, the moment I made progress, I was sent back to that Quonset hut. From this clean, British hospital, I was heading back into the toilet.

I didn't recognize any of the men who were passed out, asleep, or just quiet in the ward. All the POWs here, I was told, were TB patients—some were malnourished, some had vitamin B deficiency. The man next to me had a blanket over his head. He could have been dead, for all I knew.

I lay down and stared at the cracked ceiling. The man next to me started to stir. He threw his blanket down to the end of the bed and said, "They must have turned the heat on in this fucking oven."

I did a double take. "Zip!" I exclaimed.

"Huh?"

"Don't you recognize me?"

"Oh, my God! Is it really you, Ralph?"

We got out of bed at the same time and threw our arms around each other.

"What the hell happened to you? You must have lost ninety pounds," Zip said.

"Look who's talking," I answered. Zip looked like a skeleton with skin drawn over his cheeks. POWs—whether or not they vocalized it—were always comparing how they looked, who was worse off and who was ready for the barn.

Zip and I sat back down on our beds and told each other what had happened since we had been together at the bicycle camp.

"I didn't see you get on the plane in Singapore," I told him.

"We were in the back. Who can recognize anyone on a stretcher anyway?" Zip said. It felt good to have Zip beside me again.

During the next few days, Zip and I bitched about the food, the water, and the stench that was all around us. We swapped stories about diseases, monkeys, and snakes. But I didn't tell Zip about Louie. I couldn't do that. Zip would have thought I was crazy. Zip believed I was too smart to lose my mind. I didn't want to admit to him that I had broken down, that something had come over me, that I wasn't the same guy he had known before. I also felt that after Circus John died, a little bit of Louie died too.

Zip and I agreed that if we remained in this dump, we would go home in steel boxes. There were no American doctors or officers in the entire ward. Fed up with the do-nothing doctors who were afraid to get close to us, who refused to draw our blood, who had no X-ray machines or other hospital equipment, Zip and I dragged ourselves over to the administrator's office, demanding to see an American officer. The young, dark-skinned girl behind the desk said that she didn't know any American officers, only Indian doctors. The Indian doctors were just kids from medical school anyway. They didn't know anything.

After we had badgered, insulted, and threatened the Indian medical staff, one of the doctors visited us in our ward. He became agitated and said that this was the only place that would accept POWs with TB: "I believe the Americans know where you are, but they will do nothing to help."

When the doctor said this, we crawled out of our beds and surrounded him. Zip got in his face. "We want to see an American medical officer in this place in three hours or we are going to burn this fucking place to the ground! Now you get the fuck out of here!"

For the next two hours, anyone who dared to step into our ward was greeted by a riot. We all waved our protection knives in the air, screaming and wailing at the top of our lungs. I only had one working lung, but I sure as hell used it to full capacity. Half an hour later, two American officers walked in. We lowered our knives. We stopped acting like animals so we could be treated like humans.

Zip and I explained the horrible conditions as best we could to the colonel and medical officer, who promised us that we would be moved within twenty-four hours. The C-54 medical plane was waiting for us the next day.

As I packed my belongings, however, I noticed that I couldn't find my piece of shrapnel. I must have lost it when I had been shuttled to that British hospital.

Without it, I felt like I had again lost my identity. I suddenly became afraid, as if I were cattle being led into an unknown environment. I didn't know if I was being taken to be exterminated or treated.

When we stopped to refuel in Karachi, several more POWs had died along the way. They had come from Singapore. Zip's bunch. At least they saw freedom, I thought. At least they would have a military burial in the United States.

I asked Zip if he knew any of those fellows, and he told me that he knew them all.

"They were in bad shape," Zip said. "I wondered how they made it this far."

No one seemed to know where we were going next. Perhaps, we thought, there was a reason they weren't telling us.

"Gentlemen, make yourselves comfortable," said the captain when we reached twenty-five thousand feet. "We are now headed to the northern coast of Africa."

The captain turned off the lights, and Zip was lying just across from me, but I couldn't hear a word he said because everyone was talking.

"Where in the hell are they taking us in Africa? To the Casbah?" I heard one fellow say.

"We must be going on R and R on a stretcher," said another.

Everyone had a good laugh, but it was nervous laughter.

After dinner, half of the men started vomiting into paper bags. Our stomachs were not accustomed to hamburger. The doctors and nurses were also afraid to give us any strong drugs. They didn't seem to know how to treat us. They didn't know what they were dealing with.

We landed in Tunis in the morning. Wrapped in blankets because of the vast change in temperature from the tropics to the cool, Mediterranean air, we were carried out on stretchers. I could see the blue waters of the sea, and in the distance stood a U.S. Army hospital, built on the crown of a hill. The hospital had been built during the war as a way station for the wounded. I hoped it had tile floors and clean sheets.

The scenery was beautiful, and so were the nurses. I hadn't been with a woman in almost four years. I had no urge either. I didn't even think about it. Who would find me attractive?

"I see it's about time for a shave and a bath," one of the nurses said. "You boys look like death warmed over—and you smell like it too."

"Where in the world were you fellows living the past few years?" said another woman. "It must have been hell to get so beat up."

All of us were washed and had our heads shaved because of the lice we had acquired in Calcutta. After my shower, I felt like a plucked chicken. Every hair on my body was gone. I weighed one hundred pounds.

All the fellows were starving, and we were served meat, potatoes, and green beans. I hadn't eaten food like this since the shortwave radio gig in Batavia. We all ate fast, but the aftermath was disastrous. Everyone was calling for bedpans or throwing up into our hands as the nurses and doctors were running to assist us. No one had told the kitchen that our menu had to be baby food only.

The following morning, all the POWs were ordered to remain in bed. The doctors asked us a series of questions about our life in the prison camps—what we ate, what we did, and how we survived. These questions brought back some of the horrible treatment we suffered. A few guys broke down. I had tears in my eyes when I was interviewed. I tried not to cry, but this was the first time I had been around Americans other than POWs, and I felt safer around my own people but still lost, like I was a curiosity to them.

We were supposed to stay a few weeks in Tunis to gain some weight and grow some hair, but the head of the medical staff told us that he lacked the facilities to handle our needs. I quickly concluded that these doctors were unfamiliar with and afraid of treating TB and other diseases of the Far East. We were in American hands, but they didn't know what they had on their hands. They were just transporting us, washing their hands of us. No one knew what to do with us.

When the plane left Tunis, half the POWs were crying into their flight pillows. One man wanted to jump out of the plane and had to be sedated. I think we all felt that way. I kept wondering if the people back home would treat us like fools who had been captured. I wondered if they would ask us why we had worked for the Japs. The C-54 could have dumped us into the ocean and all my fears would have been gone. I got my courage up to ask one of the attendants how Americans viewed POWs.

He looked at me and didn't hesitate. "You fellows are heroes," he said. "You made it through the war."

I sort of smiled at him, thinking he was some kind of bullshit artist. Having been lied to for so long, I didn't believe a word people said.

"What the hell kind of hero am I?" I thought. "What did I do? I didn't fight. I was shot down. I'm no hero! I have no pride. There's nothing to be proud of. I'm a liability."

I cried, trying to ignore what lay ahead.

We made our last stop in Newfoundland. We were on the ground for about two hours while the plane was refueled. I chatted with Zip and a few others about dealing with this new world. I had never really cried in the camps, but I sure broke down now. My weakness, my tears—sobbing in front of my fellow POWs—surprised me. I thought I must have been getting soft to allow my feelings to show like this. My shield was built for POW camps, not for an airplane, for fuel stops, for nurses, for questions. It was for war. "What would I be like in peacetime? Where were they going to hide us?" I thought. Canada? We'd freeze to death.

"Put me down!" I heard a frightened POW shout. "I wanna stay here. Put me down! I don't want to go home!" The doctors gave the man a shot so that he passed out and then carried him back onboard.

We encountered extensive turbulence on this final flight to New York, and the doctors kept us doped up for 90 percent of the trip. I remembered how on *Dolly*, our B-17, we would rock all the time, but this was an enormous plane with more than fifty people aboard, and this thing was rocking wildly because of the headwinds. We couldn't see anything except for some flashes of lightning in the darkness. But the storm outside was nothing like the storm taking place inside my head. I conjured up all kinds of torture. Since I didn't have long to live, maybe they'd take me down to the operating theater and open me up, look at my organs, and work on my skin. Maybe they'd discover some cure for diseases if they ripped out my heart and lungs to see what had kept me alive. Maybe they'd feed me some new kind of medicine to see if I'd live. Hero? No, I'm a dog who's about to go under the knife in the name of science.

Again, the medical staff reassured us that we would be put in separate wards in New York until we got well, and then our families would visit us.

Everyone had tears in their eyes as we crept closer to home. The wheels hit the runway.

"Gentlemen, this is your last stop," said the captain. "We are entering the state of New York. We had a very difficult ride through the storm, but fortunately we all made it with very little damage. You are finally home."

The plane was dead silent.

⋆ 37 ⋆

"Try a Little Tenderness"

September 1945

I KNEW WE WERE HOME FOR CERTAIN WHEN I HEARD THE BAND PLAYING THE "Star Spangled Banner." I covered my face with a small pillow, but the tears continued to flow. When I was carried out of the plane, the first face I saw was that of a medic. He had a concerned look. My eyes rolled back, and I saw the clouds. It smelled like rain. There was no cheering, but I noticed many servicemen standing at attention, saluting us as we were placed in the ambulance. Sirens blared, and the convoy began.

When we arrived at the naval hospital, the doctors and nurses were waiting for us. Many wore smiles, but they couldn't hide their stares of disbelief. They avoided making eye contact; they pointed and nodded directions. "Send the garbage over there," I thought.

I was taken to a large ward along with the other nineteen POWs who were left. My personal belongings were placed under my bed. For the next seventy-two hours, we were X-rayed and had our blood tested. After the doctors heard our tales of horror, one of them commented, "We should have killed all those Japs with the atom bomb. They're inhuman bastards." When we heard this, all the POWs clapped and whistled. We now felt comfortable; we knew we were in a safe place.

No one was allowed out of bed unless he could make it to the toilet on his own. I was still on oxygen, as were about half of the other POWs with advanced cases of TB.

The next afternoon, a young woman in civilian clothes came to my bed. She was very pretty but pale. "Your father and mother have arrived," she said, stunning me. "They would like to visit with you for a short time."

"What? Wait. No!" I said, terrified. I thought I was going to have a heart attack.

The woman tried to calm me, saying that one of the doctors had suggested this little visit.

"They will be here in five minutes," she said as she left my bedside.

Tears welled up, and I began to cry. How was I going to gain eighty-five pounds in five minutes? How could I grow my hair back that quickly? How could I change my gray skin to a healthy pink?

That doctor had no permission from me. He had lied to me. He lied. They all lied.

A few minutes later, my parents walked in. A nurse appeared at my side and propped me up with a few pillows. My father was dressed in a dark brown suit with his hat in his hand. My mother wore a long black dress and a matching hat. They were holding hands. Both of them looked older and tired. Even though they both had white masks on, I could see the tears streaming down their faces. The ward was silent. My heart was pounding.

My mother reached my bed first.

"I'm looking for my son," she said.

"Who are you looking for?" the nurse asked.

"Ralph Rentz," said my mother.

"Well, this is Ralph," answered the nurse.

My mother looked confused. I saw her glance down at the end of the bed. She picked up the medical chart and turned it toward my father.

Then my mother came closer, bent over, and kissed me on the forehead. Some of her tears fell on my face, and she wiped them off with her handkerchief. My father then reached for my hand and squeezed it. His hands were as I always remembered them, hard and rough. My father had lost most of his hair, while my mother's head was almost entirely gray.

After my parents stared down at me for what seemed like an eternity, my father pulled my mother back from the bed very gently.

"That isn't my Ralph," I heard him whisper to her. "They must have made a mistake. Let's find out from the doctor where our son is located."

"Dad," I said. "I know I don't look like my old self, but I am your son."

They both started to cry, standing there like broken people.

"How did you get into this hospital so quickly?" I asked, breaking the silence.

"We were told after your landing that we could see you in a few days," replied my mother. She could barely get the words out of her mouth. The head nurse suddenly appeared and escorted my parents out of the ward. I was weeping softly as another nurse came to console me.

"Sergeant, that was a good meeting for the first time in four years," she said.

I looked over to my right and one of the fellows had a pillow over his head. I guess he was thinking what it would be like when his folks visited.

All the other fellows either had tears in their eyes or were blowing their noses.

I hid myself under the bedsheet for the next hour. I couldn't take it. I kept replaying the scene.

"This isn't my Ralph," my father echoed in my head.

"This isn't my Ralph."

"This isn't my Ralph."

"This isn't my Ralph."

If my father doesn't recognize me, who am I, then? Where did I come from? That's all I could think about: my father doesn't recognize his own son. My parents saw an animal. I looked somewhat like a person, but I was an animal, a wounded animal.

When the doctor allowed my parents to see me, I couldn't believe anyone anymore. Ever. They all were a gang of liars. I got angry at the head nurse and cursed her out, but I didn't say anything to the doctor. I was afraid he'd take me downstairs and open up my head.

When the doctor came in later that night, I said to myself, "Here comes the brother of Satan. I wonder what he's going to do to me next."

This doctor told me that all the POWs in the ward should be quarantined. I thought they were going to put us in cages—that's what *quarantined* meant to me. And that was fine with me. I didn't want anybody to see me. I'd rather be put down in a hole and have food thrown at me than be seen by anyone who knew me. I'd rather be like a monkey in a cage with a bed. Just put a lock on the door. Give me a toilet and sink and leave me there.

Two days later, my sister, Sylvia, and my younger brother, Zeldan, surprised me with a visit. Zeldan, who was dressed in an officer's uniform with flight wings on his chest, was now in the Army Air Corps. Sylvia still had a slender figure with soft brown eyes and light skin.

Sylvia looked at me and started to cry. Then I cried. She didn't say a word.

"Go outside and fix your makeup," Zeldan told her. Sylvia left and didn't come back in.

"Mom and Dad told us that you got beat up and starved pretty bad," Zeldan began. "They're very happy you made it but are concerned about your health. I know you'll pull through. Just stay tough."

This reunion was easier than the one with my parents. I smiled and said, "I'll be back to my old self in a few months." I knew I was kidding myself, but I didn't want Zeldan to worry about me. He looked great.

"You know Joe is stationed in Indiana," Zeldan told me. "He's a master sergeant."

I didn't answer. "Oh, Dad, I'm sorry. I'm so sorry," I thought. That's all I kept thinking about—my poor dad.

Zeldan didn't stay long, but when he left the ward, one of the fellows said, "You sure have a good-looking sister. She has a beautiful figure."

It was like Halloween in the ward at night—nightwalkers, guys crying, howling for half the night. We waited for the animals to come out. My mind was wild. I couldn't control my thoughts. We took sleeping pills to get two or three hours of sleep, but I would often see the little camp commandant from Camp Bandung. He was strutting around, banging his sword. We all waited for the first guy to scream, cry, or shout. One night it would be me, the next night Zip. We didn't even know we were screaming. There were two nurses on the ward around the clock. The nurses would stick you with a shot when they heard you hollering. Then you'd shut up.

The next day, a new doctor arrived and reviewed my medical chart, keeping his head down as he addressed me.

"You sure had a long visit in hell, didn't you, Sergeant?" he said. "First, you were shot down, then beriberi. Beatings. TB. Three operations. Wow. Now you want me to put you back together?"

The doctor's bedside manner put me at ease. He came closer with his stethoscope.

"Who stabbed you?" he asked referring to the scar on my chest.

"You should see the one on my shoulder."

"I think we will move you to a semiprivate room so we can give you more attention."

"Did the nurse tell you I've been having nightmares?" I asked him.

The doctor nodded.

I was moved the following morning to a small room that contained two single beds and a restroom. A nurse entered early to take a blood sample. She took out a hypodermic needle.

"What are you gonna do with that?" I asked.

"We're gonna test your blood," she said.

"You're gonna test my blood?"

"Yeah, take some blood out of your arm."

She found a vein.

"I don't mind the pain," I said, "but are you gonna stick that thing straight through me?"

"No, just a surface puncture."

"I don't believe you," I said.

The nurse called in a medic to hold me down. I didn't understand this system of medicine. Why take my blood? That means I have less blood to live off of. Is this some experiment? Are you trying to kill me? My thinking was monstrous.

About an hour later, a patient was rolled in with a mask on his face. "My name is Rentz," I said after the nurse put him into the other bed.

"My name is Zummo," the man replied.

I popped up in bed. "Dammit, Zip, I just can't get rid of you."

Zip got out of bed, and we hugged each other. "Here we are," Zip said, "together again."

Zip told me that his parents had passed away. He had four brothers, but they never came up to visit. They were waiting for him back home in Texas—too busy, I guess. Zip was fine with that. He didn't want to go through what I had been through.

We talked about military doctors, our illnesses, and hundreds of other things until Nurse Madison tried to break up our reunion.

Nurse Madison had spent twenty-eight years in the Navy. She looked like a man. She must have weighed 175 pounds, and she probably could have picked us both up and thrown us against the wall. I think she wore a brown wig.

Madison took control immediately, demanding that our bedsheets be spread without a wrinkle. She hated men, and she let us know it. Her parting words to us that first day were, "You two are back in the army now."

After she left, I turned to Zip and said, "We have to find a way to fix her clock or she is going to make us miserable."

Zip nodded, and it wasn't long before we cooked up something good.

We waited a few days until Madison thought she had us trained. Then one morning she screamed at us to get out of bed to stand at attention. That lit our fuse. Zip and I decided to put our little plan into effect immediately.

Madison had already told us that we shouldn't buzz her unless it was important, so this morning we called for the old broad, and we could hear her thick shoes clopping on the wooden floor. Zip and I then sat up in bed with our twelve-inch protection knives in our hands. As soon as Madison turned into the doorway, Zip and I threw at the same time. His knife hit the molding on the right side of the door, and mine rattled on the left, boxing her in. It nearly took her wig off. Madison was stunned. She turned to the right, then to the left, then fainted.

One of the nurses walking down the hallway saw Madison on the floor and hollered for help. Meanwhile, Zip and I yanked our knives from the molding, dropped them into our bags, and then jumped back into bed, pushing the buzzer for the nurse's station, as we had planned.

Seconds later, there was a huddle of nurses around Madison, trying to revive her. Finally, Madison awoke and started to babble incoherently, pointing at us. Zip and I looked as innocent as two choirboys, and no one understood what the hell she was saying. It wasn't long before an officer and two marines examined the molding and found the evidence. They demanded our knives. We surrendered them. Two marines with guns were now posted at the door.

The following morning, two doctors and four attendants arrived. They put us in straitjackets and stuffed us into wheelchairs.

"Where are we going?" I asked as they rushed us down the hallway.

"In an airplane far away from here," said one of the doctors.

"Did you hear that?" I said to my partner. "We are going on an airplane, but he doesn't know where they're sending us. Sounds familiar, huh?"

"They're gonna dump us in the ocean," Zip said.

Zip and I were shoved into an ambulance and then whisked inside a DC-3. Removed from our wheelchairs, we were buckled in when a major appeared. He looked furious. "What the hell are you doing to these POWs?" he shouted at the medics. "These men are stretcher cases. Take those straitjackets off of them immediately."

We appreciated the officer's concern, and when we were gaining altitude, the major came to check on us. We chatted about how we had been captured and what a gang of bastards the Japs were. The major told us we'd be fed as long as we behaved.

That evening, we landed at Lowry Field just outside of Denver, Colorado. An ambulance was waiting, and we were taken to Fitzsimons Army Hospital, where we were brought to the head doctor. He examined our medical files, but he was confused about our transfer. Once Zip and I told him about Madison and our little circus act, he almost fell off his chair laughing.

"Fellows," he chuckled. "You are in the ward for the insane."

Zip and I looked at each other and started laughing.

☆ 38 ☆

"I Can't Escape from You"

August 1946

AFTER DINNER AT LEFTY'S STEAK HOUSE, MY PARENTS DECIDED TO TURN around and head back east to Lansdowne. I felt bad that we had to cut the trip short, but I think it hurt my parents more than it plagued me. We drove in silence for much of the way back until Bob, a doctor himself, started going at me again.

"What were the doctors like in Denver?" he asked.

"They asked a lot of questions," I told him.

"Naturally," Bob said.

I told Bob that even though the doctors might have admired us as survivors, they believed that we were shell-shocked. They couldn't comprehend what we had been through. They gave us a cocktail of sleeping pills and vitamins for all our ailments. None of these pills, however, did anything to stop the nightmares. The nurses couldn't understand why our pajamas were soaked in sweat almost every night. They were told not to ask us about our nightmares—the doctors were afraid that questioning would rile us up even more.

"The doctors didn't know what the hell they were doing," I told Bob.

Whenever the American doctors thought they had one problem under control, another—dysentery, skin ulcers, beriberi—would give them fits. Zip and I advised the hospital to obtain the services of Dutch doctors who had been in the Jap prison camps, but our suggestion was shot down.

"Tell him about your feet, Ralph," my mother said, obviously listening to me while keeping her eyes on Izzy and on the road.

"What happened to your feet?" asked Bob. "I thought it was your lung."

"It was," my mother countered. "But he had his feet operated on in Denver, too. Tell him, Ralph."

"My feet had small stones and sharp particles embedded in them," I said.

Bob looked intrigued. For a second, I thought he was going to ask me to take off my socks so he could examine them.

"They grafted skin from cadavers onto the bottoms of my feet," I said. "Our feet looked like horses' hooves from working barefoot in the jungle."

"They're as soft as a baby's bottom," my mother added.

Yes, I had new feet, but no future, I thought.

"That was just after the time we came out to see you, huh, Ralph?" my father asked.

I nodded. It had been in November.

✴ 39 ✴

"Put Your Dreams Away"

November 1945

My parents were ushered in as a nurse set up two chairs near my bed in ward 26, which consisted of twenty-six beds. Dr. Gibson had put Zip and me in this new ward that had been set aside for POWs with TB. Dr. Gibson also told us that some of the POWs here in Denver with severe mental problems would be sent on to Albuquerque, New Mexico. Zip and I still wondered if we would be sent there because of the knife-throwing stunt we had pulled.

"You've gained some weight, Ralph. You look much better," my mother said, trying to steady her voice. I remember feeling her lips through her white mask as she kissed me on the forehead and held my hand.

I had been a mere 100 pounds when my parents had last seen me in New York, and now I was up to 127 pounds. I had learned to eat a basic American diet again. My hair had grown in the past six weeks, and thanks to the breathing exercises and the booze, I had some color back in my face. The doctors didn't know which drugs would work on us, so they tried alcohol, too.

"What are you drinking?" my father said after he greeted me.

"Look under the bed," I told him.

Twelve quarts of bourbon were stashed under my bed. My father looked at me confused.

"You've been drinking in here?"

"It's part of my medication."

"You're getting drunk every day?"

"Well, I got pain."

"Well, they got medicine for that."

"I don't want to get addicted to that."

"You can get addicted to booze, too, you know?" my father said as he smiled and pulled up a chair.

"I know you both are concerned, but don't worry about me," I told them. "I'll gain the rest of my weight back and be out of here in a few months."

My parents looked at each other, wondering what type of hospital this was. I asked my father about my brother, Joe, and learned that he was out of the Army Air Corps and would be attending Temple University the following semester.

"At least you got one of us in college, huh, Dad?"

My father squinted. I read more into that squint than he knew. I felt that he was thinking, "Ralph, look what you did to your life when you joined the National Guard. See how you screwed up your life?" My father wanted me to be like Joe.

My mother couldn't stand seeing the crooked smile I had put on my father's face, so she quickly changed the subject. My mother was very observant. She asked questions about my high school days, which was really the only period of my life I still couldn't remember very clearly.

I didn't recall some of the names my mother mentioned, and she could sense I was searching to make connections. "Where did he live, again?" I would ask her, and my mother would walk me through everything. Every name, every street corner, every detail. My mother was acting like Circus John, filling in all the gaps.

"How's Nana doing?" I asked her.

My mother lowered her head and looked away, swallowing hard before she spoke. "She passed away three years ago."

When my parents, Sylvia, and Zeldan had said nothing about Nana in New York, I had begun preparing myself for this news. My father now told me that Nana had just fallen over one day and died suddenly of a heart attack. I thought of saying a quick prayer for Nana, but I didn't.

"You lied to me in New York," I said to my mother.

"I had to. You were very, very sick," my mother answered. "We didn't know if you were going to live or die. Why would I tell you then?"

"Son, what do you think you'll do when you get home?" my father quickly spoke up.

"It's too early to think about that now," my mother cut in. "He must get well before he can decide what his future will be, Izzy. I told you it's too early for any of those discussions. Why don't you just keep quiet about that subject?"

I didn't dare ask my mother about Lynda. I wasn't ready to take that hit now, too.

My parents stayed only a week.

Later, when I was recovering from the operation on my feet, I started to take in a little air in my right lung, and Dr. Gibson was pleased with my progress. I had to use the oxygen mask at night, but I could breathe freely with my one lung, which was just slightly perforated. Zip's lung had a hole in it. With TB, many men lost their appetites, but I took twenty-one vitamin pills a day along with four square meals. I thought Zip and I were going to make it.

With Zip and me improving, Zip made a point to drag me to church one day. I knew more about the Catholic religion than about my own Jewish faith because of Ruth, Father Marque, and all the people in Lansdowne, but this trip didn't rekindle my interest in God. I knew Zip wanted to go, and they wouldn't let a man go by himself, so I joined him. I admired Zip because he remained a believer even after all he'd been through. He had given up his interest in boxing but not in God.

Once I could put pressure on my feet, Zip and I were up and walking around the place. We would put on white masks and visit the other POWs. The medical staff appreciated that we could help these men who were just hanging on. We tried to lift their spirits, ease their minds, encourage them to fight to stay alive. Guys were getting "Dear John" letters all the time. Some cried, some said they'd find other girls. Others were depressed and didn't want to talk about it. They went to see the psych doctor a little more often.

There was one Italian fellow—Tony, we called him—who handled it all really well, I thought. Tony had the biggest penis I had ever seen in my life. He wasn't a big guy—about five feet, ten inches tall and slim. Whenever a nurse would come in, Tony would get up, and his pants would fall off. I'd never seen anything like that before. I imagine if Tony got a hard-on, it was a yard long. I don't know how he walked with that thing. Tony said he had a problem getting an erection, though. He had no vitality. But once Tony did get that thing going, he needed a nurse right away, but they ran from him. He'd screw anything on two legs.

The waiting to get healthy again, though, was what really brought on the depression and the nightmares, the night sweats. My only solitude was listening to the big bands on the radio during the day. That perked up my spirits.

"You play the notes beautifully, but you play them without feeling," I remember Yasha telling me as a child. "I can tell by your eyes you're not in love with the music. You must be in love."

I remembered telling Lynda that one day, I was going to be the best clarinetist in the country. She believed me. Now I often wondered if I would ever be in love that way again, if I would ever feel the notes.

⋆ 40 ⋆

"Polka Dots and Moonbeams"

February 1946

THERE WAS GROUP OF YOUNG WOMEN WHO VISITED THE POWs IN WARD 26, although the doctors told them to keep away from the very ill patients. Since neither Zip nor I was married, we spotted two cuties and decided to make our move. Soon Carlita and JoJean were visiting us three times a week.

Just after I met Jo, my right lung began to open up a little more every day. Encouraged by my recovery, Dr. Gibson gave Zip and me permission to go outside for the first time.

Carlita and Jo were attending a small college just a few miles away, and both were also studying fashion design. As we walked the trails under the sheltering trees, Zip and I wore our white masks and newly decorated army uniforms. Zip would reach for Carlita and I would grab Jo, and then we would split up. I nestled up beside a tree and held Jo close to me. I knew that I could not kiss Jo because I had TB, which, of course, was contagious, but the companionship was all that mattered. It had been so long since I had felt like a man. With Jo beside me, though, I felt things weren't impossible. I didn't even know this young girl, but her fresh smell and soft touch made me believe—just a little bit—that I could be myself again.

Jo and I started spending all our time together, and I think falling in love with her further accelerated my recovery because the results of my next test for TB were negative. It felt good to be wanted again.

One time, when Dr. Gibson gave me a weekend pass, Jo and I went with Zip and Carlita to Colorado Springs, at the base of Pikes Peak. We stayed in a secluded cabin near a long stream. While the women drove into town for food, Zip and I fished for trout. We didn't catch anything, but the snow-capped peaks were idyllic, the air was cool, and the smell of the fresh pines pleased my lungs. I could have stayed there forever.

Jo and I made love that night. I went into the bathroom first and put on my pajamas. I always wore my top when I was in bed with her. She never saw the scars on my shoulder and chest. I wouldn't allow it. And when I kissed Jo, I kissed her on her neck, her back—never on the mouth. I also made her take a shower immediately afterward. If we starting kissing on the mouth, Jo would surely catch TB.

I had been concerned that I couldn't perform like I had before. It had been ages since I had been with a woman, and because of my lung, I wasn't sure what would happen. I struggled, but I made it. Jo never asked me about my POW years, and I was happy that she wasn't the curious kind. Jo really wanted to get married—that was always on her mind.

The four of us were having such a good time together, though, that Zip and I forgot to look at the return time on our weekend passes. Consequently, when we got back to the hospital, they threw us into lockup. We had been considered AWOL. When Zip and I confessed to Dr. Gibson that we had let the girls hold onto our passes, he laughed like hell. Soon, our excuse became legendary around the hospital.

Days later, Dr. Gibson called me into his office to discuss my recent chest X-ray.

"Ralph, the lung pleura stiffens like a piece of leather around the lung, and it will take at least five years for this tissue to soften so you can breathe normally again," he said.

The doctor explained that my lung wasn't expanding enough. That made sense to me, because my breathing was still labored. My hands got clammy and my throat tightened before I asked him the only question that mattered to me: "Will I be able to continue my career as a musician, Doctor?"

Dr. Gibson looked at me evenly, staring into my eyes with a blankness that only a doctor can master. "You will have to find some other work, Ralph," he said. "Your right lung will only improve to 80 percent capacity. You will never be able to go back to the woodwinds."

Tears came to my eyes, and my nose started to leak.

"I had to tell you the truth about your condition, Ralph, because I heard you tell Zip that you would be ready to play in a few months. I know this information is a big shock to you, and I am very sorry to be the one to tell you this, but you must make other plans concerning your future."

Devastated, I sat on the end of my bed. I was constantly having nightmares, and now I had to battle this news.

I buried myself in my bed for twenty-four hours. I'm just a thing, not even a human, I thought. God is torturing me again for the indiscretions I committed in my youth. He wants me to suffer, but I will not ask God for forgiveness, because He does not exist. I will do what I think is right, and if I make mistakes, fuck it—they will be mine. Why should I cry over my misfortunes? They happened. I did it, and God had nothing to do with it.

Suddenly, I got out of bed and turned to Zip and said, "The doctor told me I won't be able to play in the bands anymore because of my lung."

Zip nodded, as if he had already known this.

"I don't know right now what I'm going to do, Zip, but I've become an atheist, so I don't expect God to help."

Zip looked at me and started to laugh.

"That information the doc gave you was a real shock to your brain, huh, Ralph? Now you're an atheist? Wow, that news really got you by the balls."

"I mean it, Zip."

"You'll change your mind one day, Ralph," Zip said, still smiling. "But stay with what you think for now, because you really are a smart man—I think."

We both started to laugh, and then the nurse came in and gave me more pills than usual. I didn't ask what they were for—I just took them.

I knew Jo was a great catch, but having my music taken from me sent me spiraling into an even deeper depression. Jo received her father's permission to marry me, but it was too early for me to make a commitment to her or to anyone, so I broke off the relationship.

Zip thought I should marry Jo. He thought it was a cushy deal—her father owned a ranch in Wyoming—and that I should jump at it. But I needed to be on my own. I wasn't ready. I was too sick, both mentally and physically. But honestly, I was also leaving the door open for Lynda. I didn't write to her because I was angry that she had not called or written to me. I expected Lynda to make the first move.

A few weeks later, a captain from the Army Air Corps tried to force me to sign honorable discharge papers, which meant I wouldn't receive 100 percent disability. I was shocked that army services would try to exploit me like that, and I adamantly refused to sign and then consulted with Dr. Gibson about my dilemma.

"Ralph, if you sign those papers, you will be out on your own," the doctor cautioned me. "Remember, you enlisted in the Army Air Corps—you were not drafted. You are still in the service, and you qualify for 100 percent disability. Ralph, say no to everything until you get what you deserve."

I thanked the doctor two or three times before he told me I could stay at the hospital as long I wished; he also reminded me to forget that our conversation had ever taken place. I understood and agreed completely.

Later that evening, I called my father.

"Tell that captain to go fly a kite," my father said, coming to my defense in a hurry.

It was comforting to hear his voice, and I could tell he appreciated my asking his advice. I knew even before talking to my father what I intended to do, but I wanted to include him, to make him feel proud again to be my father. I had disappointed him so much.

The next day, I called the hospital librarian to obtain a book on discharging regular army personnel. It was a painstaking and tedious process to document my medical history, and just one ill-chosen word in a doctor's report could have resulted in the rejection of my application, but I received my 100 percent disability, and I helped Zip do the same. I was discharged on June 18, 1946.

After I thanked Dr. Gibson and received my travel orders and funds owed to me, I said my farewells to the men in the ward and packed my duffel bag and arranged all my clothes for the next morning. I no longer had that four-inch piece of shrapnel, and my protection knife had been taken from me. I hadn't wanted to lose those items—I had wanted to show them to people. But I realized now that losing them was a release. They were prisons, prisons without bars.

When I climbed into bed that night, I became very serious about my new life even though I didn't trust the outside world. I knew that what Van had taught me was for the prison camps, and I had to build a new shield now. "Don't think about where you've been or what you've done," I told myself. "Talk about what you're going to do now." I was healing. I was getting well. And getting well was a matter of telling myself that I was going to get well. Still, I didn't know what I was going to do with my life, and I worried about that.

"Look. He's so cute," one of the nurses said when they came around to say good-bye. "Let's get under the sheets with him."

"I have a big day tomorrow," I said, laughing. "I'm really tired."

"Right. Sure," said the other nurse. "We heard all about you and Zip having those girls taking care of you, being AWOL for six hours. Who do you think you're kidding?"

The nurses toyed with me some more and then gave me kisses on each side of my face and said, "Have a safe trip and a loving life."

The next morning, I took a walk with Zip, and we made promises to keep in touch by phone. It was a difficult breakup because of all we had been through together.

"Buddy," Zip said. "I'll see you later, whether it be upstairs or downstairs. Have a little faith." We hugged each other, and that was that.

I purchased a ticket in a sleeping car for the trip home to Philadelphia and slept on and off during the train ride. I got a couple of books, but I didn't finish them. Mostly I lay in bed, watching broken-down houses or mountains passing by. I had my uniform on and hated it—everything was made of wool.

One night I had dinner with a young lady who was going back to Bryn Mawr. I told her I had been wounded. She didn't ask me anything else about it. She did most of the talking.

Occasionally, I would walk from one train car to the next—there were eight cars altogether. I was just trying to get some exercise and to clear my mind. I had pressing fears about what everyone would be asking me back home:

"Hello, Ralph, how you been?" they might say. "Tell me why you look this way."

Or they might say something like, "You've lost a lot of weight. You don't look the same, Ralph."

Or "Well, don't worry. Minnie will straighten you out, Ralph. She'll fatten you up a bit."

I was ready to hit any son of a bitch who crossed my path down those train cars. I just wanted to be by myself. "What does this fucking guy know?" I would say to myself when a stranger passed by. "He doesn't know anything." These fears of what people might ask me and of what they might really be thinking made me sweat even more at night. But I still wanted to see my family.

I knew my parents weren't going to argue about me going back to college. They were going to let me float around a bit. But I knew I wasn't going to stay in Lansdowne long because of the weather. My lung required a warmer climate. Also, I knew I wanted to be my own man, not a child living with my parents.

My ideal homecoming would be to sit around the dinner table and ask them about their lives, not talk about my life. The store, my brothers' experiences in the service, Sylvia's love life (if she had one)—anything about them. Anything. Not me. Them.

As the train pulled into the station, I saw my parents waiting at the platform. My mother started to cry as soon as she saw me, and so did my father. I didn't hesitate at all. Using all the wind I had in me, I ran into their arms, and I started to cry like a baby, my face plastered between theirs.

"Are you all right, Son?" my father asked me.

"Yes, but I'm very tired. It was a long trip," I said, smiling through my tears. It felt good.

* 41 *

"I'll Be Seeing You"

August 1946

IT WAS A VERY LONG CAR RIDE BACK TO LANSDOWNE. THE LAST 250 MILES were especially quiet. I think Bob was upset that he didn't get to see California.

I thought of calling Jo in Denver, but I didn't. Then I thought of calling Lynda once I got back home. "What the hell's the matter with you, Ralph?" I thought. "You know Lynda's married. You know you're not healthy. Dr. Gibson told you it's going to take five years for that lung to get better. You know she's looking for sex the way it used to be, and she's not going to get it. Don't call her, Ralph. Don't."

I looked at my reflection in the car window to make sure I wasn't talking to myself. My lips weren't moving.

I don't know why I was in such a rush to get back home again, anyway. I had nothing waiting for me there except my bedroom. And for the next three days, I stayed there in a drug-induced sleep. I increased my sleeping pill dosage from five to ten milligrams a day.

Two weeks later, in an effort to pry me out of my room, my mother suggested that we visit Parvin State Park in New Jersey. I knew Parvin State Park as Union Grove, the place we used to go on summer weekends. Both my parents were deeply concerned about my state of mind and inactivity; perhaps they thought that connecting with some happier childhood memories would be therapeutic.

A forty-minute ride from our home, Parvin State Park used to be a wooded area with just rowboats, but now it was a tourist attraction with paid admission, a new dock, sailboats, and plenty of shops.

As I walked along the shore with my parents, I stopped and remembered the spot where my mother first taught my brother Joe and me how to swim. We used to take off our rubber shoes and toss them into a rowboat.

"Okay, let's go," my mother would say as she paddled out.

Joe and I would swim after her, going from one end of the lake to the other. When we got tired, we had a little routine:

"I can't swim anymore," I would yell first.

"I can't either," Joe would then shout.

Then I would scream, "I'm going to drown!"

"Well, then I'll have one less son," my mother would joke.

Now, all the splashing and screaming children made me uneasy. This park was too crowded. Noisy. We headed for a little food shop along the lake to get something to drink. As I walked in with my mother, I heard a kid shouting in Japanese. I turned around and saw a Jap couple with a little boy who was jumping up and down, pointing at some candy. His high-pitched screech infuriated me. My rage swelling inside me, I rushed at them.

"Shut up, you little bastard!" I said to the boy. "Get that goddamn kid outta here before I kill it!"

The little boy's father was shocked, and the couple immediately grabbed their child and ran out of the store.

My mother grabbed me and shook me. "Ralph, you can't do this to other people," she shrieked. "Forget it. The war is over."

During the car ride home, my father was livid. As he was driving, he looked over his shoulder and said, "Don't you have any feelings?"

"I don't know," I murmured.

As we drove in silence, I felt absolutely ashamed of myself. I felt ashamed of being a POW. I was no hero. I felt like a convict every day. When people looked at me, I thought they were thinking, "Look at that goldbrick. He sat out the war in a POW camp. That goldbrick sat around in Java for three years and seven months. He played cards. He had a good time."

In fact, I learned from my mother that Eubank had sent a letter to my folks while I was POW. He told them that Java had plenty of food and that they should have no worries, I'd be taken care of. He made it sound like some resort.

I was stuck. Stuck between the sweat and the shit. I didn't want to explain what I had been through, and I couldn't stop people from thinking what they were thinking. I couldn't correct their thinking because I didn't want to talk about it. There was no way out.

When we returned home, I went upstairs to hide in my room again. As I reached the second floor, though, I saw Sylvia's open door. Nana had slept in the room with Sylvia, but the room had been completely redecorated—new beds, curtains. But my sister's vanity table remained.

Something compelled me to enter the room, and I sat down where Nana had slept. If Nana were alive, she would put her arm around my shoulder. She wouldn't be afraid to touch me, I thought.

"Nana, why didn't I listen to my father? Why? What if I hadn't joined the National Guard? I could have finished school. What if I hadn't joined the Army Air Corps? Then maybe I would've been sent off to Europe. What if I hadn't been selected for that mission, Nana? I could have gone to cadet school. But I really wanted to go back to my music. And I wanted Lynda, too. Why, Nana?"

I looked up, and my mother was standing at the door.

"What are you doing in here?" she asked.

I didn't answer her.

"You know, Ralph, your father and I are really worried about you. We're going to have to put you in an institution if you keep up like this."

I didn't answer her.

"You are strong, Son. You have a new life to look forward to. The future is up to you."

My mother turned and went back downstairs.

What was my mother talking about? I had no future. All I had ever wanted to be was a musician. Oh, I had been so happy-go-lucky then. I would give anything for those days again.

I got up and went down to the dining room, and I quickly picked up the phone and dialed. It rang several times.

"Hello."

"Harry!" I said. "It's me. Ralph."

"Hey, Kid. You're back."

Harry said he had called the house once during the war, and my father told him that I was missing in action. I wasn't going to tell Harry about what I had gone through as a POW, and he wasn't the kind of guy to ask. Harry didn't give a shit about anything as long as he had a gig and a girl.

"I just got back from Europe," Harry said. "I was on a ship in the Mediterranean for three months. Spain is terrific. They love jazz over there. And the women are out of this world."

Harry mentioned that he had spent four years in the entertainment section of the service, playing all the USO gigs—two weeks here, two weeks there. Always moving. On the road.

"What are your plans now, Kid?" he asked.

"I don't know, Harry," I said, then I told him about my lung and that I couldn't play my instruments anymore.

"Well, I won't be playing horn all my life," he said. "I'll be doing something else. When it comes, it comes. But right now, I'm having a great time. I'm single, and I love traveling."

I couldn't move my mouth. Harry filled the silence.

"Well," Harry said with a smile in his voice. "We sure had plenty of good times, Ralph, and you'll have those memories the rest of your life."

The tears were starting to run down my face. "Good-bye," I said, then hung up the phone.

My knees were wobbly, but my feet led the way into the enclosed porch. I turned on the radio. Talking to Harry sent my mind back to Havana—the jam sessions, the women dancing on our laps. Siesta. The booze. The smoky back rooms. The brassy horns. The mem'ry of all that _____

Losing my music was truly the worst thing about my recovery. I had nothing to go back to. And nothing could replace my music. When I played, I was out of this world. It was an elixir of happiness. When I thought of my music, I saw people dancing. I was playing for them. Oh, the sounds that came out of my instrument. People were happy. It felt wonderful.

As I sat there on the enclosed porch, it was bittersweet to know that Harry was living the life I wanted. I also knew the nightmares would still come, never letting me forget what I had survived. Maybe my strange odyssey had somehow allowed Harry to enjoy the life he had.

Now, staring at the glow of the soft, amber light on the Motorola, I realized that I was still a prisoner, a prisoner of the music, held captive by what was and what could never be.

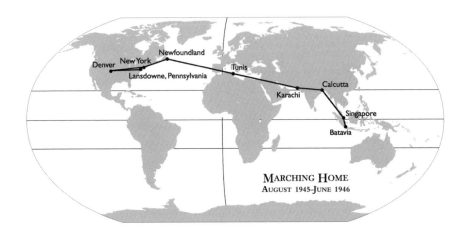

Denver New York Newfoundland Tunis Karachi Calcutta Singapore Batavia
Lansdowne, Pennsylvania

MARCHING HOME
AUGUST 1945–JUNE 1946

EPILOGUE

"I Could Write a Book"

THREE MONTHS AFTER RETURNING HOME TO LANSDOWNE, PENNSYLVANIA, I decided to move to California. I joined up with a classmate from high school who was starting his own business producing sun visors for automobiles. A month later, I met and shortly thereafter married my first wife, and we had three children. Marriage initially suspended some of my nightmares, but they soon came back with a vengeance: cold sweats, screaming in the night, and even a diabolical episode where I found myself strangling my wife while I was asleep. Somehow, I thought she was the Japanese commandant at Camp Bandung.

After this incident, I sought help from the Veterans Administration Hospital in Westwood, but they didn't provide much psychological assistance. In 1946, medical professionals knew very little about post-traumatic stress disorder, which affects many POWs as well as those who have suffered from physical abuse or have witnessed horrific acts of death, destruction, or human violation. Many doctors could only prescribe heavy doses of drugs and aspirin for my ailments, along with the same advice: "Put it out of your mind." If only it was that simple.

While I was being treated for my disorder, my sun visor partner abandoned the business and commandeered my car in the process. Later, after taking a proficiency exam, I enrolled in college to study accounting, with my education financed by the GI Bill.

Soon afterward, I started my own accounting business, which was successful. However, two tragedies occurred in my family: my wife died suddenly of a brain hemorrhage, and my son suffered a prolonged illness and death from diabetes. I also endured professional loss during this time—the U.S. government indicted me for fraud. After several lawsuits, I appealed my case, and the verdict was overturned. Later, I had another battle with the U.S. government in 1956 when the Veterans Administration reduced my disability to thirty percent. Again, I fought back, and my 100 percent disability was reinstated. I still maintain that status today.

Zip Zummo died of tuberculosis only a year and a half after he left the hospital in Denver. Lieutenant James Frerry knocked on my door one afternoon in 1948 when I wasn't home. My wife invited him inside, but he did not feel like waiting. He never came back. As for Harry, I never saw him again, either—and the same goes for Lynda.

A golf buddy introduced me to a beautiful, caring woman named Ellie on Labor Day 1989. Ellie's husband had died two years earlier, and she and I dated and then I moved into her condominium. We married on August 25, 1991. Single-handedly, Ellie encouraged me to write this book.

Ellie has a married daughter, Cathy, and a son-in-law, Randy, and I am crazy about both of them. In 1992, Cathy and Randy had a little girl, Alexandra, and I became her Papa. I have been so happy since Alexandra came along. She is a joy.

In 1996, I received an invitation to my sixtieth high school reunion. I had not returned to my hometown since my mother's funeral. I did not want to attend the event because I had very little recall of my high school days, but Ellie convinced me to go. While we were eating, a man walked over to me and introduced himself. I told the man that the only person I remembered from those years was a kid who had a very special Lionel train set on his porch.

The man smiled. "Ralph, that's me," he said. "I'm Jack McSherry, and I'm still running those trains in my home."

I smiled at my old friend. It's fascinating how the human mind can be derailed and then brought back on track.

Before we returned to the West Coast, Ellie and I drove through my old neighborhood. There were torn blankets hanging from the windows of our old store. The building was crumbling. That was the last time I went back to Lansdowne. I was so proud of that little town in my memories.

Even though I have a Purple Heart with two stars, I still wrestle with the shame of being a POW to this very day. And I often wonder why I am still here. Perhaps I'm starting to believe in God again. A little bit. Just a little.

And as for Louie, I have discovered from writing this book that he was a mixed blessing. He was a monster, yet in a strange way he protected me; he saved my life. Maybe we all have a Louie somewhere deep inside us.

At eighty-five years old, I am retired, and other than the nightmares that still visit me every once in a while, I am glad to be alive.